The
MIDDLE AGES

1000 TO 1600

Published by The Reader's Digest Association Limited
London • New York • Sydney • Montreal

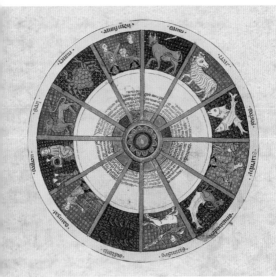

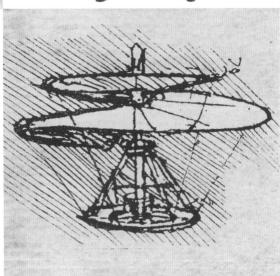

Contents

Introduction

In AD 1000, Chinese technology far outstripped that of Europe. Islamic science was in full flower, with scholars like the Persian Ibn Sina (Avicenna) making major contributions to philosophy and medicine. Before long, though, Europe was resurgent as a wave of creativity swept across the continent in the 15th and 16th centuries. At the same time Protestantism emerged as a religious force to be reckoned with. Evolving from centuries of debate on doctrinal matters, the Lutheran Reformation converted large sections of the Christian communion reinvigorated with the ideas of Humanism.

Buoyed up by the newly acquired knowledge, Europeans embarked on audacious voyages of exploration. Meanwhile, a high tide of new inventions was reached at home. The shoulder collar, for example, enabled draught horses to exert their full power without choking, massively increasing agricultural output. The magnetic compass and the sternpost rudder made possible the great voyages of discovery. The windmill helped to feed a growing population and brought new land into use. The cross-ribbed vault enabled architects to reach for the sky in soaring Gothic cathedrals. The cannon, meanwhile, changed the face of war, bringing new levels of destruction.

From the modern scientific method, pioneered by the English scholar Roger Bacon in the 13th century, to Gutenberg's invention of the printing press, the technological revolution was well and truly underway by the time of the Renaissance. Imitation and improvement were driven by the exchange of ideas between scientists and by competition between Europe's emerging nation-states. In art, the rapid spread of oil painting – heralding greater realism and later giving rise to different modes of expression – developed from the simple notion of diluting pigments in linseed oil. Leonardo da Vinci epitomised the Renaissance collaboration between art and technology. In many ways, the 15th and 16th centuries represented a golden age of innovation, but not everyone was yet ready to renounce the long-held beliefs of the past.   *The editors*

To the glory of God
The cloisters of Gloucester Cathedral display fan-vaulting in ornate late Gothic style, known in Britain as the Perpendicular and in France as the Flamboyant. By the time Gloucester Cathedral neared completion in the 14th century, construction of cathedrals had been going on up and down the land for more than two centuries.

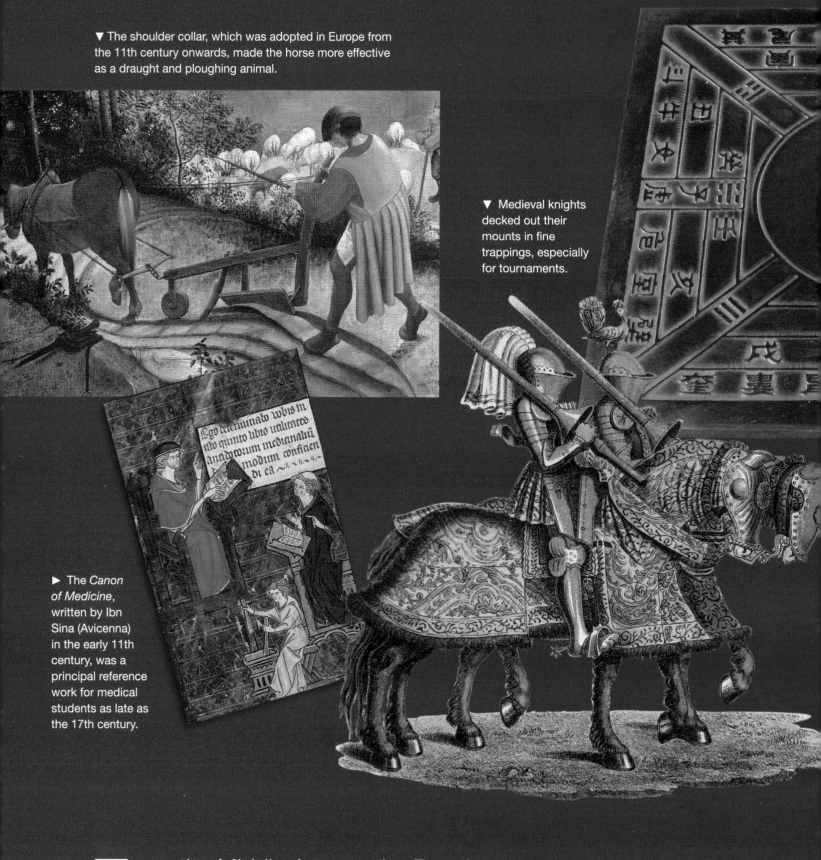

▼ The shoulder collar, which was adopted in Europe from the 11th century onwards, made the horse more effective as a draught and ploughing animal.

▼ Medieval knights decked out their mounts in fine trappings, especially for tournaments.

▶ The *Canon of Medicine*, written by Ibn Sina (Avicenna) in the early 11th century, was a principal reference work for medical students as late as the 17th century.

From the Middle Ages to the Renaissance, a seismic shift took place in human consciousness. The world, once such a narrow and confined place, suddenly opened up at a dizzying pace, as explorers ventured to far-off lands and pushed back the frontiers of

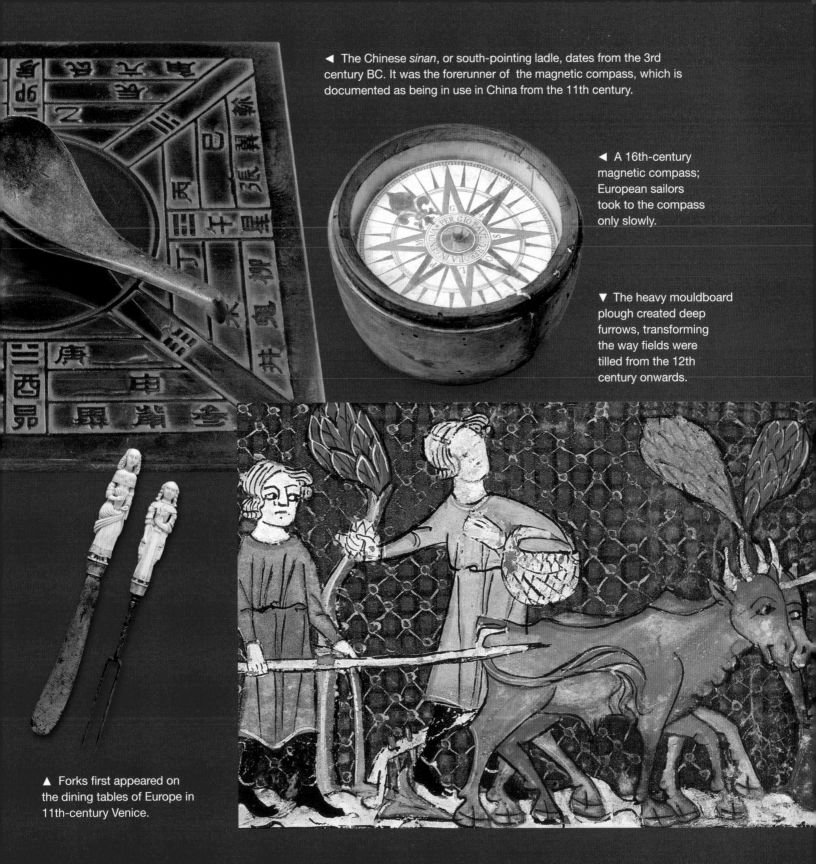

◄ The Chinese *sinan*, or south-pointing ladle, dates from the 3rd century BC. It was the forerunner of the magnetic compass, which is documented as being in use in China from the 11th century.

◄ A 16th-century magnetic compass; European sailors took to the compass only slowly.

▼ The heavy mouldboard plough created deep furrows, transforming the way fields were tilled from the 12th century onwards.

▲ Forks first appeared on the dining tables of Europe in 11th-century Venice.

knowledge. Nor did this spirit of adventure stop at the most famous 'discovery' of the era: the New World. At home, new inventions came thick and fast, changing the way people lived and bringing further innovations in their wake. It was not just the

▼ The sternpost rudder, known to the Chinese since the 1st century, only caught on in Europe from the 11th century onwards.

◄ Horizontal-axle windmills were widely adopted in medieval Europe.

► Cranes came into use in the early 15th century.

unimaginable distances involved in voyages of discovery or revelations about the heavens that made heads spin; the whole mental and physical landscape of the Middle Ages was, it seemed, on shifting sands. No sooner had a stable point been reached than

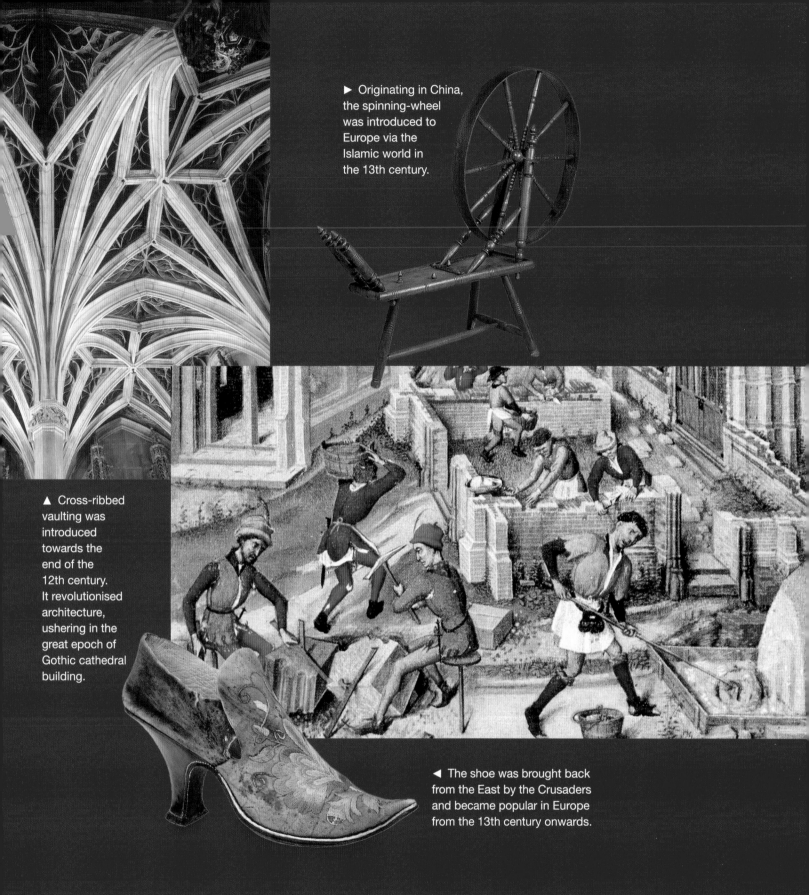

▶ Originating in China, the spinning-wheel was introduced to Europe via the Islamic world in the 13th century.

▲ Cross-ribbed vaulting was introduced towards the end of the 12th century. It revolutionised architecture, ushering in the great epoch of Gothic cathedral building.

◀ The shoe was brought back from the East by the Crusaders and became popular in Europe from the 13th century onwards.

some new development would set the kaleidoscope in motion once more. The great humanist agenda was to gain a comprehensive grasp of all things, great and small. Convinced that human beings should become masters of their own fate,

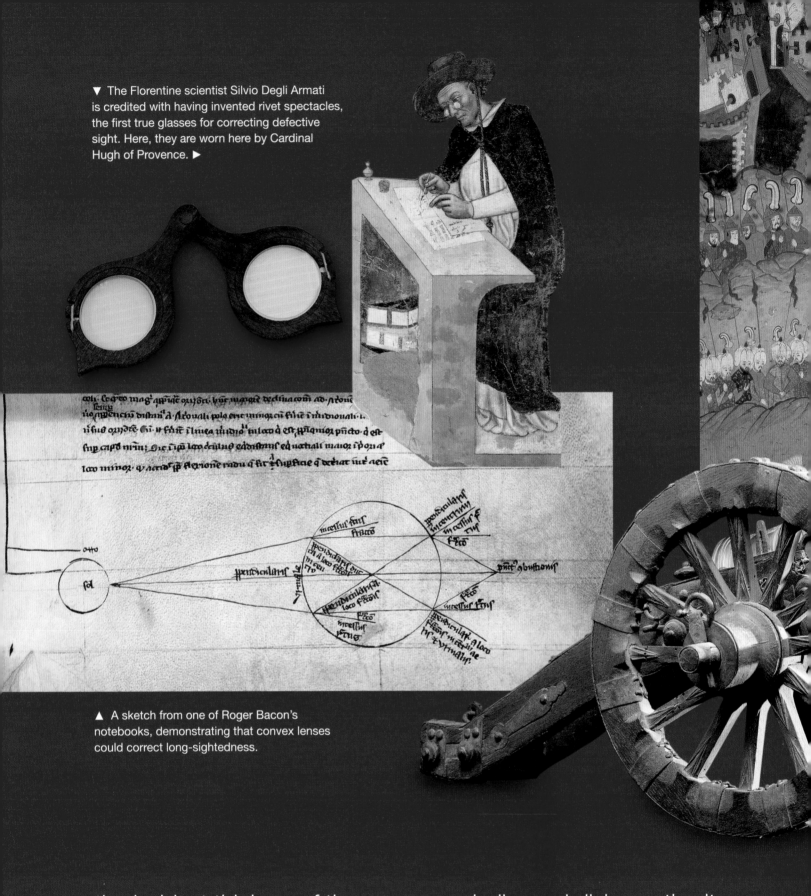

▼ The Florentine scientist Silvio Degli Armati is credited with having invented rivet spectacles, the first true glasses for correcting defective sight. Here, they are worn here by Cardinal Hugh of Provence. ▶

▲ A sketch from one of Roger Bacon's notebooks, demonstrating that convex lenses could correct long-sightedness.

the boldest thinkers of the age even challenged divine authority over the secular world. This headlong quest for knowledge was fraught with danger, and no more so than for those pioneering scientists and philosophers who dared to question Aristotle and

◄ The cannon, widely adopted by European armies from the beginning of the 14th century, revolutionised warfare and played a key part thereafter in military strategy.

▼ Painting in oils was pioneered by Jan van Eyck, who added oil highlights to a base of egg tempera. Oil painting really came of age in the work of the Venetian master, Giovanni Bellini.

◄ The mechanical weight-driven clock first appeared in Europe in around 1335.

Ptolemy's conception of a central fixed Earth. Scanning the skies with ever more powerful instruments, astronomers were forced to the realisation that Earth was just one of several planets orbiting the Sun – an insight that set them on a collision course with the

▼ Some artists used a portable camera obscura to project as accurate an image as possible of their subject onto the canvas.

▶ A replica of Johannes Gutenberg's printing press, in operation from 1450.

▼ Single-point perspective, which was rediscovered at the beginning of the 15th century, completely changed the way paintings were composed.

Church. Though Tycho Brahe clung to the notion that the Earth was the centre of the universe, his data paved the way for Kepler and Galileo's more radical – and accurate – understanding of planetary motion. By the time the Inquisition forced Galileo to

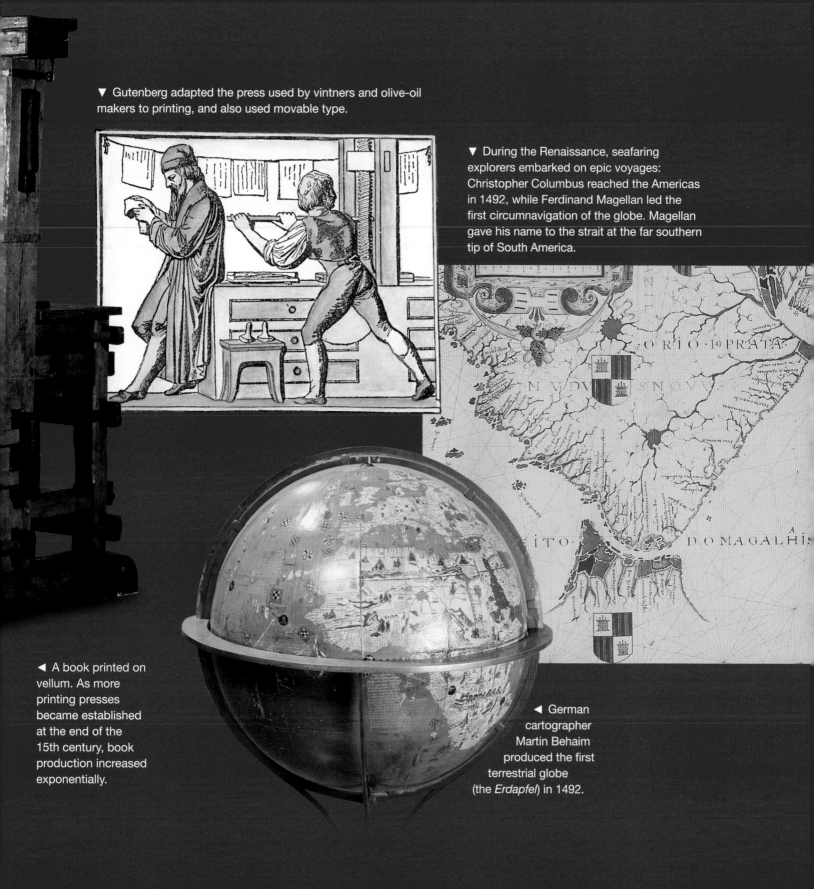

▼ Gutenberg adapted the press used by vintners and olive-oil makers to printing, and also used movable type.

▼ During the Renaissance, seafaring explorers embarked on epic voyages: Christopher Columbus reached the Americas in 1492, while Ferdinand Magellan led the first circumnavigation of the globe. Magellan gave his name to the strait at the far southern tip of South America.

◄ A book printed on vellum. As more printing presses became established at the end of the 15th century, book production increased exponentially.

◄ German cartographer Martin Behaim produced the first terrestrial globe (the *Erdapfel*) in 1492.

recant his defence of a heliocentric universe in 1633, the genie was long since out of the bottle. In the late 13th century, Roger Bacon had stressed the paramount role of inductive reasoning and experiment; astronomy was just one of many fields of scientific

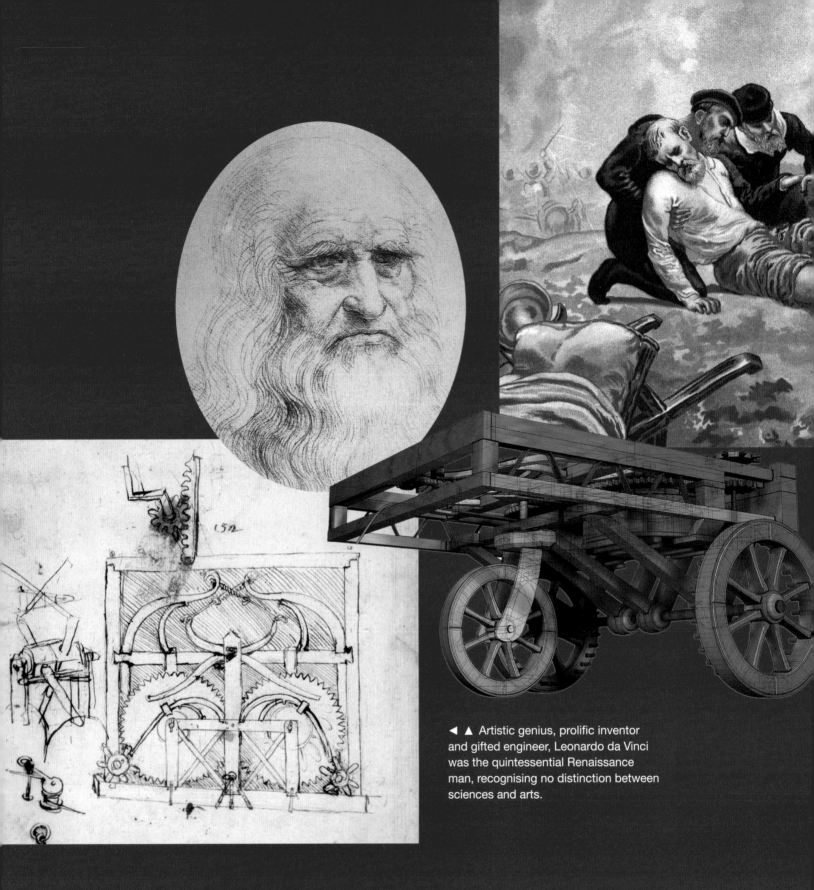

◄ ▲ Artistic genius, prolific inventor and gifted engineer, Leonardo da Vinci was the quintessential Renaissance man, recognising no distinction between sciences and arts.

enquiry that now focused on measuring the world and fixing humanity's position within it. Key inventions reflect this urge: sophisticated maps and nautical charts, the terrestrial globe, the magnetic compass and even the rediscovery of single-point

◄ Ambroise Paré, the founder of modern surgery, performing an urgent operation on the battlefield in about 1560. Paré also invented the first jointed artificial limbs.

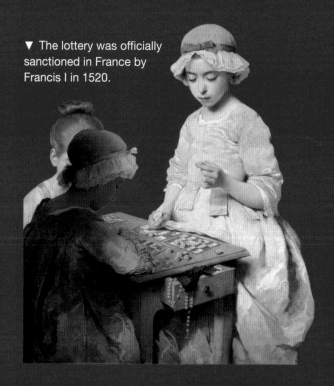

▼ The lottery was officially sanctioned in France by Francis I in 1520.

▲ French potter Bernard Palissy first created his unique form of enamelware in around 1545. Among his many talents Palissy was a keen naturalist, and incorporated lifelike casting of animals, like this rabbit, into his pottery.

perspective in painting. Parallel with this mastery of physical space, the invention of the mechanical, weight-driven clock gave human beings the measure of time. The epitome of the Renaissance mind was Leonardo da Vinci, polymath par

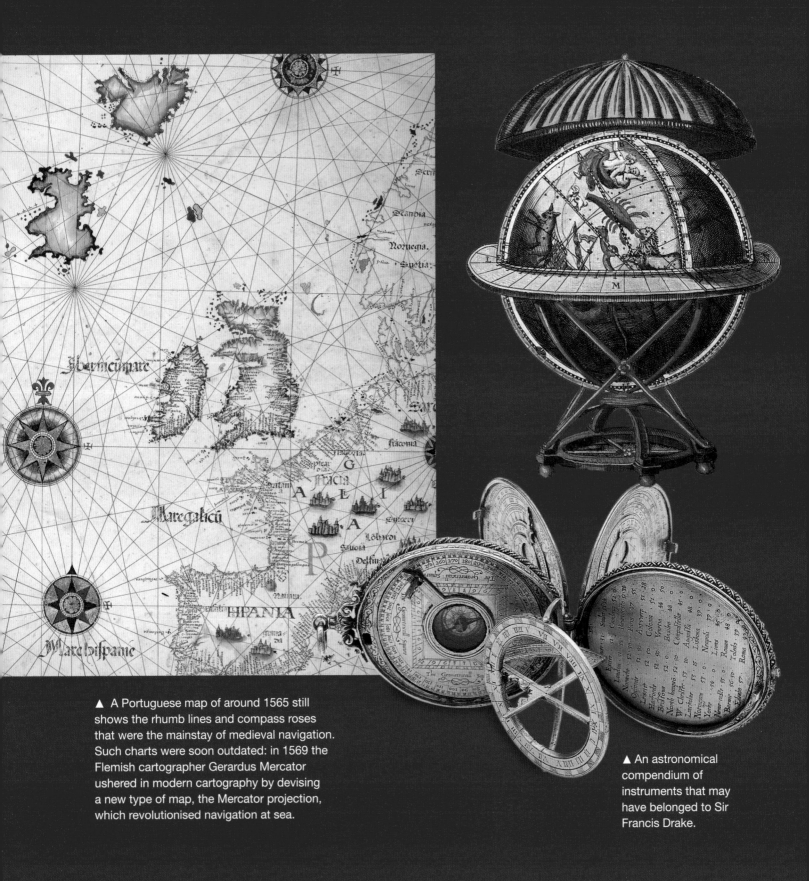

▲ A Portuguese map of around 1565 still shows the rhumb lines and compass roses that were the mainstay of medieval navigation. Such charts were soon outdated: in 1569 the Flemish cartographer Gerardus Mercator ushered in modern cartography by devising a new type of map, the Mercator projection, which revolutionised navigation at sea.

▲ An astronomical compendium of instruments that may have belonged to Sir Francis Drake.

excellence, whose interests spanned portraiture, landscape painting, anatomy, military architecture, civil engineering, mechanics and aerodynamics. While the Renaissance rekindled interest in classical learning and took its models from ancient

◄ From 1571 to 1599, Danish astronomer Tycho Brahe charted the position of hundreds of stars on this brass armillary sphere. His astronomical sightings were all done with the naked eye; optical instruments like the telescope had yet to be invented.

◄ The thermoscope, invented by Galileo in the late 16th century, was improved a few years later by his compatriot Torricelli when he developed the modern alcohol-filled thermometer, with a graduated scale.

◄ England pioneered prefabricated buildings, the first such structure being erected on Old London Bridge in 1577. In the 19th century, Joseph Paxton's cast-iron and glass Crystal Palace (left) was a groundbreaking feat of design and engineering.

◄ The graphite pencil first appeared in 1565, gradually replacing the lead pencil which had been in use since ancient times.

▲ 16th-century Venice grew rich on its trade with the East, enabling it to build the most powerful fleet in the world and be at the very heart of Renaissance inventions and discoveries.

Greece and Rome, it was far from being just a nostalgic re-creation of the past. Through its emphasis on the dignity of humanity and the creativity of the human mind, the movement may be said to have laid the foundations of our modern world.

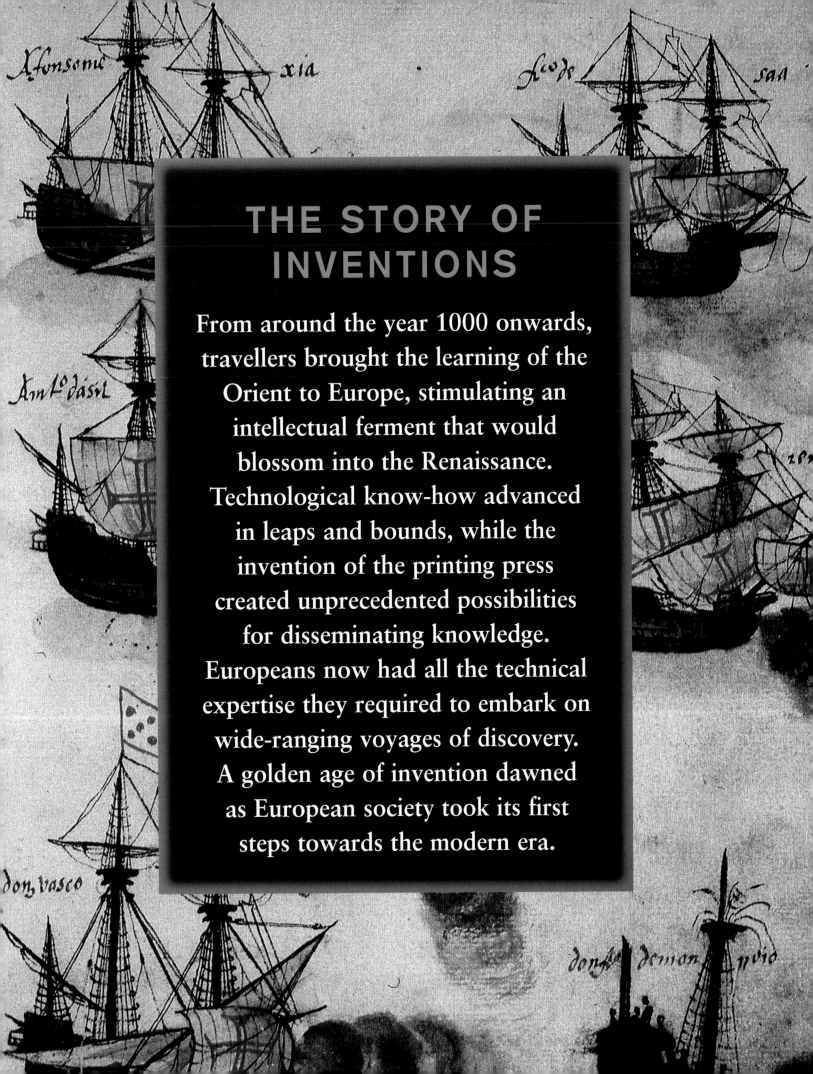

THE STORY OF INVENTIONS

From around the year 1000 onwards, travellers brought the learning of the Orient to Europe, stimulating an intellectual ferment that would blossom into the Renaissance. Technological know-how advanced in leaps and bounds, while the invention of the printing press created unprecedented possibilities for disseminating knowledge. Europeans now had all the technical expertise they required to embark on wide-ranging voyages of discovery. A golden age of invention dawned as European society took its first steps towards the modern era.

Harnessing horsepower

The invention of the horse collar and new forms of harness during the Middle Ages enabled people to exploit the pulling power of the horse to the full, be it for ploughing in the fields or pulling carts along the roads. From China to medieval Europe, the history of the horse collar is synonymous with that of the working horse.

HITCHING UP DOGS AND LLAMAS

Horses were unknown in the New World prior to the arrival ofEuropeans from about the 1520s onwards. The only draught animals were llamas in South America and sled-dogs in the snowy regions of North America. Both could be harnessed, but as with camels, onagers and donkeys in Mesopotamia and the Middle East, harnesses had to be strapped either around the animals' bellies or their hindquarters.

Ever since the first harnesses appeared, in the form of wooden yokes in Mesopotamia in about 3000 BC, it was oxen that provided the pulling power for transport and ploughing. Although horses – which were domesticated around the same time – were far faster, they were put to more exalted uses, such as hunting and warfare. Among both the Assyrians in *c*2000 BC and the Hyksos in Egypt some 300 years later, the horse-drawn chariot was a fearsome weapon of war. The bridle and bit, already used by horsemen at that time, along with a primitive form of harness comprised of flat straps around the animal's neck and chest, were all that was needed for horses to pull these extremely light vehicles.

Greek and Roman chariots, which were used both in war and for hunting, still employed this 'throat-and-girth' harness. But as soon as anyone tried to make horses pull heavy loads or exert real effort, the arrangement choked the unfortunate beasts, so when heavy hauling tasks were called for, people opted for cattle yoked in pairs. Furthermore, a large proportion of the goods transported at the time were carried on pack-saddles slung on the backs of donkeys, mules or camels, all of which were ideally suited to negotiating uneven tracks. As a result, from

antiquity right through the Bronze, Iron and Dark Ages, no real thought was given to improving harnesses for horses. This state of affairs endured well into the medieval period.

Advent of the shoulder collar

The shoulder collar first appeared in Europe on northern farms, where it helped to till the heavy soils. At the end of the 9th century, Alfred the Great, ruler of the Anglo-Saxon kingdom of Wessex (871–899), recorded his astonishment at seeing working horses while on a visit to Norway. The new collar shifted the strain onto the animal's skeleton frame – especially the breastbone. The arrangement revolutionised animal traction, effectively increasing the horse's pulling power by more than 60 per cent and enabling it to take on roles formerly performed by much slower oxen. The use of horses in farming soon became widespread.

For the collar to be used most effectively another innovation was necessary: the single, heavy draw-bar connecting the harness to the implement being pulled was replaced with twin shafts. Whereas the yoke required that two animals, at least, be hitched up side by side, one or more on each side of the drawbar, horses could be harnessed 'between the shafts', either singly or in tandem – that is, one behind the other. Horse owners soon realised that the pulling power of horses in line was far greater than that of horses side by side. Another advantage was that they were easier to control when harnessed in this way. The arrangement would endure right up to the mid-20th century.

A Chinese invention

Yet the origins of the shoulder collar lie much further back in time. As with so many other

Ploughing for the Conqueror
The earliest known representation of the horse collar is on the Norman Bayeux Tapestry (left), which was embroidered in around 1080.

KNIGHTS AND THEIR CHARGERS

In the 11th century, western Europe witnessed the rise of a feudal nobility – the knightly order, whose vocation was fighting on horseback. Only after a long apprenticeship in the martial arts were young men dubbed knights in a solemn investiture ceremony. In many countries, they became a hereditary caste and were feted in literature. Horses were key to a knight's power, so noblemen chose their mounts with care. Strong, agile horses from Castilian or Aragonese stock that could withstand the rigours of jousting and carry a heavily armoured knight were in great demand. The knight and his charger formed a powerful team; the epic poem *The Song of Roland* (*c*1150) relates how Vaillantif, Roland's horse, refused to let anyone else ride him. It also notes with contempt how the traitor Ganelon got his comeuppance: 'to shame him, they saddled him up on a beast of burden'.

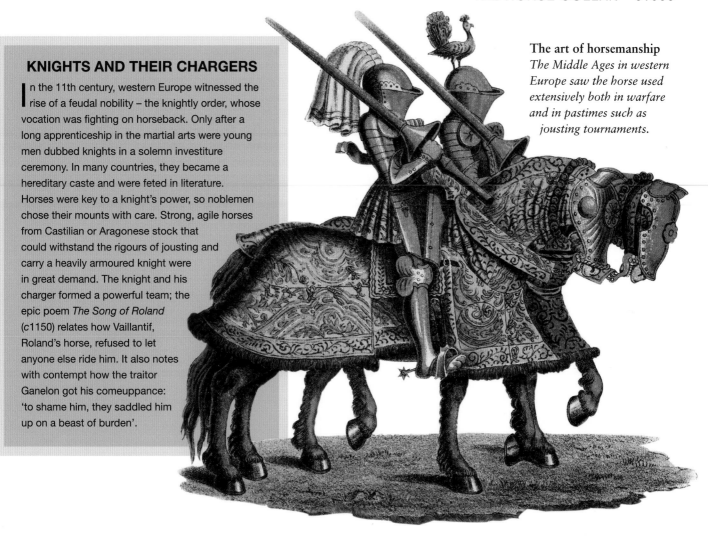

The art of horsemanship
The Middle Ages in western Europe saw the horse used extensively both in warfare and in pastimes such as jousting tournaments.

Tilling the land
A ploughman driving a horse equipped with a shoulder collar in The Fall of Icarus, *a painting by Pieter Brueghel the Elder, (c1558).*

inventions, it was the Chinese who were the first to introduce a type of collar and harness for working horses. From around the 6th century BC, they used a leather harness with straps that fitted around the animal's breast. This ensured that horses could pull loads without throttling themselves. This 'breastcollar' harness was the ancestor of the breast harness used in the West from the Middle Ages right up to the 19th century.

The reasons why the Chinese hit upon the idea of improving the harness were probably twofold. Firstly, they already had wheeled vehicles with shafts. Secondly, the people living on the fringes of the Gobi Desert found that whenever their horses tried to pull any sort of load, they were constantly getting bogged down in soft sand, which must have made the search for a more efficient harnessing system more compelling. Their solution may well have been inspired by Chinese bargemen, who man-hauled their boats along the country's many waterways using harnesses that strapped around the chest and collarbone.

The strapped harness arrived in the West in the 8th century by the same route as the stirrup, which was introduced by the Avars, a nomadic Caucasian people who invaded Hungary in 568. The Bayeux Tapestry, created in the 11th century, provides the earliest record of this type of harness being used in Europe.

The first collar harnesses

From at least the 1st century BC, the Chinese were also familiar with the rigid collar harness, ancestor of the shoulder harness. The first collar harnesses were designed to secure a

21

yoke. Unlike oxen, horses do not have a horizontal spinal column with a hump protruding above the shoulders, and the padded collar served in some measure as an artificial hump onto which the yoke could be fitted. The Chinese quickly saw that the collar could be deployed differently, by tying the straps that held it onto the shafts of vehicles. Camels were also used extensively in China at the time, the camel drivers using pack-saddles that comprised a wooden hoop padded with felt. It may well be that the collar harness had its origins in these simple pack-saddles.

In any event, the invention was to have a far greater impact in medieval Europe than at home. Ultimately, the horse saw only limited use in China, with water buffalo doing the bulk of farm work, especially for tilling the paddyfields. Meanwhile, in the realm of military logistics, most troops and arms were ferried along China's many waterways.

Horses or oxen?

Even in Europe the collar by no means supplanted the yoke, which retained its devotees and continued to evolve in its own right. From around the 11th or 12th century the withers yoke, which makes the animal take the strain on its shoulders, gave way to the bow yoke, placed over the neck, and the head yoke, both of which are still in use today.

Contrary to popular belief, the pulling power of oxen and horses is much the same. And although the horse is faster, more efficient and more resilient, it cannot replace cattle in all circumstances. The strength and stolidity of oxen, for example, makes them ideally suited to forest clearance work. Economic factors also played a role: not only are horses more expensive to buy and more tricky to rear, they are also three to four times dearer to feed than cattle. In southern climes, where oats cannot be cultivated easily, the horse never became established as a beast of burden.

A question of performance

Up to the 19th century, the collar was used at riding schools, on plough-horses and on horses that hauled heavy goods wagons, canal barges or minecarts – in short, all those tasks that called for slow, steady pulling. Thoroughbred horses were rarely used for this kind of work, since owners feared

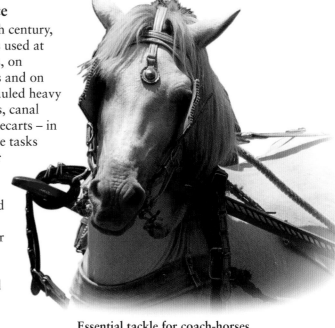

Essential tackle for coach-horses
A light collar harness is used for horses hitched in pairs (above). In a typical Hollywood Western scene (below), a team of paired coach horses tries to outrun an attack.

that it would damage their manes. Breast harnesses were preferred for this type of horse and one advantage of the arrangement was that a postillion could mount up and ride the lead horse of a mail coach or other carriage.

The question of whether the collar or breast harness was more effective was settled in 1910 by the Paris General Omnibus Company. Using a dynamometer – a pulley for measuring force, first devised in 1802 – retired cavalry officer Richard Lefebvre des Noëttes compared the pulling power of teams of horses harnessed respectively with a collar and a breast harness. The result was clear: with the collar, horses could draw three times the weight of horses equipped with the breast harness. The findings resulted in the breast harness gradually being abandoned in favour of the collar by all the various trades using working horses.

From the mid-19th century onwards, first the advent of the steam engine, especially on the railways, then the combustion engine and motor cars posed serious competition to the horse. All told, it took less than a century for the engine to completely eclipse horse-drawn transport. Yet even in the machine age the horse was not entirely forgotten: when the British engineers James Watt and Matthew Boulton calculated the power output of their steam engines, they set the base unit of measurement as 'one horsepower'. The term still serves as a reminder of the days when the horse was the chief means of motive power.

Horse trials and competition
A two-man gig pulled by horses in breast and shoulder harness at the annual French carriage driving championships at Chantilly.

MADE TO MEASURE

To ensure that a horse can achieve its full pulling power, it must be fitted with a sturdy, well-padded and properly adjusted collar to avoid risk of injury. Every animal has a different bone structure and musculature, so it is vital that saddlers make harnesses to measure. In the 19th century, the skill and ingenuity of these craftsmen was unsurpassed: the collars they fashioned ranged from unpadded types made of sheet metal to ones made from plaited rye straw or bulrushes lined with serge cloth. There were even collars made of solid rubber and inflatable ones, like pneumatic tyres.

Equine artistry
The modern art of saddlery is evident in this shoulder harness, which is light and yet extremely strong.

Persian polymath

The wide-ranging scholar Ibn Sina, who became renowned in the Christian West as Avicenna, epitomised the great blossoming of sciences in Islamic culture during the medieval period. His fame vied with that of Galen, the celebrated Graeco-Roman physician, in the medical faculties of European universities right up to the 17th century. His works were also highly influential in the rise of philosophy in the West.

In the year 997, according to the Christian calendar, Abu Ali Hussein ibn Abdalah ibn Sina was summoned to the palace of Nuh ibn Mansur at Bukhara, the capital of the Persian Samanid Empire. Ibn Sina was only 17 years old, yet even at this early stage the breadth of his knowledge and his growing reputation as a physician had so impressed the prince that he was prepared to put his life in the young man's hands. For Ibn Mansur was gravely ill.

Avicenna the doctor

Ibn Sina examined the prince in an attempt to diagnose from the visible symptoms – specifically pain, fevers, secretions and skin lesions – what was afflicting him. In doing so he was drawing upon the lessons that his tutor, Issa bin Yahya, had taught him. Ibn Sina, a Shiite Muslim, had learned his profession from a Christian. This was by no means uncommon, since Nestorian and other Christians were settled in the Middle East from Syria to Persia, in what had now become the Muslim world. They had been responsible for introducing to the region the medical writings of Greek and Roman physicians, such as Hippocrates, Paul of Aegina, and Galen. Their works were translated into the Syriac language from the 6th century onwards. Prior to this, medical knowledge in the region had also been greatly enhanced by Persian and Indian scholarship.

From his tutor, Ibn Sina had learned that illness was an outward sign of a disruption of equilibrium between the four 'humours' defined by Hippocrates: phlegm (or lymph); blood; yellow bile; and black bile. The humours were respectively associated with coldness, warmth, humidity and dryness, so Ibn Sina would have tried to ascertain whether the prince demonstrated an excess or deficiency of one or another. His diagnosis unfortunately has not been preserved, but the course of treatment prescribed would almost certainly have involved a special diet, plus medicines derived from plants and animal

Fanciful portrait
With the look of a dreamer and the countenance of a prophet, this medieval portrait of Avicenna reflects an idealised Western view of the Islamic scholar.

AVICENNE

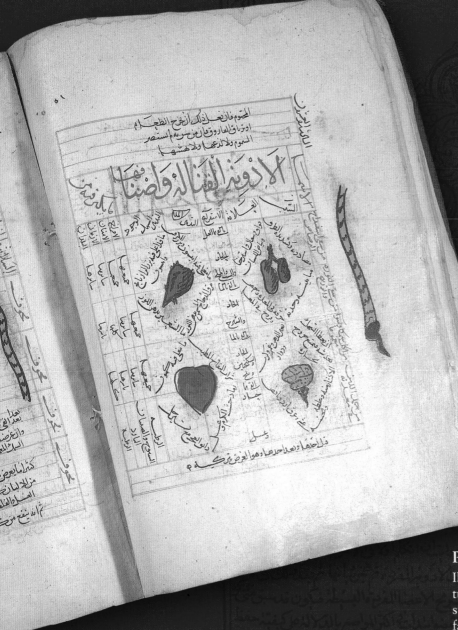

A TRUE POLYMATH

No modern scholar would dare to claim knowledge in as many different disciplines as Avicenna. The subjects of his published treatises include mathematics, logic, medicine, metaphysics, philosophy, psychology, Canon law, physics, the natural sciences, meteorology, astronomy, music and zoology. In doing so, he systematically collated, interpreted and transmitted not only all the knowledge of the ancients but also that of his own age.

grasping its meaning. Perhaps he found the source of his enlightenment browsing in the prince's library. In any event, it was a commentary on the *Metaphysics* by the philosopher al-Farabi, who was dubbed by his contemporaries the 'second master' (after Aristotle) and died *c*950, that finally brought everything into focus for him.

Politician and academic

Ibn Sina's career suddenly took an unexpected turn after the episode in Bukhara; in quick succession first the prince and then his own father died. As political unrest swept Persia, Ibn Sina embarked on a life of travel. Initially he took up a teaching post in Gorgan, on the Caspian Sea, before moving west to settle first in the town of Rai, near modern Tehran, and then in Hamadan, where he was appointed vizier to Shams al-Daula, the Buwayhid emir of Khwarezm. When the city fell to Mahmud of Ghazni in around 1012, Avicenna fled to Isfahan, the capital of western Persia, which was controlled by the Buyid dynasty. Once there, he again found himself in the service of a prince, Abu Jafar ala Addaula, a post he retained until his death.

While mainly devoting his energies to public life, Avicenna still found time to teach philosophy and, helped by his followers, to burn the midnight oil compiling treatises. He published more than 240 works, covering practically every field of knowledge. Two of these are still cited today: the *Canon of Medicine* and his studies on the soul, known collectively as *De Anima*. These were both translated into Latin by the Italian scholar Gerard de Sabloneta in the 13th century.

Avicenna's magnum opus The *Canon of* Medicine *remained a standard work on medicine for many centuries. The pages reproduced here contain a description of various human organs.*

products. The patient rallied and Ibn Sina not only saw his reputation greatly enhanced, he was also granted the freedom to consult the prince's extensive library whenever he wished.

Prodigious learning

Since the age of 10, when he had learned to recite the Koran by heart, Ibn Sina had been imbibing all the current knowledge of his age, both through conversations with his father Abdullah, a high-ranking government official, and his elder brother, and through his own reading. In addition to medicine, in which he was formally trained, he mastered every other branch of learning. There can be little doubt that he was an exceptionally gifted individual, but his wide-ranging erudition was typical of the intellectual climate of his age, where knowledge was not rigidly separated into different disciplines.

Even so, Aristotle's *Metaphysics* caused Ibn Sina considerable difficulties. Reportedly, he re-read the work 40 times without truly

AVICENNA THE GEOLOGIST

Like many earlier Islamic scholars, Avicenna took a keen interest in geology. His ideas on the origin of mountains prefigure both the rival 'Plutonist' theory (rocks formed by fire) and the 18th-century 'Neptunist' theory (rocks formed by sedimentation). He correctly saw the presence of shells in many types of rock as proof that the land had once been covered by sea, and he was one of the first to realise that the action of wind and dripping water erodes different rocks at different rates. Other ideas of his were less accurate: he thought that the continents had been formed by intense heat from beneath the ocean floor.

Rock formations

Avicenna put forward some bold theories to explain geological formations such as natural basalt columns (above) and the presence in rocks of fossilised ammonites. Many of his ideas were later proved correct.

Parallel text

A 14th-century edition of the Canon of Medicine *(right), written in both Hebrew and Arabic.*

Avicennism

Although it covers a wide range of learning, including physics, logic, and metaphysics, *De Anima* is mainly studied for its philosophy. Avicenna set out an entirely original synthesis of the teachings of Aristotle, Neoplatonism and Ismaili Shiism. He asserted that human beings derive from a single entity – namely, God – but that the intellect (the 'sensory soul') takes its ideas from a totally separate intelligent entity, which is not to be confused with God. In acquiring greater knowledge, a person effectively grows closer to that external intelligence and attains a higher spiritual state.

Learning from the master
An illustration from a 14th-century edition of the Canon of Medicine *(right), shows Avicenna (in red) teaching his students.*

Here, Avicenna was trying to square philosophy with mysticism, knowledge with revelation, reason with faith.

In the West, Avicenna's fame as the leading Islamic philosopher was rivalled by Ibn Rushd of Córdoba, (aka Averroës, 1126–98) who developed the materialist and rationalist aspects of Aristotelian thought. Yet Averroism, which distinguished between rational and revealed truth, upset the Christian Church, while Avicennism was to have a major influence on the writings of St Thomas Aquinas (1225–74), the key figure in medieval Christian scholasticism, which sought to reconcile ancient philosophy with Christian theology.

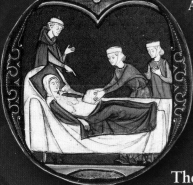

Illustrated version
A 13th-century Latin edition of the Canon *contained a wealth of illuminations.*

The *Canon of Medicine*

In the same period, the name Avicenna became familiar to students of medicine in Europe as his *Canon of Medicine* became a standard work of reference alongside the writings of Galen. Avicenna had begun compiling his overview of medical knowledge during his time in Gorgan. The work is certainly comprehensive: in five volumes, he set down everything known at that time about the workings of the human

body and also expounded his own theory on health, founded on the doctrine of the four humours. He lists and describes, organ by organ, every known disease and ailment, from pleurisy and meningitis to melancholy, suggesting simple or compound drug remedies for them. He lists 760 simple pharmaceuticals.

Avicenna's *Canon* was a huge achievement. Translated into Latin in the 12th century, it established the framework within which medicine was taught and practised throughout the Middle Ages. Following the invention of printing in the 15th century, the *Canon* would go through more than 30 editions. But it would not set the standard forever. In 1527 in Basel, Switzerland, a young professor of medicine threw a copy of the book into one of the braziers lit for the Feast of St John; by this bold, controversial gesture, the doctor, alchemist and teacher Paracelsus (1493–1541) signalled his rejection of what he saw as outmoded scholarship that stood in the way of a true understanding of living nature. It was not going to be quite that simple to consign the venerable work to oblivion. It remained the standard work of reference in medical schools right up to the mid 17th century.

AVICENNA'S IMPETUS DYNAMICS

In *De Anima,* Avicenna made an important contribution to dynamics, the study of bodies in motion. Aristotle had postulated in his work *Physics* that a projectile continues to travel through the air after being thrown, rather than instantly falling to Earth, because the projector – be it hand or bow string – somehow transfers its motive power to the air itself. And yet we know that air actually resists movement.

Refuting Aristotle's view, Avicenna suggests that some kind of incorporeal driving force passes directly from the projector to the propelled object. To explain this hypothesis, he introduced the concept of impetus: the natural impetus of an object to regain its state of rest is counteracted by a violent impetus – or acquired force – which imparts movement to it. Avicenna's ideas were picked up by the 14th-century French philosopher Jean Buridan in his theory of impetus, which defined the force exerted in propelling an object in terms of its velocity and mass. Buridan's theory helped to explain certain phenomena, from the impossibility of throwing a feather as far as a stone to the rotation of the stars and planets.

Sailors get their bearings

The magnetic compass first appeared in China in the 11th century. Several centuries later, it was to revolutionise the art of navigation, enabling sailors to venture forth on the high seas in search of new and distant lands. Alongside the growing science of cartography, the compass made it possible for navigators to set a precise course and stick to it, giving them confidence that they would return safely.

Feng Shui **compass** *Made in China in the 3rd century BC, this 'south-pointer' compass, or sinan, used a ladle-shaped magnetite lodestone to indicate north and south. It was used for divination for centuries before its potential as a navigational aid was realised. By the 16th century, compasses had taken on their more familiar form, as shown in this French illustration of 1583 (opposite).*

Imagine the port of Venice in the 15th century, a veritable hive of activity. On one of the merchant ships sailing back and forth to Alexandria the captain is busy overseeing the installation of a new instrument which should allow him to chart a course far more accurately than before: a magnetic compass. The trickiest part is magnetising the needle, which has been cut from the finest tempered steel. Not trusting anyone with this delicate task, the captain places a magnetic lodestone on the centre of the needle, taking care to get the correct polarity. Then, with the solemnity of a religious ritual, he moves the stone gently from one end of the needle to the other, ignoring the magnetic force that tries to pull the needle with it.

Roots in divination

The story of the compass began in 3rd-century-BC China, where people first discovered the properties of magnetite, an iron ore that naturally aligns itself with the Earth's magnetic field. From the 1st century AD, this characteristic was exploited in geomancy, better known as *feng shui*, a form of divination used to aid the siting of houses and tombs so that they 'cooperated and harmonised with the local currents of the cosmic wind'. To the great amazement of Westerners, the Chinese oriented themselves towards the South Pole, which formed a key element in their cosmic symbolism.

One of the main feng shui devices was the 'south-pointer' – a square divination table made of bronze, which represented the Earth, with a circle in the centre symbolising the heavens. Around its edge were engraved the eight principal directions, together with divination symbols. The philosopher Wang Ch'ung described a south-pointer in the *Lun-Cheng*, a work that appeared in AD 83, stating that if a lodestone was placed on the south-pointer, it would always align itself along a north–south axis. The magnetite object was carved in the shape of a ladle – the name given by the Chinese to the constellation we know as the Plough (*Ursa major*). Attempts to re-create such devices have shown that the 'magic' works only if the baseplate is highly polished.

The first true compasses

Almost 1,000 years elapsed before the Chinese abandoned the magnetite lodestone in favour of magnetised iron. It is thought that they probably knew about the principle of transferring the magnetic properties of magnetite to iron and steel from as early as the 4th century AD, but this is not known for certain; in the 17th century, Jesuit missionaries to China burned most of the manuscripts relating to geomancy, so destroying centuries' worth of precious information. As a result, the first scientific description of the magnetic needle is in Tseng Kung-Liang's *Wu Ching Tsung Yao* ('Complete Compendium of Important Military Techniques') of 1044, which describes a 'fish pointing to the south'. This 'fish' – in fact, a needle cut from a very thin sheet of iron that had been magnetised – floated on a bowl of water and aligned itself along a north-south axis; it was the ancestor of the magnetic compass. Whether in the form of a wooden fish containing a piece of magnetised metal floating in a bowl of water, or a turtle made of magnetite and wood pivoting around a bamboo pole, the compass soon gained a foothold in Chinese life, on land and at sea.

The respected scientist Shen Kua (1031–95) in his *Meng Qi Bi Tan* ('Dream Pool Essays', *c*1088), explained that the 'magicians rub the point of a needle with the lodestone; then it is able to point to the south.' He went on to make a further observation: 'But it always inclines slightly to the east, and does not point directly to the south'. Shen Kua had described for the very first time the phenomenon of magnetic declination, which in the centuries that followed became a major source of errors in compass readings and gave rise to the most far-fetched theories as to its cause.

CHINA'S SOUTH-POINTING VEHICLES

In the 3rd century BC, the Chinese engineer Ma Jun invented a strange two-wheeled chariot on which was mounted a jade statue of a seer with his arm outstretched; whatever direction the chariot went in, the figure would always point south. Many more were subsequently built: indeed, 'south-pointing chariots' are mentioned in Chinese works right up to the 13th century AD. For a long time, people confused the vehicles, which have nothing whatsoever to do with magnetism, with the 'south-pointing needle' mentioned for the first time by Shen Kua in the 11th century. In fact, instead of relying on a magnetic compass, the workings of the chariot were entirely mechanical. It used a gear train much like the differential gearing found in modern cars. It was this mechanism that helped to counteract changes in direction and ensure that the statue kept on pointing south.

False compass *Images of 'south-pointing chariots', like this illustration from the 3rd century AD, show that these bizarre vehicles really did exist. Recent studies have proved conclusively that they had nothing whatever to do with magnetism.*

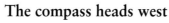

The compass heads west

No trace of the magnetic compass can be found in Europe before the 12th century. In 1187, an English scholar and cleric named Alexander Neckam wrote in his *De Naturis Rerum* ('Concerning Natural Things') that 'when the sky is obscured by clouds, then the sailor makes use of the twirling needle to show him the cardinal point

Guardian angels
A 17th-century engraving of cherubs using navigational aids hints at the aura that surrounded the compass (bottom). The ivory compass below, from the same period, was made for show. For early mariners, the robust, gimbal-mounted compasses (bottom right) were life-savers.

to which the prow of his ship should be turned'. Precisely how the compass came to Europe is a mystery. It may have been brought to the Near East by Arab traders, who regularly sailed from the Persian Gulf across the Indian Ocean to the East Indies, where they would have had contact with Chinese sailors. In turn, the Venetians could have encountered the compass in their dealings with Arab traders from the ports of the Levant. Another theory holds that it may even have been invented quite independently in Scandinavia.

Whatever the case, the first magnetic compasses comprised stalks of straw, for buoyancy, through which were pushed pieces of magnetite or a magnetised needle; each straw was then floated on a shallow dish of water. By the 15th century, the compass had developed into a true maritime navigational instrument. The magnetised needle was mounted on a pivot so that it hovered beneath a circular disc marked with the cardinal directions; the whole apparatus was contained in a sturdy wooden case mounted on gimbals to keep it level and steady in heavy seas.

Henry the Navigator

A great leap forward in the art of navigation took place in the early 15th century, and was largely the work of

one man. Captivated by tales of the gold of the Sudan and the 'Spice Isles' in the Indian Ocean, Portugal's royal *infante* (heir-apparent) Dom Henrique set about transforming Sagres, a desolate promontory in the Algarve, into a Naval Academy with a library, an observatory, a celebrated school of navigation and an arsenal where a new type of vessel was built to tackle new challenges – the caravel. All this earned him worldwide fame and the title by which he is known to posterity: Henry the Navigator (1394–1460). As a result of Henry's inspiration, Portugal became the world's first centre of maritime exploration.

Henry commissioned a 'Manual of Nautical Instructions' containing information on all the latest navigational and cartographic techniques, including the effective use of the magnetic compass. His efforts paid off: after his death, Bartolomeu Dias, Vasco da Gama and other Portuguese captains became the first to sail round the southernmost point of Africa into the Indian Ocean; Diaz named it Cabo das Tormentas ('Cape of Storms'), but we now know it as the Cape of Good Hope.

Work of the devil?

In the western Europe of the Middle Ages, popular belief ascribed strange powers to magnetite, including the ability to cure all kinds of illnesses. Sailors associated magnetic needles with black magic and the instruments

THE PROBLEM OF MAGNETIC DECLINATION

Early navigators were at a loss to explain why compass needles pointed north, or why there was a discrepancy between the direction indicated by the needle and True North; the angle between them is called the 'magnetic declination'. Columbus was the first to note the coordinates of the line of 0° declination, in mid-Atlantic, which he passed on 13 September, 1492. Over a century later, the English physician William Gilbert put forward the first theory of magnetic declination. Based on his experiments with a magnetised model, he concluded that the Earth's core was magnetic. Shortly afterwards, the German scholar Athanasius Kircher instigated the first worldwide measurement of magnetic inclinations – the 'dip' angles that a magnetic needle makes with the horizontal plane at specific locations. Kircher published three tables containing 260 measurements, 198 of them taken at sea. In 1634, by comparing two sets of data collected at the same place (Deptford) but 12 years apart, Henry Gellibrand made the key discovery that magnetic declination changes over time. Over 54 years declination varies by more than 7°, between 11°3' and 4°1'.

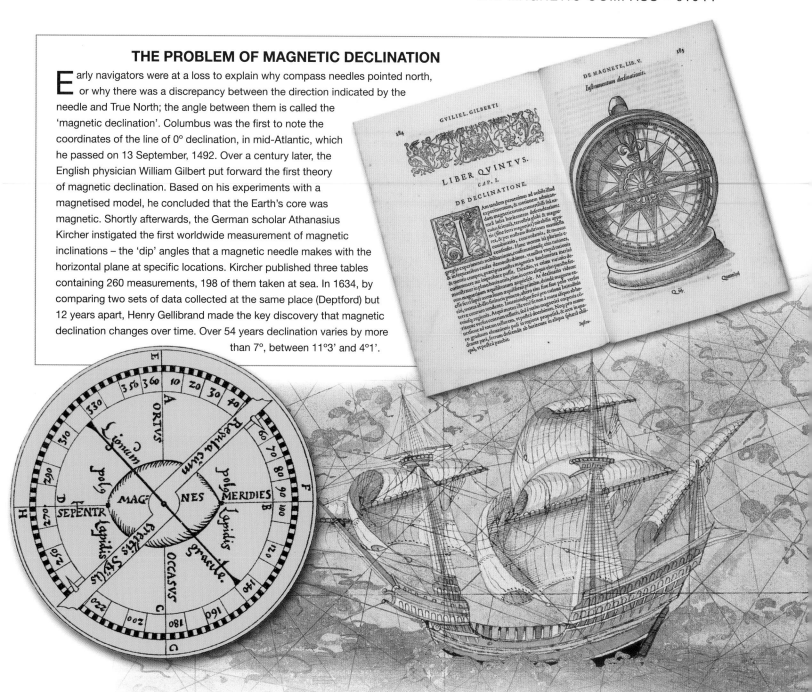

took some time to become accepted. At first, captains who used compasses were careful to consult them only in the privacy of their cabins. Every ship's master had his own foibles aimed at minimising the risk of error, and so ensuring a safe return home. Ferdinand Magellan, for example, took on board no fewer than 35 compass needles when he set off on his circumnavigation of the globe in 1519.

Incremental improvements

Adoption of the magnetic compass as a navigational aid was neither instantaneous nor universal. It caught on quickly in the Mediterranean, making the portolan charts of coasts and harbours in the region – already more detailed than those covering the Atlantic and the North Sea – even more accurate. In

the Indian Ocean, where the monsoons arrived with predictable regularity, mariners continued to navigate by the prevailing winds. In the North Sea and the Baltic, sailors put their faith mainly in plumb lines; by dropping a line over the ship's side at regular intervals they could tell how deep the water was and also (by putting tallow on the base of the weight) whether the seabed was sandy or muddy. They used the compass only as a back-up.

Along with the sternpost rudder, the compass was one of the key technologies that drove the Age of Discovery. Constant efforts were made to improve it: the 19th century in particular brought several major advances. The liquid compass, in which the needle is housed in a container filled with a liquid that cannot freeze (usually a mixture of water and

Conquest of the oceans
Three vital steps in sea-going exploration included William Gilbert's treatise on magnetism (top); the freely pivoting compass needle, shown here (above left) in a sketch by Peter Peregrinus of Maricourt (1269); and the caravel, developed in Portugal in the 16th century (above).

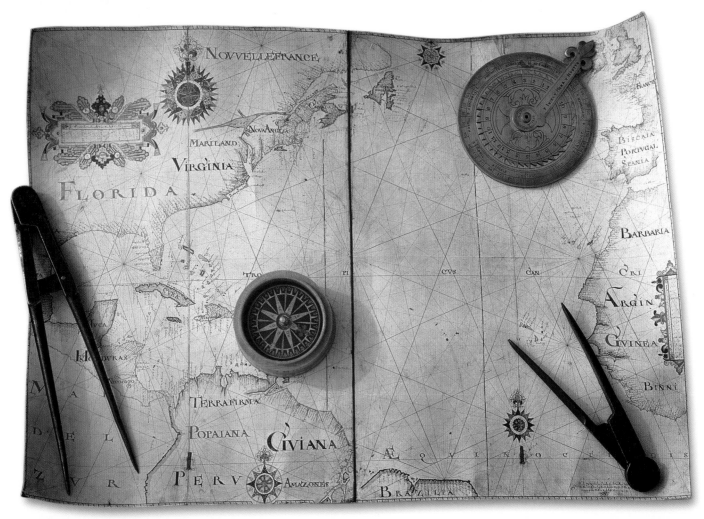

Navigators' tools
Pre-requisites of the mariner's trade in the 17th and 18th centuries were a magnetic compass, nautical dividers, an astrolabe and portolan charts.

alcohol), gradually supplanted dry-mounted compasses. The liquid also allowed the needle to stay steady by damping shock and vibration.

A more serious problem was compass error caused by the increasing use of iron in ships. The first to attempt a solution was the English explorer Matthew Flinders, who suggested using a 'counter-attractor' in the form of a vertical soft iron bar in a tube on the foreside of the compass binnacle (the mounting). In the

1880s, the 'Flinders Bar' was supplemented by Kelvin's Balls: two iron globes set on either side of the binnacle, named for their inventor William Kelvin, Lord Thomson. From the early 20th century on, the magnetic compass was eclipsed by the gyroscopic compass, which works by an electrically-powered fast-spinning wheel. Unlike its magnetic predecessor, it has the advantage of always showing True North and is unaffected by external magnetic fields.

A modern gyrocompass
Invented in 1908 by the German Hermann Anschütz-Kaempfe, the gyrocompass was perfected and marketed, along with a gyrostabilisation system for large ships, by the American engineer Elmer Sperry around the time of the First World War.

THE MYTH OF THE MAGNETIC MOUNTAIN

A persistent legend among medieval sailors told of a magnetic mountain somewhere on Earth that was the source of all magnetism. Mariners unwise enough to sail too close to it would suddenly see nails and other metal fittings of the ship torn out and drawn towards the mountain, causing the vessel to break up beneath their feet.

The Eastern tradition originally located this peak somewhere in the southern hemisphere, but by the 13th century,

as European navigators began using the magnetic compass, it had shifted to the North. Charts made around 1569 by the celebrated Flemish mapmaker Gerardus Mercator pictured the mountain rising from the ocean above the Bering Strait, cleverly set to one side of the North Pole to take account of magnetic declination. In 1600 William Gilbert, personal physician to Elizabeth I, tried to scotch all this 'nonsense and moonshine' by claiming that magnetism in fact came from the Earth's core. Yet the myth clung on for a long time thereafter.

The fork c1080

The ancient Egyptians used forks, but these were very different from the eating utensils we are familiar with today. Resembling pitchforks rather than delicately pronged implements, they were used for fishing pieces of meat out of the bottom of large cooking pots. The Egyptians made no attempt to adapt this cumbersome tool to table use. Nor did the Romans, in their turn, devise a fork for eating.

The fork as we know it first appeared in the second half of the 11th century, in Venice. Theodora Doukas, the Greek wife of Doge Domenico Selvo, had retained the custom of her birthplace Constantinople of using a dainty golden fork with two tines to pick up food. Her eating habits caused quite a stir in her new home, but failed to catch on. Quite the contrary, in fact; despite her exalted status, the citizens of the Most Serene Republic considered the new Dogeressa to be lacking in refinement for eating her meals in this way.

Golden forks crop up frequently in inventories of medieval noblemen's possessions, but they were by no means widespread: these utensils were only used to spear pieces of meat on a communal platter. When dining, guests continued to use what they considered to be the most efficient implements of all – their hands, which they had no qualms about dipping even into dishes with sauces. Even when forks did appear, inveterate users of hands and finger-bowls tended to regard those who insisted on using them as rather effete.

In Europe, it was under the reign of the French king Henry III (r1574–89) that the fork – at this stage still with just two tines – finally came into its own. In introducing use of the fork to his court, the king may have been influenced by his mother, the Italian noblewoman Catherine de' Medici, or he could have encountered it on a state visit to Venice. Fashion probably also have played a part; one distinct advantage of the fork over hands was that elegant gentlemen could lift their food to their mouths without spattering their extravagant ruff collars.

The fork was probably introduced into Britain early in the 17th century, when the wealthy would bring their own cutlery with them to the table. A century later the fork (now with the four tines customary today) had found its place in polite society. Yet even then, unlike the knife or the spoon, many people still regarded it as superfluous. In many Asian countries chopsticks are used in preference, while in other cultures, especially in Africa and the Indian subcontinent, people continue to eat with their hands.

Luxury utensils
A 17th-century ivory-handled knife and fork (left): such items were the preserve of princes at this time.

Acquired habit
During the 18th century fork usage became more widespread, reaching the lower classes, as shown in this contemporary painting of a peasant woman by the artist Tiepolo. Etiquette had yet to dictate the polite way to hold it.

An agricultural revolution

The introduction of the mouldboard plough had just as momentous an impact on farming as its predecessor, the ard, had done in the 4th millennium BC. Invented by the Celts, the plough was adopted only gradually and patchily until the start of the 12th century, but thereafter its use spread rapidly throughout Europe.

Timing the tilling
Ploughing is the subject for the month of March in the Limbourg brothers Très Riches Heures du Duc de Berry *(above). It is also shown among the farming tasks for the month of April in this detail from an Italian 15th-century fresco (right).*

One of the exquisite illuminations in the medieval book of hours known as the *Très Riches Heures du Duc de Berry* (1416), representing the month of March, shows peasants tilling the fields; in the background is the castle of Lusignan, in the Poitou region of western France. In the foreground, a labourer dressed in a smock is depicted using a goad in his right hand to control his team of two oxen, while his left hand grips the stilt of a wheel plough. Incorporating a coulter (a vertical iron blade in front of the share), a metal ploughshare and a mouldboard – a device that turns over the clods of earth in a continuous strip to form a furrow and aerate the subsoil – this basic type of plough continued in use in some parts of Europe right up to the 20th century.

The heavy mouldboard plough was first documented at the beginning of the 12th century. It was the end result of a series of refinements, over many centuries, to an extremely ancient tool: the ard. As often seems to be the case in the history of technology, the transition from one to the other was by no means instant. Nor did the plough completely supplant the ard, which is still used in some Mediterranean regions and also by many cultures around the world that have, out of necessity, clung to ancient, virtually unchanged agricultural methods. The plough arose when it was found that the ard – which was designed for light, sandy ground – was unsuitable for tilling the heavy, waterlogged soils of Northern Europe, with its rainy continental climate.

From the ard to the plough

The difficulty of working such soils saw the ard evolve in various stages from its basic form. To begin with, in the 1st century AD, the Romans in Gaul fitted a front axle and two wheels and hitched the ard to a pair of oxen. These important innovations steadied the implement and kept it level in the soil. Later, they attached an additional blade – the coulter – to the front of the sole, which 'prepared' the soil by breaking up large clumps of earth before the ploughshare (also made of iron by this stage) passed over them.

It was in the German-speaking regions of central Europe, from the 6th to 8th centuries AD, that this 'improved' ard really developed into the modern plough, with the introduction of a laterally mounted ploughshare. Onto this had been fitted the new component, the mouldboard, which lifted up and turned over the ploughed sod and opened out the furrow. Because the ploughshare and mouldboard were both located on the same side of the sole, the soil could be turned over alternately to the left and right of the furrow as the ploughman moved up and then back down the field. This ploughing technique, which came to be known as 'ridge and furrow tillage', had the advantage of helping to drain waterlogged soils, as well as grubbing up the roots of perennial weeds. Ridge (or asymmetrical) tillage changed the face of the rural landscape, since it encouraged the growth of strip farming, a system whereby fields were divided into narrow bands called 'selions', each of which was cultivated by a different farmer.

Slow acceptance

The mouldboard plough gained acceptance only very gradually. Its spread was no doubt hampered by the social and political upheavals of the great population migrations in the Middle Ages. Cost was another crucial factor; unlike the ard, this plough required livestock

FIELDS FROM FORESTS

Between the 10th and the 13th centuries, the population of western Europe mushroomed from 45 million to 75 million. This demographic explosion was a prime impetus behind the extensive land clearances undertaken at this time, which radically altered the rural landscape. New farmland was carved out from forests, moorland and marshes, while poor coastal scrubland was enriched and transformed into the arable fields known as polders in Flanders and the East Anglian fens. Originally instigated by individual landowners, from the early 12th century the clearances increasingly came under the aegis of the Church and feudal lords. It was only such wealthy individuals or institutions that could afford the outlay involved in scrub clearance and drainage. On the downside, the clearance programme destroyed huge tracts of woodland, which were vital in maintaining the region's ecological balance, and also turned too much unsuitable land over to cultivation, which in the event yielded disappointing results. Clearances slowed from the 13th century on, even though population growth continued apace. The lack of available land, plus the inadequacy both of production methods and financial support, all contributed to the major famines that would sweep through Europe in the 14th century.

ENRICHING THE SOIL

Agricultural output is closely linked to the type of soil in the fields and the fertilisation methods used. Although farmers in the Middle Ages already knew about improving the soil by burning stubble or by digging in marl or lime, animal husbandry was still in its infancy and was unable to supply manure in sufficient quantities to make a real difference to the quality of the soil. To give the ground time to recover and regenerate its nutrients, farmers followed a system of three-field crop rotation. This entailed dividing a parcel of land into three parts: one would be sown with winter wheat or rye in the autumn for harvesting in spring; the second was planted in spring with barley or oats for harvesting in autumn; the third field would be left to rest and lie fallow until the next year. The system allowed farmers no more than three harvests annually on average, or five in exceptional years.

The introduction of new strains of cereal, such as winter-sown oats or wheat in the 11th to 13th centuries, enabled farmers to reduce the time that a field had to lie fallow and significantly increased yields. Manure – organic matter from animal waste – remained the main way of fertilising the soil until the development of the first artificial fertilisers (initially superphosphates and later nitrogen-based compounds) by the German chemist Justus von Liebig in the 1840s.

Traditional fertilisers *Breton peasants collecting seaweed to spread on their land in around 1910 (top) and dung-spreading in modern Vietnam (left).*

Harrowing
The mouldboard plough was not the only farm implement that needed to be hauled by horses. The harrow – a spiked frame dragged over fields to break up the clods of earth – was in widespread use on farms in England in the 1340s, as shown in this contemporary illustration.

to pull it. Even after it was firmly established in central Europe, it took several centuries more to really catch on in eastern Europe. But as its popularity grew, the plough became one of the mainsprings of the agricultural boom that began in the 11th century. Population growth had created an urgent need for more cultivable land and improved yields. In the absence of fertilisers, fields had to be left fallow for one year in three, and the inefficient performance of old farming implements, notably the ard, meant that yields were low.

Improvements in harnessing

The gradual replacement of the ard by the plough went hand in hand with major advances in other areas of farming equipment. The throat-and-girth harness, in use since antiquity, had the major drawback of choking draught animals; it was supplanted by the shoulder collar, which utilised the full pulling power of horses. Further enhanced by the practice of harnessing horses in tandem, these innovations really came into their own when ploughing narrow strips of land. Methods of

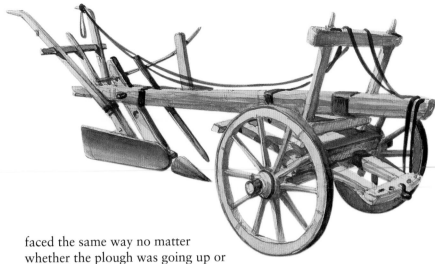

harnessing oxen also advanced, as the traditional withers yoke was replaced first by a yoke attached to the animals' horns, and then – in around the 13th century – by the head yoke; each improvement brought an increase in tractive effort. The plough was a heavy contraption made up of weighty components, such as the iron or sometimes timber mouldboard. But pulled by one or more large draught animals it proved its worth, making short work of reclaimed tracts of land that would have taken backbreaking effort to cultivate by hand.

New farming techniques

Improvements in other farming implements also helped the plough become more widespread. The harrow, for instance, completed the process of breaking up the soil begun by the plough. It was used to prepare the ground as a seedbed for sowing and thereafter to cover the newly sown crop with a thin layer of soil. Finally, the field was tamped down with a roller.

Meanwhile, the pack-saddle was being supplanted by the wheeled cart, which was far more efficient at transporting goods. The sickle gave way to the long-handled scythe, which was easier to use and cut a bigger swathe. Most farming tools that had hitherto been made of wood were now made of metal. The period also saw the development of the windmill and wine-press, along with new techniques of cultivation and livestock rearing, which up until then had been limited. These included gathering hay into stooks for winter fodder, stabling of farm animals over winter and using their manure on the land.

Larger tracts of land began to be worked ever more efficiently; they were better fertilised, although still generally cultivated on the three-field crop rotation system. By the early 1500s farmers in Waasland in Flanders were pioneering a four-field rotation using wheat, turnips, barley and clover. What they did not know was that clovers, like other legumes, enrich the soil by 'fixing' nitrogen from the air in nodules on their roots.

In the mid 16th century the turn-wrest plough was already coming into use; the major development was that the mouldboard and coulter could be moved from side to side, so that all the furrows

faced the same way no matter whether the plough was going up or down the field. Other innovations included the whippletree (a horizontal bar that helped to distribute the pull of the draught animal evenly on the plough), plus a mechanism for adjusting the depth of the ploughshare by moving a peg in a series of holes along the length of the sole. Finally, in certain regions where the soil type allowed, lighter ploughs which had the front wheeled axle replaced by a single runner or caster were used in preference to traditional ploughs.

Blessing the plough

In medieval England the benefits of the plough were so greatly appreciated that the first Sunday after Epiphany was celebrated as Plough Sunday. All the ploughs of a parish, bedecked with ribbons, would be hauled to church to be blessed. On the following day, Plough Monday, the teams would parade their ploughs around the village, seeking contributions for an 'ale' or night of revelling at the tavern. Plough Tuesday would usually

Ongoing development
Manufacturers of farm implements were constantly looking to improve the plough, in particular to make it more manoeuvrable and easier to handle. Innovations included the turn-wrest plough from the 18th century (above) and the 20th-century reversible plough (below).

State of the art *The Industrial Revolution had a major impact on farming. Steam power gradually replaced draught animals – the Howard Steam Tractor of 1875 is shown below – while precision engineering saw the emergence, in the early 20th century, of versatile new ploughs such as the Double Brabant (above), which had two mouldboard ploughs mounted back-to-back.*

be spent recovering before work began in earnest. The blessing of ploughs still takes place in many rural churches today.

Agriculture and industry

A second phase of innovation began in England in the 18th century, intimately bound up with the Industrial Revolution and geared to applying industrial methods to farming in order to raise production. The massive growth of industry in cities drained the available manpower from the countryside just as the demand for agricultural produce skyrocketed, and the extensive farmlands owned by the landed gentry became the laboratories of agricultural innovation.

At the same time, animal husbandry and manuring methods also evolved; the aim was to dispense entirely with the fallow-field system in favour of a more sophisticated four-field method of crop rotation. England was also the place where,

in around 1760, large-scale production began of a revolutionary iron swing plough designed by Dutch inventor Joseph Foljambe. Named the 'Rotherham plough' after its place of manufacture, it teamed a metal coulter and share and an iron-sheathed mouldboard with a wooden frame; the result was both lighter and more robust. During the last quarter of the 18th century, the growth of the iron and steel industry also prompted the widespread introduction of the all-metal ploughshare with integral mouldboard.

Constant innovation

The pace of development accelerated in the 19th century. In 1808 the British engineer Robert Ransome introduced the first completely cast-iron plough, with parts that could be dismantled and replaced. In 1837, during America's expansion westward, a Vermont blacksmith named John Deere realised that cast-iron ploughs were ill-suited to the loamy soils of the Midwest and was inspired to invent the world's first steel plough.

A later invention, the Double Brabant plough, delivered huge savings in ploughing time and was nothing short of a sensation. The device comprised two entire plough bodies, set one above the other; simply by pressing a lever the ploughman could rotate the plough through 180° when he got to the end of a furrow and turn round. All elements on the

Double Brabant were duplicated – coulters, shares, mouldboards – along with two skim-coulters to clear stones off each sod before it was turned. In addition, the Double Brabant had a self-adjusting front axle, which meant that the stilts could be dispensed with and replaced with a couple of simple handles. The great advantage of this was that it took just one person to steer this powerful implement.

Improved pulling power

Yet no matter how sophisticated ploughs became, they still depended on animal traction. From as early as 1860, some major landowners started to experiment with a new source of power – steam. Even so, due to the costs involved, it took a long time for mechanical pulling power to oust animal traction on farms. At the outset, a stationary steam engine ('ploughing engine') was used to draw the plough across a field by means of a cable winched onto a drum; the process was laborious and worked one-way only, as the plough had to be dragged back across the field every time it had completed a furrow.

Before long wheeled traction engines, the precursors of modern tractors, began to appear on the scene, but they were cumbersome vehicles and found it hard going on heavy or soft ground. The real breakthrough came in the 20th century, with the development of tractors driven by the internal combustion engine. These were sufficiently light to cross

A PLETHORA OF PLOUGHS

Alongside the heavy mouldboard plough, other types of plough appeared, designed for specific tasks such as ploughing between trees or rows of vines. A plough for use with vines was usually mounted on a chassis with a single wheel and asymmetrical handles to offset the slope on many vineyards; it had the drawback of being less stable than normal ploughs, so a heavy iron bar had to be mounted on one side of the sole as a counterweight to the share. They were later supplanted by the universal rotavator, an economical solution that equipped farmers with a multi-purpose tool at minimal cost. As need arose, the rotavator could be fitted with a turn-wrest for working on slopes, a potato hopper or a rake. The chisel plough, fitted with either rigid or flexible blades (shanks), is suited to hoeing compacted soil, while the rotating hoe is ideal for preparing a seedbed.

rough terrain yet powerful enough to pull a plough. Running first on oil, then petrol, then finally diesel, and fitted with ever more efficient gears and pneumatic tyres, tractors totally eclipsed draught animals throughout the developed world. Modern tractors are used in conjunction with increasingly sophisticated ploughs, stripped down to a basic chassis on which can be mounted a variety of different shares. These are raised and lowered hydraulically, while the depth of the furrow is altered at the flick of a switch. When working ground that is stony or full of tree roots, farmers today can use ploughs equipped with anything from one to eight concave, swivelling discs, which lift automatically if they encounter a serious obstacle.

Agribusiness
Powerful modern tractors coupled with multiple-share balance ploughs, like the one pictured below, enable modern farmers to cultivate huge tracts of land.

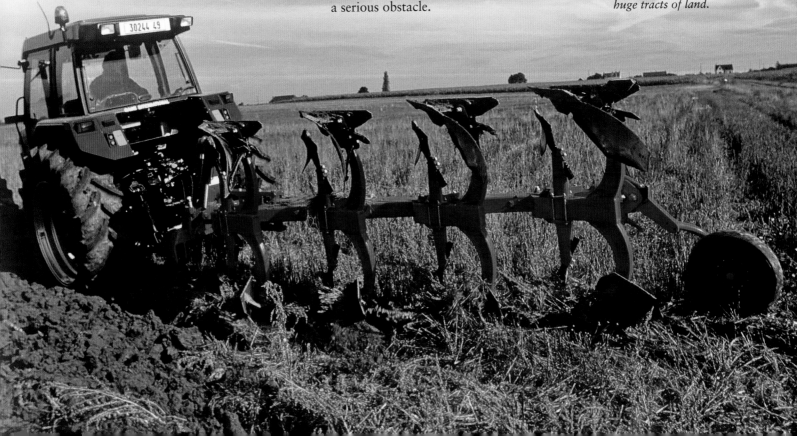

Steering a safe course

From the 12th century onwards, the rudder – a simple piece of wood mounted on the sternpost of boats and ships – would radically change the history of navigation. It was held in such reverence that the oldest collection of maritime laws, the Rolls of Oléron compiled in 1160, treats it almost as a sacred object. Above all, it made long-distance voyages a possibility.

Bound for the Holy Land
Twin-masted vessels like the one shown below carried the Crusaders to Jerusalem. It is equipped with a lateral steering-oar.

The popular image of seafaring in olden times is of the ship's captain, one hand gripping the tiller and eyes fixed on the horizon, steering his vessel and crew through conditions good and bad to reach their destination port in safety. In fact, the cliché is completely false: medieval captains, like modern ones, set the ship's course but left the physical business of steering to a helmsman, who was just another sailor following orders. Yet that hands-on control of the rudder has remained imbued with a mystique that has lasted right up to modern times. On the maiden voyage of the Transatlantic liner *France*, on 11 January, 1962, journalists and guests insisted on photographing the captain at the helm, despite his protestations. Centuries after the first appearance of the rudder, it remains a symbol of command.

From the steering-oar to the stern-rudder

In the early days of river and coastal navigation, some 8,000 years ago, boats were steered with oars. For craft of up to a few metres long, two or three oarsmen were sufficient to change course or turn a boat around within its own length. But on longer and heavier boats steering was difficult, especially when running against the current and a headwind. Accordingly, sailors learned some subtle skills of oarsmanship. Letting their oars go with the flow of the current, they discovered

Chinese innovation
Stern-mounted rudders were first used on ancient Chinese river junks (above right) and the technology is still steering Chinese junks today (right).

that they could change course most effectively by holding the blade at an angle rather than vertically. Tilting the blade slightly was enough to change the direction of travel. A wide range of oar-powered and sail-powered craft – from dugout catamaran canoes used by Polynesians to ancient Egyptian vessels and broad-beamed Phoenician 'round boats' – were steered in this way. Two wide-bladed oars mounted on either side of what would come to be called the sternpost – the continuation of the keel at the rear of the vessel – served as lateral rudders.

Yet in heavy seas, these steering oars proved largely ineffectual. With the exception of the intrepid Vikings, who

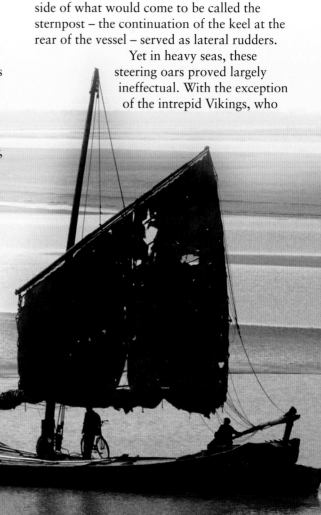

ADMIRAL ZHENG'S FLEET

As a result of Chinese advances in navigational technology – chief among them the magnetic compass and stern-mounted rudder – Chinese mariners were the first to embark on long-distance voyages of exploration. Between 1405 and 1433, under the reign of Zhu Di, the Yongle Emperor of the Ming Dynasty, Admiral Zheng He undertook seven great ocean-going missions. On successive voyages he gradually extended his range through Indonesia and Sumatra to India, Ceylon (Sri Lanka), Hormuz and the Maldives, reaching the Arabian peninsula and the east coast of Africa. Some claim that he rounded the Cape of Good Hope into the Atlantic, some six decades before the Portuguese navigator Bartolomeu Dias.

More controversial is the claim – not supported by any records – that on his sixth voyage, which set sail from the estuary of the Yangtze River in March 1421, Zheng He headed not for the Indian Ocean but the Pacific and 'discovered' Australia, New Zealand, the Americas, the Arctic and Antarctic, and even rounded Cape Horn a century before Ferdinand Magellan. Whatever the destination, the sixth voyage was the last under the rule of Zhu Di, who died in 1424. The seventh voyage, from 1431 to 1433, would be Zheng He's last; he died in 1435 and China's ventures in ocean-going exploration came to a close, leaving the Portuguese, Dutch and later the French and British to gain mastery over the waters of the world.

A mixed flotilla
These 15th-century prints show the huge variety of vessels that Admiral Zheng He assembled for his voyages. His fleets consisted of up to 100 teak-built junks, each some 300m in length, plus merchant ships and river boats, needing a total crew of up to 30,000 men.

pitted their *drakkar* longships against the might of the Atlantic, most early ships did not venture far from the coast.

Chinese ingenuity

In around the 1st century AD, the Chinese were the first to replace lateral steering-oars with a centrally mounted stern rudder. The oldest-known depiction of this device is on a Han Dynasty terracotta model of a junk.

The square shape of the hulls of Chinese junks, which also had very high sterncastles, made it impossible to use lateral oars. So their shipwrights came up with the solution of mounting a rudder on the centreline of the ship. Although the device took a variety of different forms, it became known generically as the sternpost rudder (even though junks in

fact had no sternpost), because this was the part of the ship to which it was attached. Small boats had a simple, straight rudder, whereas heavier ships were equipped with a wedge-shaped rudder, which flared out at the base away from wooden jaws or sockets that attached it to the vessel's hull. This arrangement meant that Chinese sailors were able to manoeuvre their ships with the minimum of effort. From around the 13th to 15th centuries some junks were fitted with fenestrated rudders (with holes cut in them), which further improved manoeuvrability. This innovation would eventually be adopted in the West in 1901, on a torpedo boat.

The greatest innovation was undoubtedly the movable rudder, which was used both on seagoing junks and smaller river craft. Rather

side of the ship. Although these rudders could move only in a restricted way, they were ideally suited to steering longboats. Then, over the course of the 11th and 12th centuries, the shape of ships began to change, as the stern grew wider and they became broader in the beam. Official seals from the coastal towns of Pevensey in Sussex and Dunwich in Suffolk, dating from the early 13th century, portray clinker-built ships of the Nordic *knarr* type, with high aftercastles (raised areas above the stern) and lateral rudders. Although this type of rudder was moved progressively further forward towards the bow of the ship, it was not up to the task of steering larger vessels.

From the 12th century onwards, on ocean-going ships that plied Atlantic coastal waters from Scandinavia in the north to Portugal in the south, the lateral rudder had begun to be replaced by the centreline rudder, hinged from the sternpost using a pivoting pintle-and-gudgeon arrangement and operated from the deck with a horizontal tiller. The oldest-known depiction of such a vessel is on the font in Winchester Cathedral, dating from the end of the 12th century. City seals from the Baltic cities in the following century attest to the fact that the stern-mounted rudder was widespread there fully 200 years before it was adopted in the Mediterranean. By the 15th century, the caravels of explorers such as Bartolomeu Dias, Vasco da Gama, Columbus and other pioneers of the Age of Discovery, as well as the warships and merchants vessels of the period, were without exception fitted with sternpost rudders.

Universally adopted
Caravels docked at the quayside in Seville on the Guadalquivir River in the 16th century; all display a sternpost rudder.

Working boatmen
Rowers and helmsman, in a sketch by the Italian Baroque artist Annibale Carracci (1560–1609). In reality, the helmsman's job was more strenuous than implied here.

than being mounted on pintles (hinges), movable rudders were suspended over the stern on two ropes attached to a winch. Sailors would raise or lower the rudder by means of cables or chains, according to the depth of the water below them and the displacement caused by the amount of cargo they were carrying.

The changing shape of ships

In the early Middle Ages, ocean-going ships in Europe were based on those that had taken the Vikings across the Atlantic; they were equipped with a single rudder, in the form of a steering oar mounted on the starboard (right)

Vital yet vulnerable

Even so, shipbuilders took a long time to devise a truly robust sternpost rudder. Mishaps were commonplace, with the most serious of these – the total loss of the rudder – leaving a ship at the mercy

THE RUDDER TAKES TO THE SKIES

No sooner had the first balloons been constructed, in the late 18th century, than their intrepid builders were seeking ways to steer them. Early theoretical studies in aeronautics took their vocabulary and methods from maritime navigation, describing the air as a 'fluid' through which the flying machine would glide.

The seminal year of 1784 saw would-be aeronauts attempt a variety of different solutions for steering, using rudders, paddles and sails – with decidedly mixed results. On 2 March, the whole of Paris turned out to watch Jean-Pierre Blanchard lift off from the Champ de Mars aboard his 'flying boat', slung beneath a hydrogen balloon. Seated in the craft's gondola, he energetically operated two sets of oars and a rudder, but failed to convince the onlookers that he was making any headway against the wind in his free-floating balloon. On 11 July that same year, two abbots named Miolan and Janinet failed to get airborne from the Jardin de Luxembourg in their hot-air balloon, which was equipped with a large fin-shaped rudder; enraged by the failure, the disappointed crowd set light to the balloon and destroyed it. Four days later, the Duke of Chartres and the Robert brothers fared somewhat better, but another whole century would elapse before the first true steerable dirigible took to the skies. On 9 August, 1884, the powered airship *La France* of Charles Renard and Arthur Krebs made its maiden flight just outside Paris. The era of aerial navigation had finally dawned.

Beyond control
In a vain attempt to control their craft, the inventors of the first flying machines – such as Jean-Pierre Blanchard (1753–1809), pictured right in his balloon-powered craft, and Guyton de Morveau (1737–1816), whose hydrogen balloon is shown below – tried fitting all kinds of different steering mechanisms, including the stern-mounted rudder.

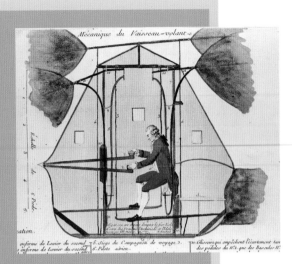

of the waves. If a lateral rudder broke, it was easy to replace, but this was not the case with a stern-mounted rudder – in heavy seas it was almost impossible to mount a new rudder on its pintles (the pins that pivot on the circular gudgeons) and repair the iron fittings.

Broken rudders are common in naval history. Following defeat by the English in 1588, storms maimed many of the fleeing ships of the Spanish Armada; *La Gironda* was one of many that ran aground in Ireland. Her rudder was mended at Killeybegs, only for the ship to be wrecked at Lacanda Point in County Antrim. There are numerous accounts by seafarers and shipowners bemoaning the difficulty of steering ships and the general inadequacy of rudders, especially in heavy seas. A particular problem for shipwrights was how to make rudders large enough to keep pace with the steadily increasing size of vessels.

Steerage methods were another constant source of concern. While most rudders in the 15th and 16th centuries were still powered by human muscle, by the 1600s rudders had grown so large and weighty that a tackle and pulley system was needed. Ultimately, some form of remote-control mechanism had to be devised and the 17th century saw the introduction of the whipstaff, a long rod attached to the tiller to facilitate steering.

Yet steerage still remained far from perfect. In the early 18th century the English invented the ship's wheel, which is still in use today. In 1854, to solve the problem of steering iron steamships which had rudders weighing several tonness, the French engineer Joseph Farcot devised the world's first servo-motor, the prototype of all power-steering mechanisms. This invention finally made rudders reliably responsive to the commands of the helmsman. And so, some 800 years since its adoption in the West, the rudder remains a vital element for the navigation of ships.

Simply effective
The rudder on the replica of the Santa Maria, *Columbus's caravel.*

Sails in the wind

Making its appearance later than the watermill, the windmill was a brilliant invention of medieval times that has remained in use, in different guises, right up to the present day. Harnessing the power of the wind was a formidable challenge; millers exploited lift, a mysterious force that would later play a key role in getting aircraft off the ground.

Prominent features
Set high on hillsides or in flat fenland, windmills have long been a feature of the European landscape. The drawing of a post mill (right) is from a 13th-century manuscript. The line of windmills (bottom) is on the plain of La Mancha in Spain, where the fictional Don Quixote famously tilted at windmills (below).

'Look, your Grace,' said Sancho, ' those things that appear over there are not giants but windmills, and what look like their arms are the sails that are turned by the wind and make the grindstone move.'

'It seems clear to me', replied Don Quixote, 'that you are not at all well-versed in the matter of adventures: these are giants, and if you are afraid, then move aside and start to pray while I enter into fierce and unequal combat with them.'

Almost everyone must be familiar with the comic encounter with windmills in Miguel Cervantes' 1605 novel *Don Quixote*. The episode has even entered the English language, in the phrase 'tilting at windmills'. The actual origins of the windmill itself are far less well known. Although it arrived on the scene much later than its water-driven counterpart, which dates from the end of the 1st century BC, the first windmills were clearly inspired by their tried-and-tested predecessor, since they operated by using drag rather than lift. Although there is a reference to a windmill in Persia as far back as AD 644,

the earliest known windmills date from the 10th century at Seistan in Persia. Such early examples took the form of a roofless brick tower supporting a vertical pole, to which lightweight, vertical sails were attached by horizontal struts. Only the sails on one side of the vertical axis were exposed to the wind at any given time. When the wind hit and turned them, the pressure set in motion a drive shaft attached to a small millstone – around 90cm in diameter – which was used to grind cereals. This type of windmill, known as a panemone, is fixed in one position and so is most suitable for sites where the wind blows constantly from one direction.

Supplementing water power

The first mention of a windmill in Europe is in a Papal Bull of 1105, granting a concession to the abbot of Savigny to build windmills in the Normandy dioceses of Évreux, Coutances and Bayeux. Thereafter windmills spread rapidly throughout western Europe; from the 13th century onwards they are found in every windswept region, from Brittany in France to England, the Low Countries, Denmark and Bohemia. By the 16th century, they had spread as far as Poland and Sweden. Windmills were in practically every location with plenty of wind, where the lack of slopes meant the absence of fast-flowing water, or where watercourses froze in winter, notably in the coastal regions of northern Europe. In an age where the mechanisation of labour was rapidly becoming essential, the windmill and watermill formed an ideal combination within certain clearly defined climatic zones.

A typical medieval windmill comprised four canvas-covered sails in a cruciform arrangement. The sails were mounted on a driving axle supported by a framework which itself pivoted around an upright central post – hence the designation 'post mill' for this type of mill; the entire body of a post mill could turn through 360 degrees. A tailpole fixed to the frame and stretching down to the ground allowed the mill to be rotated by hand to face the prevailing wind.

Setting the sail drive shaft horizontally was the major innovation brought to the technology by western Europeans. (Strictly speaking, the shaft was not exactly horizontal, being inclined at an angle of 10 to 15 degrees.) At the far end of the drive shaft, away from the sails, a wooden gear wheel engaged with a cage gear (or lantern pinion); this converted the force driving the sail shaft into energy for turning a mobile millstone (the 'runner stone') against a fixed base stone (the 'bedstone'), via a vertical axle several metres in length.

While the only motive force driving panemones was direct thrust from the wind,

GENGIS KHAN'S WINDMILLS

When the Mongol conqueror and ruler Genghis Khan (1162–1227) invaded Persia, he was so taken with the windmills there that he had local millers taken back to China to build identical mills there. Windmills are still in widespread use in China today.

Defining landmark of the Low Countries
Classic Dutch landscape paintings often feature a windmill, as in this winter scene by Hendrik Avercamp painted in 1630.

Meudon windmill
In the 1700s this windmill (right), southwest of Paris, was not used for milling grain but to power a water pumping station.

From playthings to power generators
An 18th-century street vendor selling windmills as children's toys (below). Some 200 years later, wind turbines (background) have come of age with the need to reduce the use of fossil fuels and are playing an ever-increasing role in generating electricity.

the post mills built by medieval carpenters employed a practical application of lift. This force, well known to sailors of the period, arose from the difference in pressure exerted by the wind on the front surface of the sail to that (far lesser) exerted on the back. The resulting suction billowed out the sails to create at least as much forward thrust as the actual wind blowing into them. One of the more dangerous parts of a miller's job entailed clambering out along the sails to adjust the canvas to match varying wind strengths.

A shared enterprise

With the exception of a few rare instances, the construction of a windmill in feudal Europe was way beyond the means of peasant farmers. What usually happened was that the local squire would invest in a windmill and then, invoking common law, require all the farmers who worked his estates to have their grain milled there. In return, it was usual for landlords to tax peasants to the tune of one sack of flour in every ten or twelve.

The millstones in a windmill generally weighed around 1.5 tonnes for a 1.5-metre diameter stone (double this for larger stones) and turned at up to 60–80 revolutions per minute. The grinding surfaces wore down over time and would be recut with hammers and chisels, a process known as 'redressing'.

Millers became prominent members of their local communities. They were responsible not only for the upkeep of the mills but also for the safekeeping of the grain entrusted to them, and so they lived *in situ*, set apart from the rest of the community. Millers were in the pay of

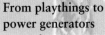

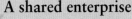

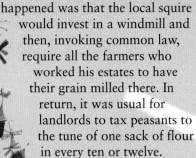

landowners and were not beyond occasionally using brutal methods on farmers to exact payment for their services. Not surprisingly, they were often mistrusted or even hated. Medieval literature usually paints them in vivid colours.

From the 1490s onwards, a rival to the post mill appeared – the tower mill. Not only were tower mills built predominantly of brick or stone, but they also worked in a different way: only the cap – the part to which the sails were attached – moved, rather than the whole structure. On advanced tower mills, the cap rotated by means of a roller and track mechanism installed at the top of the tower. Usually, this system was more rough and ready, with just a thick layer of grease to ease the friction between the cap and the walls.

Symbol of the Netherlands

The ideal test-bed for the development of all types of windmill was the Netherlands. Nowhere else were so many mills concentrated within such a small area. In the 17th century, no fewer than 900 windmills were built along the River Zoon alone. They were used not just for drainage and grinding grain but for all manner of functions, including sawing timber, pressing oil, winding cloth and making paper.

Windmills reached the pinnacle of their development in the 19th century. The simplicity of their construction was much admired (heavy components were easily transported to a site by canal), as was their capacity for powering a whole variety of small pieces of machinery, none requiring more than 3 horsepower (hp). Their efficiency also increased over time. On windmills at the end of the 18th century, it is estimated that 60 per cent of the total 40hp transmitted to the main vertical drive shaft was wasted. A century later, that figure had fallen to 20 per cent, thanks in the main to the combined use of cast iron and wood in the gearing system.

Engineers expended most of their efforts on improving the design of the sails. In Britain, from the late 18th century, canvas sails were

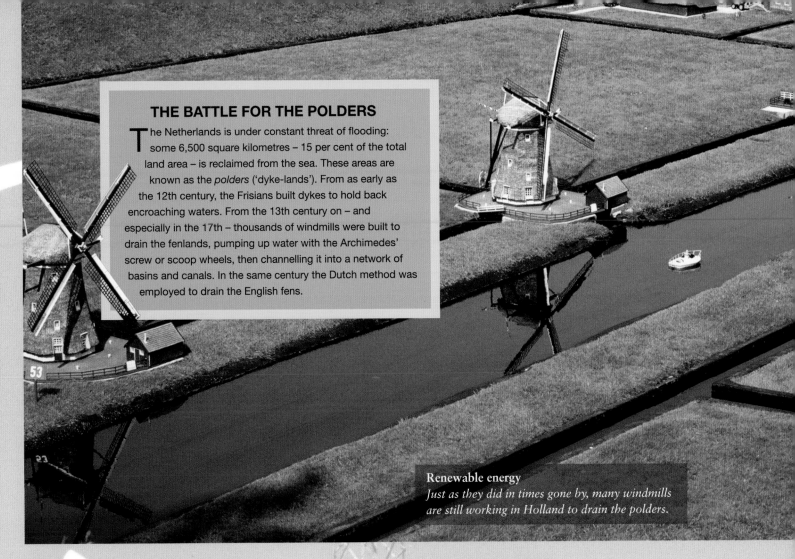

Renewable energy
Just as they did in times gone by, many windmills are still working in Holland to drain the polders.

replaced by wooden shutters; in 1772 the Scottish millwright Andrew Meikle invented the spring sail of parallel wooden slats held shut by springs. When the wind gusted hard, pressure forced the slats open, thus creating less resistance and preventing damage. Spring sails were efficient, but the mill had to be stopped every time a sail needed adjustment. In 1789 English inventor Stephen Hooper introduced roller reefing sails, in which roller blinds took the place of shutters, and he devised a remote control so the blinds could be simultaneously adjusted by means of a chain while the mill was in operation. Further improvements came in 1813 with the patent sails invented by Norfolk civil engineer William Cubitt; these combined the shutters of the spring sail with the automatic adjustment of the roller reefing type. Similarly, the French Berton sails of 1849, with overlapping longitudinal shutters, could be adjusted from inside the mill by a series of levers and pulleys.

Yet for all these innovations, by the beginning of the 20th century the windmill's heyday was past. The growth of steam power followed by the internal combustion engine, and the rise of large industrial flour mills, sounded the death knell for local windmills, which ultimately depended on an intermittent energy source. A few traditional windmills survive as tourist attractions; the Greek Aegean island of Mykonos, for example, is famous for its windmills with their ship-like sails. The windmill also lives on in another guise, typical of the American Midwest: the metal structures with angled vanes called Halladay mills, which are used to pump up groundwater for livestock and irrigation. In recent times, these have been joined by huge wind turbines for electric power generation.

WIND TURBINES – POWER STATIONS OF THE FUTURE?

As a free and inexhaustible source of energy that does not emit heat or harmful greenhouse gases to damage the ozone layer, wind power has huge advantages. Modern utility companies have been keen to exploit that power, erecting a vast and still rapidly growing network of wind turbines. Today, there are already some 400,000 turbines across 40 countries, generating an annual power output in excess of 10,000 megawatts – the equivalent of Denmark's entire yearly energy consumption. In Denmark itself, which pioneered wind power generation, turbines already account for 10 per cent of the country's energy needs. Yet the technology has its limits: even the most optimistic forecasters estimate that at most only about 20 per cent of world energy requirements could be met by wind power.

The Gothic revolution in architecture

The consecration of the new chancel in the Abbey Church of St Denis, just outside Paris, in 1140 marked the beginning of Gothic architecture. The characteristic barrel vaults of the Romanesque style were superseded by cross-ribbed vaults, as builders of great churches and cathedrals vied with one another to create soaring structures full of light and space.

From the moment they set foot in the nave of St Denis, Louis VII and his wife Eleanor of Aquitaine, together with the assembled noblemen of France and the country's five archbishops and 14 bishops, were captivated by the ethereal light that surrounded them. Tinged with blue and red, it flooded in through the stained-glass windows of the ambulatory aisle that encircled the chancel and altar. As the dignitaries shielded their eyes to gaze upwards, the secret behind the amazing light became clear: from the top of the pillars that formed the wall of the ambulatory, arches soared upwards to form a roof the like of which had never been seen before.

In place of the low, heavy, rounded arches of Romanesque churches were lofty arches supported by ribs that rose to cross diagonally at the top of a high, airy vault. The elegance of the structure was only enhanced by the fact that its bare bones were plain for all to see.

Medieval methods
At Guédelon, in the French region of Burgundy, a castle is being constructed today using 13th-century techniques. The photograph above shows the oak framework for a cross-ribbed vault in one of the towers.

Surpassing the Romans

After the end of the first millennium passed without the onset of the expected Apocalypse, a spate of religious building occurred throughout the Christian West as an expression of relief. The prevailing style was Romanesque, which

A BARBARIAN ART FORM?

Gothic architecture spread rapidly from France throughout western Europe, reaching England, Germany, Hungary, Bohemia, Holland and Sweden. Later it was also adopted in Spain and Portugal, while the Crusades even exported it to the Holy Land. Italy withstood the Gothic tide, preferring to hark back to the glories of Byzantine art and its own classical history. The Renaissance painter and writer Giorgio Vasari shunned the technical brilliance and boldness of the Northern style, calling it a 'Barbarian' art form and referring to it disparagingly as 'Gothic'.

Soaring ambition
The techniques pioneered in building the magnificent nave of the Abbey Church of St Denis (left), a masterpiece of Gothic architecture, have echoed down the ages and still influence modern building methods.

Late Gothic
The fan vaulting (above) in the cloisters of Gloucester Cathedral (1337) is a fine example of ornate late Gothic style, known in Britain as the Perpendicular and in France as the Flamboyant.

LOST IN TIME

The origins of the pointed arch are not known, although some experts maintain that its traces can be identified in certain Roman ruins. During the construction of barrel vaults, it is claimed, Roman architects used wooden or brick scaffolds with pointed arches to hold the structures in place; sometimes, these would be left *in situ*, embedded in the masonry and covered with a coat of render.

Load-bearing skeletons

The truly revolutionary aspect of Gothic architecture was to shift the weight of the building away from the curtain walls and instead make the whole masonry skeleton load-bearing. This remarkable innovation was based on the principle of balancing opposing forces: the curved segments of arches meeting on the diagonal, for example, exert an equal force on each other which bore down on the keystone of the vault, thereby locking the whole structure in place. Pointed arches were known as 'ogival', a term coined by Villard de Honnecourt, a 13th-century itinerant master-builder from Picardy. The stone ribbing of these vaults was strong enough to support the entire edifice. Walls become nothing more than infill, which could therefore be punctuated with huge openings for stained-glass windows.

Once the new engineering principles had been adopted, there was nothing to stop vaults rising ever higher. Flying buttresses outside the building helped to counteract the outward thrust of the ribbed vaults and gave lateral support to the walls. Using this method, the builders of the church of St Etienne in Beauvais (1150) raised the roof to a height of 48 metres A thousand years would elapse before architects rediscovered the basic principle behind Gothic architecture: all tall modern buildings are constructed around load-bearing skeletons of steel or reinforced concrete.

Builders' secret formulae

Medieval master-builders showed practical genius in calculating the various loads and stresses that their Gothic cathedrals would need to withstand. They were ably assisted by highly skilled stonemasons, who knew precisely what stone to use for particular tasks. Builders' 'recipes' varied from region to region, so that no two cathedrals were constructed by identical methods. Yet the results are broadly the same: the light and elevated interiors of Gothic cathedrals made for an awesome new sense of communion with God.

recalled the architectural forms of ancient Rome – notably, the simple stone barrel vault or groined vault, formed by the intersection of two barrel vaults. Yet these types of vault put huge lateral pressure on the supporting walls and pillars. To minimise the risk of collapse, the Romans and their successors built vaults of relatively limited spans and massively thick load-bearing walls. Any openings in the walls were narrow. As a result, even the grandest Romanesque buildings – like Durham Cathedral, whose nave is dominated by carved pillars 6.6 metres high – convey an atmosphere of solidity and relative gloom.

The age of the master builder

From the 11th to the 15th century, towns and cities the length and breadth of Europe were home to vast building sites employing a huge range of craftsmen. The soaring cathedrals that arose during this time were engineering marvels incorporating all the latest technical advances. They were above all eloquent testimony to the great piety and prosperity of the age.

Signs and symbols
Villard de Honnecourt's sketch of two flamingos (below) demonstrates his knowledge of Euclidean geometry; the curve of their necks and bodies is an 'aide-memoire' for determining a perfect right angle with a compass and straightedge (through the intersection of two circles).

Marks of a craftsman
A stonemason's tools, and examples of his work, from a window in Chartres Cathedral.

The Cathedral of Our Lady at Amiens in northern France, on which work began in 1218-20, is a prime example of medieval cathedral building. The dean and chapter were responsible for organising the funding and ensuring the supply of building materials. At Amiens they worked closely with Robert de Luzarches, the architect chosen to design and direct the building of the town's new cathedral. One thing was certain from their very first meeting: the cathedral was to be in the new 'Gothic' style pioneered in the Basilica of St Denis near Paris, which had been commissioned by Abbot Suger and completed in 1140. Luzarches would have introduced his plans in a draft made either on parchment or, more likely, on plaster panels. He may even have made a scale model in plaster, wood or stone, like those often seen nowadays in cathedral archives or museums, but any such model for Amiens has long since disappeared.

THE ARCHITECT – LYNCHPIN OF THE BUILDING SITE

By the start of the great age of cathedral building, at the turn of the 11th century, the profession of architect as conceived by the Romans had died out due to a long dearth of major construction projects. Yet the architectural learning of former times had been preserved in religious institutions, and bishops and abbots were the first to help revive the trades of draughtsman and master builder. As building became an ever more complex undertaking, it required the services of professionals – master masons who had learned their trade 'on the job', or scholars who had travelled abroad and studied building techniques. Over time, the profession of architect slowly took shape and won recognition, and the names of some architects were recorded for posterity: at Amiens, for example, the names of Robert de Luzarches, Thomas de Cormont and his son Renaud were engraved into a flagstone in the cathedral precincts.

Applied geometry

Luzarches would have been unaware of the works of the great Roman architect Vitruvius (*c*80–*c*15 BC), whose writings only became widely known in the late Middle Ages. On the other hand, along with other architects of his age, Luzarches did draw upon a long tradition of Euclidean geometry. Evidence of the influence of Euclid, a Greek mathematician of the 1st century BC, can be found in the notebooks of Villard de Honnecourt, a contemporary of Luzarches, who was either (depending on which historian one reads) a talented and well-read amateur or a master builder. Equipped with a compass, a set square and a straightedge, the architect of Amiens Cathedral based his designs on Euclidean figures such as circles, triangles, squares and rectangles. No doubt he also consulted the plans of earlier buildings, possibly including Notre Dame in Paris.

Off the drawing board

The initial ground plans and elevations submitted by Luzarches were basic outline sketches. These were later supplemented with more detailed drawings, sketched on the walls of Luzarches's 'design room' at Amiens, showing the sculptures and colour schemes that he had planned – all medieval churches were richly decorated. Using these working

Medieval church-building
A 15th-century miniature (right) depicts workers constructing a church near Paris.

Heavy lifting
A 15th-century miniature depicting the building of the Tower of Babel shows workers hoisting up masonry blocks with the aid of a crane. The technology was in common use from the early 15th century onwards.

Skilled labour
A medieval builder (bottom) equipped with an axe, hammer and trowel.

sketches as a guide, a specialist contractor called a stone-dresser would then prepare detailed drawings for the master masons, who would cut the various forms in the round (a task known technically as 'stereotomy'). The stone-dresser was responsible for the precise shaping and placement of every carved stone block in the building, and the wooden templates he created determined the profile of complex forms such as plinths or arches.

Coordinating the trades

The architect delegated tasks to the different craftsmen under his command. Quarrymen hewed blocks of stone into manageable-sized chunks. Stonecutters then smoothed these in preparation for masons to precision-fit them into the allotted space. While the stones were being set in place, the walls would be constantly checked with a plumb-line to ensure that they were vertical; spirit levels were used to keep everything straight and level. Gangs of labourers ground and mixed batches of limestone mortar, as and when it was required.

Carpenters would often precede the masons: using pre-cut templates, they erected curved wooden beams as supports for the cupola bricks that formed the ribbed arches of cross vaults. These ingenious timber frames, which joiners could easily dismantle and reassemble, enabled the stonecutters and masons to reproduce identical arches. As well as fashioning all the joists and beams in cathedral roofs, which are held in place by mortice-and-tenon joints without the use of nails, medieval carpenters also made the scaffolding and built wooden cranes. Another key group of workers on site were the blacksmiths, who forged ever more refined and robust tools.

Mechanical aids

The foundations at Amiens are 7 to 8 metres deep and had to be dug the hard way: by armies of manual labourers wielding pickaxes and wooden shovels. On the other hand, medieval builders would never have been able to erect the massive walls, pillars and vaults of their cathedrals – some of which are over 30 metres tall – if mechanical means of lifting stones had not been developed. Principally, medieval engineers devised

THE LABOUR FORCE

Europe's cathedrals were built by skilled artisans, supported by an army of unskilled labourers hired by the day or season (with some extra help from the faithful, who sometimes mucked in). Master craftsmen supervised teams of apprentices and journeymen. The former were usually paid for their work in food and lodgings. The journeymen moved from one site to another as work was available. Wages reflected not only an individual's skills, but also the hierarchy of the various trades: master craftsmen earned more than journeymen; masons and stonecutters were better paid than quarrymen or lime-mixers. Journeymen stonecutters did piecework, scratching the stones they had shaped with their personal mark for the foreman to work out their daily pay. Workers received no pay for days when they were idle, or for long spells in the winter when work was suspended. Craft guilds often lent financial support to members who could not provide for their families during hard times. These 'lodges' also took it upon themselves to ensure that work was of a consistently high standard.

BRINGING THE BIBLE TO LIFE

In an era when most churchgoers were illiterate, Gothic stained glass and sculpture were designed to narrate stories from the Bible in pictures. The artworks were as intrinsic to the design of a cathedral or church as its pillars or arches. The architect and an illustrator would sketch out the stained-glass design. A master glazier then traced it onto a table top whitened with chalk, which gave him the shapes of the glass panels that needed to be cut. The 13th century saw the introduction of grisaille glass, colourless glass on which the motifs were painted with a muted palette of colours made by mixing metal oxides and glass powder.

Sculptors took a rough-hewn block of stone and carefully marked out proportions with a set of dividers before starting to chisel the figure. In several instances, sculptures formed part of a pillar, which would be carved in its entirety in the workshop before being set in position.

Craftsman at work *A stained-glass window in the cathedral of Our Lady of the Assumption in Clermont-Ferrand commemorates the artisan builders.*

ever more efficient cranes and hoists. Some were designed to revolve, and while most were powered by windlasses, those made for lifting heavier loads were operated by treadmill. The largest cranes of the period were capable of lifting more than a tonne. The simple hook to hold the load was replaced with a claw.

Right from the outset, Luzarches had taken care to incorporate spiral staircases and walkways within the thickness of the cathedral walls. These allowed the builders to work high up with greater ease. They also worked on top of counterbalanced scaffolding, which was held fast against the wall by putlogs (wooden pegs sunk into the masonry).

A protracted process

Building a cathedral was a massive investment and a prodigious feat of engineering. No fewer than 22 were built in England between 1040 and 1540, including such masterpieces as Wells, Salisbury and Canterbury cathedrals. The great explosion in church building was driven by religious fervour and facilitated by an economic boom and a huge growth in population which provided the manpower. Yet even with the faithful donating a portion of their wealth, funds occasionally dried up and work was suspended pending the injection of more capital. Construction often dragged on over several decades.

Robert de Luzarches never witnessed the completion of his masterpiece. Thomas de Cormont and his son Renaud picked up the architectural baton after his death. The construction of the main body of Amiens Cathedral was completed in 1288. The towers were not finished until the 15th century.

Gothic glory
The soaring cathedral at Cologne was begun in 1248. Work only came to an end with the completion of the twin openwork spires in 1880.

53

The screw jack c1235

The very first depiction of the jack – a device for lifting heavy loads – is found in a 33-page sketchbook compiled by the master builder and engineer Villard de Honnecourt in around 1235. At the height of the 'Golden Age' of Gothic architecture, Villard visited a number of cathedral building sites with an eye to making a set of technical drawings for master builders. These included sketches of the new machines and devices that were being used by joiners. The screw jack consisted of a long screw turned by a capstan, which raised or lowered a nut

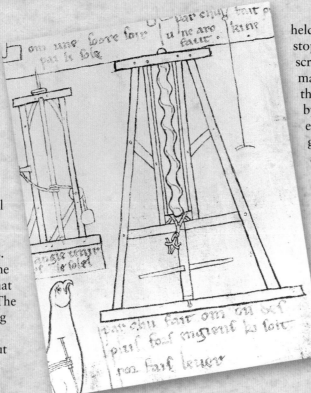

held in place by two upright poles to stop it from simply rotating with the screw. The use of the screw principle made the screw jack more powerful than comparable machines operated by levers. The jack was widely employed in cranes and other lifting gear. This is still the case today, although hydraulics have replaced mechanical systems. The most familiar tool to employ the screw-jack principle is the car jack: the force lifting the car is 50 times greater than the effort expended by the person operating the jack.

Medieval master
A drawing of a screw-jack from the sketchbook of Villard de Honnecourt, a specialist in the civil engineering equipment of the day.

Tin plate c1250

Tin plate, an alloy of steel and tin, is thought to have been first produced in Bohemia in the 13th century. The process remained a closely guarded secret for centuries: it entailed using acid to strip away thin sheets of iron, which were then dipped in a bath of molten tin. Because of the difficulties of making sheets that were thin and flat enough, and then coating them with a layer of tin that was sufficiently durable, tin plate was at first the preserve of luxury items and wealthy clients. Then gradually, as production methods improved, it began to replace tin, wood and pottery across a range of goods, including household items, farming implements, weapons and toys. Eventually, the manufacture of tin plate spread west; factories were established in Saxony in the early 1600s, and by the second half of that century plants had been set up in France, with royal assent, around the town of Nevers and in Normany. The mines of Cornwall gave England a virtual monopoly of the world's tin supply up to the end of the 19th century, when the advent of food canning saw tin plate production develop on an industrial scale worldwide. Today, millions of cans and tins for foodstuffs are still produced annually, using a base of steel coated with tin or chrome by electrolysis.

Put to new use
Tin plate is cheap and widely available; old cans are often recycled into homemade toys in the developing world, like this truck, the proud possession of a young African boy.

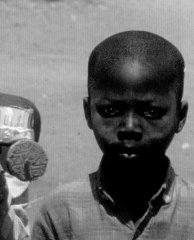
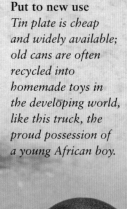

Shoes c1250

French chic
A high-heeled ladies' fashion shoe from the late 17th century.

Poulaines – long, pointed shoes that the Crusaders were reputed to have brought back from the East – became all the rage in western Europe in the 13th century. Yet such modish, impractical garb was firmly the preserve of the wealthy. For people working in the fields, which was by far the majority at that time, the most appropriate footwear was an old pair of sandals in summer and in winter leather boots worn inside wooden overshoes, or clogs, to protect them from the mud.

By the 16th century fashionable trendsetters were sporting wide-toed shoes in preference to pointed ones. When heels arrived on the scene – again from the East – shoe styles became even more outrageous. Ladies wore chopines (a high platform shoe originally from Venice) or court shoes, with a convex heel tucked under the arch to make the feet appear daintier. Heels made the going difficult on rough, unpaved streets, giving rise to the walking stick as an accessory to help people to keep their balance. By now the shoe was established as a high-fashion item, appearing in a range of colours and embellished with ribbons, rosettes, buckles and other fripperies.

Curiously, throughout the Middle Ages, there was no distinction between left and right shoes. Separate lasts for left and right were only introduced in around 1820.

Status symbols
In the Middle Ages, only a few privileged people wore 'heuse', high soft leather shoes that were the forerunners of boots. Much more common were crackowes, pointed slippers that first appeared in the 12th century.

The spinning wheel c1270

The spinning wheel was widespread in China, India and Persia by the late 13th century. It could produce yarn five times faster than the spindle and distaff. By the Middle Ages the textile industry was in full swing, not only supplying a general demand for more sophisticated garments, but also turning out acres of sailcloth for ships. Productivity had to keep improving, even at the cost of quality. The spinning wheel – first documented in the West in 1280, in guild records from Speyer, Germany – processed wool, linen and cotton with equal ease. It is still in use today in many parts of South America, Africa and Asia.

Cottage industry
Crank-driven spoked-wheel spinning-wheels like this one were widely used up to the 17th century.

TWO KINDS OF WHEEL

The large diameter spinning wheel or 'great wheel', an improved version of the traditional spindle, was almost certainly brought to Europe in the 13th century by the Moors of Spain. Yet there was also the treadle wheel, a European invention first mentioned in 1480. This had two driven pulleys, one for the spindle, the other for the 'flyer' that spun around the spindle, keeping the yarn taut. This technical innovation greatly increased the rate of output.

55

SPECTACLES – *c*1280

A clear view of the world

The great Roman orator Cicero (106–43 BC) once complained in a letter that, as his sight grew worse with advancing years, he was forced to have his slaves read aloud to him. Eye problems are as old as humanity, but it was the 13th century before help for fading eyesight finally arrived in the form of spectacles.

Early spectacles
Wood-framed, centrally pivoted eyeglasses such as this reproduction of a German model of c1350 (above), were known as 'rivet spectacles'.

Sign of a scholar
The portrait of Cardinal Hugh of Provence (above right) was made in 1352 and is the earliest known depiction of eyeglasses. It demonstrates the strong association that has existed from the earliest times between spectacles and scholarship.

'I am so debilitated by age that without the glasses known as "spectacles" I would no longer be able to read or write. These have recently been invented for the benefit of poor old people whose sight has become weak.' So wrote Sandro di Popozo of Florence in his *Treatise on Family Management* in 1289. This citation helps us to date the introduction of eyeglasses, which appeared at around the same time in Italy and China, in the final decades of the 13th century.

By that time, people had known about the magnifying power of lenses for many centuries. Rock-crystal lenses dating from around 4000 BC and found in the ruins of Nineveh are thought to have been 'burning-glasses' used to focus the sun's rays. Much later, the Roman philosopher Seneca (*c*4 BC–AD 65) observed that looking through a globe filled with water had a pronounced magnifying effect. Likewise – although he apparently drew no practical conclusions from the knowledge – the *Book of Optics* by the Arab physician and philosopher Alhazen (965–1039) gave clear descriptions of the eye, the phenomenon of refraction and various types of convex lenses. It is tempting to imagine

medieval monks, whose vocation brought them into regular contact with the written word, fashioning for themselves so-called 'reading-stones' out of rock-crystal or beryl, long before the English scientist Roger Bacon presented conclusive scientific proof in 1268 that glass shaped in a particular way could help people to read tiny characters better.

Help for the long-sighted …

Although Bacon (or 'Doctor Mirabilis', as he was popularly known) is credited with many remarkable inventions, the very earliest glasses – 'rivet spectacles' made of two lenses mounted in circular wooden, leather or iron discs that pivoted around a central rivet – probably predated him. These devices could be adjusted to fit the wearer's nose, and were held up to the face by a stick attached to the side of the frame. In English they were usually called 'eyeglasses', for obvious reasons, while the old French term 'besicles' and the modern German word 'Brille' both point to the fact that the lenses were frequently made from the mineral beryl (Latin *berillus*). Fitted with convex lenses, these were only suitable for long-sighted (hypermetropic) people and soon became widespread as reading aids among churchmen, scholars and doctors. The earliest-known depiction of spectacles appears in the portrait of Cardinal Hugh of Provence in frescoes painted in 1352 by Tommaso da Modena in the chapter house of San Nicolò Monastery, Treviso. Not only did rivet spectacles have extremely limited corrective properties, at this stage they were very much a luxury item, as the lenses had to be painstakingly ground and polished from expensive raw materials.

From the mid 15th century, the demand for spectacles increased exponentially due to the invention of the printing press and the resulting spread of the written word. The great glassmaking centres of Europe, such as Venice and Nuremberg, began to mass produce glass lenses and as a result spectacle ownership trickled down the social scale. At the same time, frames became lighter through the use of animal horn and bone, while spring-loaded mechanisms were devised to help spectacles grip the bridge of the nose.

NERO'S MONOCLE

In his *Natural History*, the Roman writer Pliny the Elder (AD 23–79) claimed: 'For the eye, there is no more agreeable colour than emerald. Indeed, stonecutters who work fine gemstones find that it is the only stone they can gaze upon without tiring their eyes.' Pliny recorded that Emperor Nero, who was short-sighted, used to watch gladiators fighting in the arena through a kind of monocle made from either emerald or beryl.

... and for the short-sighted

Even so, the simple hand-held magnifying lens was still a common sight: Raphael's 1517 portrait of Pope Leo X, for example, shows the pontiff clutching not a pair of eyeglasses but a magnifying glass fitted with a concave lens to correct short-sightedness (myopia). This important development in lens technology had begun the previous century, as indicated in the painting *Madonna and Child* by Flemish artist Jan van Eyck. Canon Joris van der Paele is depicted in the painting holding a pair of eyeglasses; the distortion of the text showing through them shows that they are fitted with concave lenses.

Clerical eyewear
This detail (right) from Jan van Eyck's Madonna and Child *of 1436 is an early depiction of spectacles.*

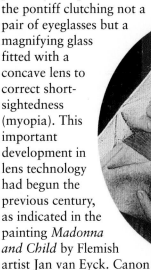

Improving frames

Groundbreaking discoveries by scientists such as Giambattista della Porta (*c*1535–1616) and Johannes Kepler (1571–1630) led to the introduction of the refracting telescope and the *camera obscura*. Yet for all the outstanding advances in optical technology in this period, spectacle lenses continued to be made from inferior glass that refracted light unevenly. Most improvements concerned new ways of holding spectacles in place. From the 17th to the 18th century, various methods were tried, including straps tied at the back of the head, strings that

Under scrutiny
A detail from a 16th-century painting showing a treasurer in one of Europe's growing cities using a pince-nez to help him to see his accounts.

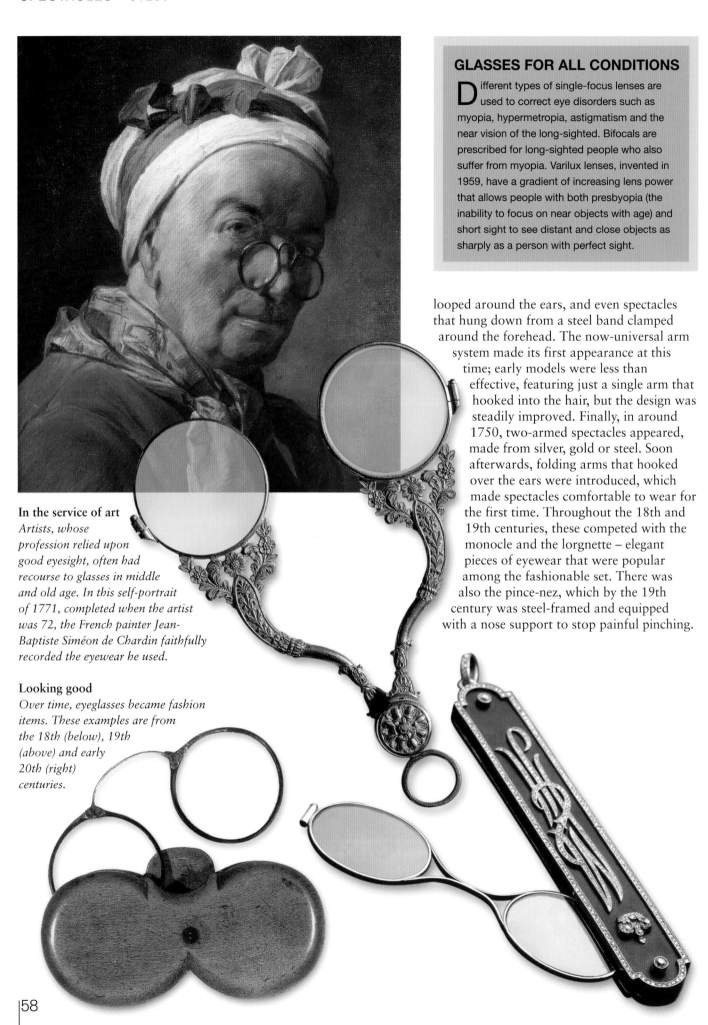

In the service of art
Artists, whose profession relied upon good eyesight, often had recourse to glasses in middle and old age. In this self-portrait of 1771, completed when the artist was 72, the French painter Jean-Baptiste Siméon de Chardin faithfully recorded the eyewear he used.

Looking good
Over time, eyeglasses became fashion items. These examples are from the 18th (below), 19th (above) and early 20th (right) centuries.

looped around the ears, and even spectacles that hung down from a steel band clamped around the forehead. The now-universal arm system made its first appearance at this time; early models were less than effective, featuring just a single arm that hooked into the hair, but the design was steadily improved. Finally, in around 1750, two-armed spectacles appeared, made from silver, gold or steel. Soon afterwards, folding arms that hooked over the ears were introduced, which made spectacles comfortable to wear for the first time. Throughout the 18th and 19th centuries, these competed with the monocle and the lorgnette – elegant pieces of eyewear that were popular among the fashionable set. There was also the pince-nez, which by the 19th century was steel-framed and equipped with a nose support to stop painful pinching.

A BRIEF HISTORY OF CONTACT LENSES

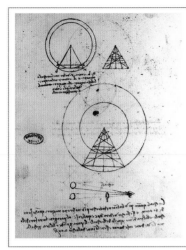

As early as the 16th century, Leonardo da Vinci speculated on the possibility of correcting vision by placing a lens directly on the eye. The first real attempt to produce a contact lens came in 1827, when the British astronomer Sir John Herschel began experiments to correct astigmatism with a lens shaped to fit exactly on the surface of the eyeball. Sixty years later,

Early optics
Sketches of the optical functions of the eye from the notebooks of Leonardo da Vinci.

Herschel's ideas inspired the Swiss physiologist Adolf Eugen Fick to make glass contact lenses. They were cumbersome affairs of thick brown glass that covered almost the entire white of the eye. It was only after the Second World War that scientists devised the first comfortable contact lenses covering just the cornea. There is now a wide range of lenses, hard and soft, made from plastic and gas-permeable (to allow oxygen to the eye), along with disposable daily-use lenses and even lenses made from a water-based silicon gel that can be worn day and night for a month.

Advances in lens technology

American statesman and inventor Benjamin Franklin (1706–90), who with increasing age was both short-sighted and long-sighted, is traditionally credited with inventing bifocals. In the early 1760s he hit upon the idea of combining the lenses from the two pairs of glasses that he used in a single frame. In the course of the 19th century, the science of optics advanced in leaps and bounds: in 1807, for example, the English scientist Thomas Young discovered the causes of astigmatism, paving the way for the manufacture of glasses with cylindrical lenses (which have different radii of curvature in different planes). The French ophthalmologist Louis Émile Javal (1839–1907) invented the keratometer for measuring astigmatism, and the German physician Hermann von Helmholtz (1821–94) put forward theories explaining both the accommodation reflex of the eye and colour vision.

Glasses to suit everyone

The 20th century brought further innovation. In 1932 the first anatomically shaped frames were introduced, curved to cover the entire field of vision, including peripheral vision to the side and downwards. These were far more effective than the simple round or square frames previously available. After the Second World War new materials such as plastics and cellulose acetate began to be used for spectacle frames. Intensive research into improving the refractive index of lenses led to the introduction, in the 1960s, of organic lenses, which increasingly began to supplant

lenses made from mineral glass, which were very fragile. Nowadays, polycarbonate lenses – thinner and lighter than classic organic lenses and offering maximum protection against UV light – are often used for sunglasses, as are Polaroid lenses. Despite competition from contact lenses, two centuries and more after spectacles first became commonplace they remain extremely popular and are now available in a huge variety of frames, tailored to suit the shape of the wearer's face, their age and individual requirements.

Bringing things into focus
A 17th-century painting of the Mannerist school depicts an elderly woman peering through her pince-nez at a young street musician.

ROGER BACON – c1214 TO c1294

The original Renaissance Man

Great changes were afoot in 13th-century Europe, as the lure of the towns began radically to reshape society. In particular, the growth of cathedral schools, with their curriculum of the 'seven liberal arts' – grammar, astronomy, rhetoric, logic, arithmetic, geometry and music – helped to foster a dynamic new atmosphere of scientific enquiry. The English scholar Roger Bacon epitomised the innovative spirit of the age, yet his lengthy imprisonment also illustrated the inherent danger of free thinking in a society still dominated by the Church.

Roger Bacon was born at Ilchester in Somerset in around 1214, the son of a noble family that had fallen on hard times. The young Roger was blessed with an innate curiosity and strong critical faculties; he went up to Oxford at the tender age of 13 to study logic and natural philosophy. He embarked on an academic career in around 1237–40 and became a Master of Arts, teaching both in Paris and at Oxford.

While there was no doubting Bacon's knowledge and persuasiveness as a lecturer, many of the ideas he expounded had a strong whiff of heresy about them. While still a student at Oxford, he had been a zealous disciple of the reforming theologian Robert Grosseteste, and in Paris he consorted with the scholar Petrus Peregrinus de Maricourt, who was accused of practising alchemy. Bacon was duly banned from publishing his works, suspended from the Franciscan Order (he had become a Friar in 1256) and placed under house arrest in Paris in 1278 on a charge of promulgating 'suspected novelties'. Some believe that he remained imprisoned right up to his death sometime around 1292–94, but recent scholarship claims that he returned to Oxford c1280.

Earth science

The Earth's magnetic field, one of Roger Bacon's main preoccupations, had long fascinated other cultures, especially the Chinese. This 19th-century geomantic compass (above) was used in the practice of feng shui, *used by the Chinese to divine the flow of currents and spirits in and on the Earth.*

In pursuit of unity

The keynote of Bacon's life and work was his unquenchable urge to establish a sense of coherence and unity. Actual errors bothered him far less than inconsistencies of reasoning. As a devout Christian, he refused to entertain the idea that a line of thought might end up refuting Holy Scripture, which for Bacon remained the final arbiter of all things. But equally he respected the teachings of the ancient masters and the Arab authors whose translations and commentaries had first made ancient wisdom known to the West. He set himself the task of rereading these texts in their original languages, which entailed learning Hebrew, Greek and Arabic. In the process, he carefully noted all the contradictions in the writings of the early Church Fathers, as well as errors in the works of Aristotle, Avicenna and Averroes. His aim was not to take issue with them; on the contrary, his aim was to piece together a frame of reference within which each was workable and to tease out the fundamental points of agreement between them.

The guiding principle that Bacon clung to was that there could only be a single truth, a unified focus of all learning, since truth was ordained by God; the same principle applied to

---

PETRUS PEREGRINUS DE MARICOURT

It is known that de Maricourt tutored the young Roger Bacon and was probably responsible for initiating him into the arts of alchemy, but beyond that details of the man and his life are scant. An outstanding thinker, de Maricourt is known mainly from his writing: in 1269 he produced a treatise on magnetism, called the *Epistola de magnete* ('A letter on the magnet'). This set out for the first time the fundamental laws of magnetism, namely that like poles repel and opposite poles attract. De Maricourt also advanced a theory on the Earth's magnetism, based on experience, and outlined a plan for a perpetual motion machine driven by the alternate attraction and repulsion of a lodestone.

intellectual enquiry, given that the human mind was a God-given faculty. Thus, he argued, theology remained the highest branch of learning and the exercise of reason – that is, the practical application of the intellect – was bound to establish unity. It was through reason that a person came to understand the truth, while the rigour of scholarship was determined by the use of mathematics, the 'innate' tool of reason. The basic principle of inductive reasoning that informs all modern scientific enquiry is already evident in Bacon's critical method.

Bringing enlightenment

While Bacon's search for the truth was driven by his thirst for knowledge, his mainspring was critical reasoning. He took a very modern approach, subjecting everything – references, sources and texts – to the cold light of criticism. But for his day, it was a radical step for him to question certain aspects of the Biblical text in current use at the University of Paris, or to cast doubt on syllogism, the deductive mode of reasoning that prevailed among 13th-century scholars.

Bacon never saw criticism as an end in itself. Rather, he used it as a foil against the unquestioning acceptance of authority. His targets were prejudices, *a priori* thinking, received ideas and pseudoscience – in short, the 'ideology of concealment' practised by those opposed to enlightenment. The tools that he employed in his critical method were the analysis and study of original texts and, in reasoning, mathematics.

Astrology and alchemy

Given the insistence upon intellectual rigour and rationality that runs through Bacon's works, it comes as something of a shock to the modern reader to discover his interest in astrology and alchemy. Yet his attitude towards these 'magical' disciplines was far from one of naïve credulity. He simply saw them as potentially valuable modes of enquiry, while keeping himself firmly grounded in reality. The authorities at the time failed to grasp such subtleties. It was an

Occult practices
Alchemy and astrology, forerunners of chemistry and astronomy, were important academic disciplines in Bacon's day. He would have been familiar with an athanor (above), a type of furnace used by alchemists, and the zodiac wheel (top). The manuscript illustration (left) shows an alchemist instructing his apprentice.

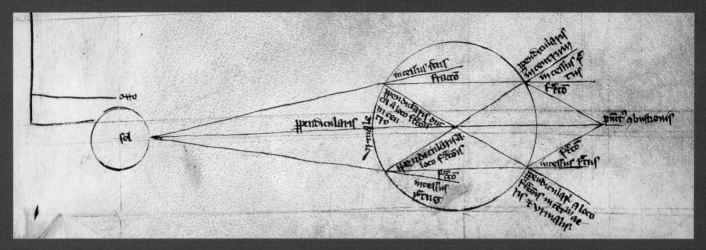

Experiments with lenses

A diagram from Bacon's Opus majus, *demonstrating how a magnifying glass works. The drawing shows rays of light coming from the Sun (on the left, labelled 'Sol') and passing through a spherical glass container filled with water. The sphere acts as a lens, refracting the rays of light and bringing them to a focal point (on the right).*

extremely bold, some would say foolhardy, move of Bacon's to edit the *Speculum astronomiae* in 1278, a work that attempted to show how the position of the stars had a direct bearing on human behaviour. Bacon persisted with this enterprise even though the Archbishop of Paris was about to issue a condemnation of astrology.

Yet the fact remains that his work on astrology yielded some extremely important findings for Bacon. For instance, it helped him to understand the precession of equinoxes, which in turn alerted him to the flaws in the Julian calendar that was then in common use. Morever, his work on the planets gave him an insight into the phenomenon of the tides, while his patient observation of the heavens benefited his research into optics, which was to advance people's understanding of the workings of the eye, vision and the use of artificial lenses. Bacon had all the requisite knowledge to have conceived and even constructed the first microscope or telescope. As for the dark and mysterious 'science' of alchemy, his involvement in it was confined to what we would nowadays call chemistry. He was the first person in the West, for example, to give the precise formula for making gunpowder.

THE BRILLIANT BACONS

Roger Bacon is sometimes confused with the Elizabethan statesman, jurist, historian and philosopher Francis Bacon (1561–1626). The two are completely unrelated, although by a remarkable coincidence the later Bacon was also a leading advocate in his day of a fresh approach to the sciences and philosophy, characterised by inductive reasoning.

The primacy of experience

Bacon was adamant that the only legitimate basis of knowledge was experience. On this key point, he once again drew heavily on the work on optics and magnetism by his early tutor de Maricourt, who first fired his enthusiasm for observation.

'I don't ask you to believe me unless you have first experienced something for yourself', wrote Bacon in 1266, before going on to explain the role of experience in people's acquisition of knowledge. 'We have three modes of understanding: through authority, experience and reasoning; however, authority does not deign to reveal to us the reasoning behind what it asserts to be true … reasoning, on the other hand, cannot distinguish between sophism [an illogical argument] and genuine proof unless and until its conclusions have been verified by experience.'

In his rigorous application of the scientific method, Bacon was a precursor of the quintessential Renaissance Man, Leonardo da Vinci. Like da Vinci, Bacon speculated on the possibility of making self-propelled vehicles (literally, 'automobiles') and various strange flying machines.

'Doctor Mirabilis'

Philosopher, theologian, scholar, inventor, physician, astronomer, astrologer, alchemist. It is hard to know which of Bacon's many roles earned him the posthumous title of Doctor Mirabilis ('wonderful teacher'). First and foremost, he was a pioneer, a rebellious spirit who opened up new paths for later scholars.

While many of his works have come down to us only in fragmentary form, they clearly show that he had an inquisitive mind keen to explore every field of learning. In 1266, he sent a letter to Pope Clement IV arguing for more experimentation in the scientific curriculum and proposing a universal encyclopaedia of knowledge. The pontiff took this to mean that

the work was already finished and asked Bacon to bring it to him. Bacon immediately set to work and in an astonishingly short space of time composed an encyclopaedia in three volumes – the *Opus majus*, *Opus minus* and *Opus tertium*. The synopses that he sent to the Pope covered such diverse topics as the causes of human ignorance; the relationship between philosophy and theology; languages; mathematics and applied mathematics; optics; alchemy; geography; astronomy; and the role of experiment in science. The death of Clement IV in 1268 was a cruel blow to Bacon, though he continued to work on his encyclopaedia.

Ultimately, the old argument about what Bacon personally invented is of little consequence. His key legacy is that he laid the groundwork for experimentation and invention. In an era of medieval scholasticism, his radical thinking prefigured the Renaissance and his place in the history of science ranks alongside that of Kepler, Newton and Galileo.

Dangers of experimentation
A fanciful 19th-century print shows Bacon experimenting with gunpowder (top). In his alchemical experiments Bacon would have used a still like this one (right), known as an alembic.

A PERSISTENT MYTH

A long-running legend maintains that Roger Bacon was the inventor of gunpowder. Although he did experiment in this field, letting off large explosions, most scholars nowadays think that he obtained firecrackers from the first Christian missionaries to visit China, from which he worked out the formula for gunpowder in around 1242.

THE CANNON – c1300

New arms for new wars

With its power to hurl projectiles over great distances, the cannon completely revolutionised warfare. From the first primitive muzzle-loaders to modern artillery pieces, the materials from which cannons were made have continually evolved, steadily extending the limits of their destructive power.

Siege bombardment
The squat bombard, precursor of the cannon, fired stone balls weighing anything from 50 to 500 kilos.

On 14 April, 1450, King Charles VII of France, enraged by the continuing English occupation of Normandy, began the siege of Caen. The governor of the city, the Duke of Somerset, sent for reinforcements from across the Channel. A force of 4,500 men was immediately dispatched, commanded by Sir Thomas Kyriel, but on arrival they were halted by the army of the Count of Clermont at Formigny, between Caen and Tréguier.

Kyriel thought he could engage the enemy according to tried-and-tested rules of combat. He ordered his archers to fire a few salvoes to clear some ground, into which the lancers would charge, followed by the cavalry. Clermont had other ideas. Loading two cannons that he had brought to the battlefield, he directed withering fire on the English camp. The French then attacked. Kyriel's force suffered heavy losses, and in no time Normandy was taken by the French. Three years later, another French victory at the Battle of

Routing the enemy
Artillery firepower helped the citizens of Ghent to defeat a French army led by Count Louis of Flanders in May 1382.

Castillon in the Dordogne brought the Hundred Years' War to an end. The victory had been set in train by just two examples of the new wonder weapon: the cannon.

A revolution in propulsion

In his *Treatise on Combustion*, since lost, Archimedes is believed to have been the first to broach the idea of using a tube to fire a stone ball. Leonardo da Vinci, who was familiar with the work, even claimed that Archimedes had built a copper cannon called the 'Architonnerre', which used steam pressure to fire a cannonball. Leonardo's account is probably fanciful. A far more likely source for the genesis of the cannon is the wealth of experience that European armies had acquired since ancient times in operating ever more powerful siege engines that worked on the principle of the slingshot – namely, the catapults and ballistas of the Romans, and later the mangonels and trebuchets of the early Middle Ages. Armourers would naturally have sought to develop new weapons capable of hurling projectiles ever further and with greater destructive force.

Their efforts only really bore fruit with the introduction of gunpowder, which had been invented in China and brought to Europe by the Moors in the 13th century. Once ignited gunpowder released gases into the gun breech, creating the pressure required to eject a projectile with great force, without any need for the complex systems of winches, counterweights, springs and ropes that characterised traditional siege engines.

SPECIALISTS IN GUNNERY

The term 'artillery', coined in the 13th century by the chronicler Jean de Joinville to denote the panoply of siege engines, comes from the Old French verb *atillier* – 'to arm'. Over time, it came to be applied to the branch of an army that specialised in operating cannons, which at first were used in siege warfare. Light, mobile field artillery was pioneered in the 17th century by the King Gustavus Adolphus II of Sweden, especially the use of canister shot against infantry. Heavy artillery played a key role in the trench warfare of the First World War, as Allied forces devised the 'creeping barrage', behind which the infantry steadily advanced.

Varied design

The first cannon to appear in Europe can still be seen at the Tower of London; it dates from 1288 and is of Chinese manufacture. Made of cast iron, it is precisely 99.06 centimetres long with a calibre of 28mm. It was apparently brought to Europe in the days of the Mongol conquests by a man named Ch'I Wu Wen. It is not the only type of early Chinese cannon. They are also known to have developed a squat weapon, similar to the bombard, in the 14th century along with another type of cannon mounted on four wheels. The close resemblance between the heavy guns that soon started to appear throughout Europe and the Chinese cannon suggests that original Eastern models were copied and steadily improved by German, Italian and French armourers.

The diversity in the manufacture of guns thereafter makes it impossible to establish a precise chronology of how this technology spread. Among the many types of cannon used in the Middle Ages, the most common included the field culverin, a light artillery piece that was supported on a fork stuck in the ground, and various related carriage-less guns, all of which were carried around on carts along with barrels of gunpowder. The bombard was a short-barrelled, small-calibre weapon that rested on a wooden plinth. The veuglaire had a barrel that was open at both the muzzle and the breech, at one end of which was fixed a box containing the powder charge

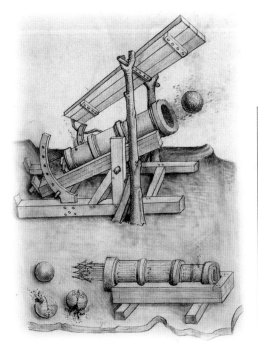

Joint operations
A 14th-century illustration shows a combined infantry and artillery assault on a moated town.

Dead-end
The arrow-firing cannon (left, bottom), invented in the 15th century, was a short-lived experiment, unlike the more conventional ball-firing weapon depicted above it.

THE PARADOX OF THE POT-DE-FER

The English defeat at the Battle of Formigny is the more surprising because, over 100 years earlier, King Edward III had deployed a primitive type of cannon in his victory over the French at the Battle of Crécy (1346). The weapon resembled a bulbous iron bottle with a narrow neck and was known as a 'pot-de-fer'; Edward had five at his disposal. The vessel was filled with gunpowder then a large stone ball was wedged in the neck. The powder was lit through a small touch-hole, and the resulting explosion would hurl the ball around 100 metres. The pot-de-fer, which was more of an 'erupter' than a true cannon, had its drawbacks: even when it did not explode and kill the operator, it was difficult to ignite the powder if it was windy or raining. Over time, the design was improved by the Genoese and the French, using Chinese know-how.

and projectile. Although the barrels of some early cannons were cast from a single piece of bronze (the first such gun in Europe was forged in Augsburg in 1378), those of small-calibre weapons tended to be made from a bundle of wrought-iron rods bound with iron straps, like the staves and rings of a wooden barrel. Projectiles included cannonballs of stone or iron and even, early on, flaming arrows.

New materials, new projectiles

The late 1400s saw a series of improvements in gun technology that produced more mobile, reliable and deadly artillery pieces. Advances in

Battlefield mobility
The 17th-century field howitzer below already represented a move towards the concept of light artillery. The illustration of 1529 (bottom) shows a bombardier, shielded behind wooden ramparts, firing a vertical cannon, the forerunner of the mortar. By the 16th century, the Ottoman army was deploying ranks of cannon (right).

metal casting led to the introduction of safe muzzle-loaded cannons made from cast iron in 1508–9; earlier attempts at making cast-iron cannon had ended in disaster, as flawed castings exploded on firing, shattering the barrel into deadly fragments. Iron cannon were more robust and cheaper to produce than copper, brass or bronze barrels. At the same time, greater mobility was achieved by mounting guns on wheeled carriages. Munitions also became more effective through the universal use of metal shot, as well as the introduction of exploding shells, which sprayed a wide area with fragments, and grapeshot – a mass of small metal balls contained in a canvas bag or metal cylinder.

In search of greater accuracy

During this same period, the elevation of artillery was improved by placing wooden wedges underneath the breech-block;

advances in ballistics from the 16th century onwards enabled gunners to work out optimal firing trajectories. Meanwhile, standardised manufacturing methods began to turn out cannonballs of uniform size, whose weight determined the calibre of early guns.

Because of their long barrels and light construction, and their ability to fire round shot at long ranges over a flat trajectory, cannon became crucial weapons in naval warfare. One of the first ships able to fire a full cannon broadside was the English carrack the *Mary Rose*, which was equipped with 78 guns when completed in 1510, increased to 91 after an upgrade in 1536.

By the 1570s, all the armies of Europe had a full arsenal of artillery pieces, including mortars that lobbed shells in a high arc and huge siege guns operated by several hundred men apiece. From the 17th century there was a general trend towards the Swedish model of lighter artillery pieces with shorter barrels;

even so, a debate continued over the strategic deployment of artillery, between on the one hand advocates of mobility and on the other sheer firepower. In the 18th century, the use of artillery was rationalised as gunnery divisions became autonomous units within armies. The extensive use of light artillery was the brainchild of Frederick II (the 'Great'), of Prussia (1740–86). Around the same time, ordnance reforms by the French Lieutenant Jean-Baptiste de Gribeauval produced a new breed of light, robust guns. These were fitted with tangent scales, breech devices that allowed better sighting, elevation and aim. Gribeauval also devised the first shells filled with musket balls, an idea later picked up and improved upon by the British artillery officer Henry Shrapnel in 1803.

An indispensable tactical weapon

After 1850 the rise of heavy industry sparked a fresh revolution in artillery technology. The most significant change was the introduction of rifled gun barrels. Rather than having smooth barrels, the interiors of these cannon were made in a helical pattern which imparted spin to the cannon ball, improving both range and accuracy. Other developments included the universal adoption of breech-loading mechanisms; a solution to the problem of recoil by the addition of a hydraulic brake (fitted most famously on the French 75mm field gun, introduced in 1897); and the appearance of new types of munitions, such as fused or exploding shells. Artillery had become a fearsome part of every army's arsenal.

Hand-held cannons
Devised in the 15th century, these portable weapons were hybrids combining features of the arquebus and musket.

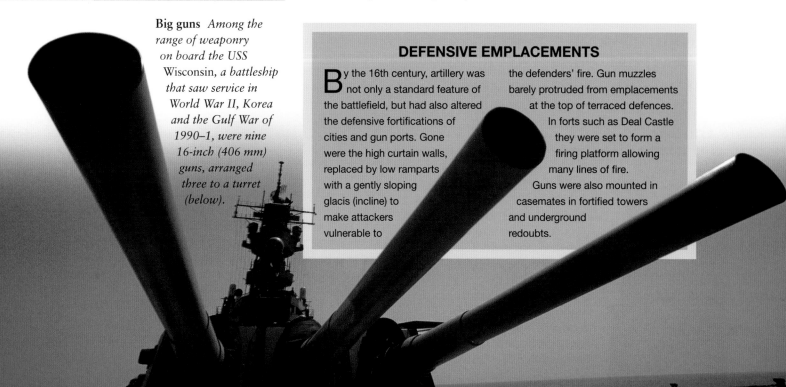

Big guns *Among the range of weaponry on board the USS Wisconsin, a battleship that saw service in World War II, Korea and the Gulf War of 1990–1, were nine 16-inch (406 mm) guns, arranged three to a turret (below).*

DEFENSIVE EMPLACEMENTS

By the 16th century, artillery was not only a standard feature of the battlefield, but had also altered the defensive fortifications of cities and gun ports. Gone were the high curtain walls, replaced by low ramparts with a gently sloping glacis (incline) to make attackers vulnerable to the defenders' fire. Gun muzzles barely protruded from emplacements at the top of terraced defences. In forts such as Deal Castle they were set to form a firing platform allowing many lines of fire.

Guns were also mounted in casemates in fortified towers and underground redoubts.

Democratising time

Originally, clocks were used to mark the canonical hours and to call religious communities to prayer, but once installed in towers and belfries in cities, clocks took on a whole new role. Starting out as little more than novelty items, they soon began to perform a real public service. Thanks to the clock, telling and keeping the time became accessible to everyone.

In 1335 Galvano Fiamma, a Dominican friar and chronicler of the city of Milan, wrote a description of the clock in the campanile of the church of San Gottardo. He was particularly impressed by the way it marked the passage of time at regular intervals throughout the day and night: 'There is a very large clapper which strikes a bell 24 times according to the 24 hours of the day and night, and thus at the first hour of the night gives one sound, at the second two strokes, and so distinguishes one hour from another, which is of greatest use to men of every degree.'

He was clearly impressed. It was not the first time he had heard the clock chime, but generally clocks chimed only on feast days and special occasions, such as marriages or burials, or to mark the hours of prayer; at night they were silent. But now the clock chime was being used to tell people the time. They still could not read the time, as early clocks had no faces, but from now on they could hear it by counting how many times the clapper struck.

Unequal hours

Milan was not the only city that boasted a public clock. In 14th-century Europe, clocks were being installed pretty much everywhere, for the simple reason that they fulfilled a genuine need. As cities grew and their industries boomed, they imposed a quite different rhythm of work on people. Formerly, on building sites, for example, there would

have been a simple sundial with four lines on it marking the beginning and end of the working day. On overcast days, this was replaced by a water-clock (clepsydra), but this too had drawbacks: the water froze in sub-zero temperatures and evaporated during heatwaves. Hourglasses were ill-suited to measuring long periods because they frequently had to be turned over. And both clepsydras and hourglasses were calibrated against sundials, which divided the period of daylight into twelve equal hours, irrespective of whether it was winter or summer.

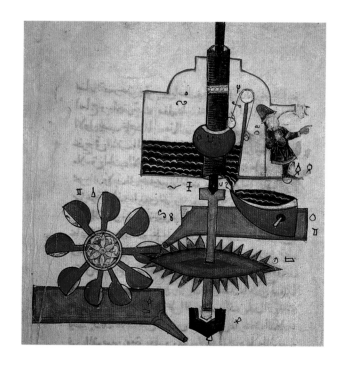

Clock power
The first mechanical timepieces, as shown in a 12th-century Arab manuscript (above), used water power. Later clocks like those at La Turbie in the French Alps (left) or Wells Cathedral, Somerset, (above right) were weight-driven.

WATER-POWERED CLOCKS

In 725, the Chinese Buddhist monk Yi-Xing built a hydraulic clock – the world's first mechanical timepiece. Standing some 10 metres high, it was driven by a paddlewheel with cups for paddles. As each cup filled, it rotated the wheel by exactly one thirty-sixth of a turn. A huge gearing system applied this motion to a celestial globe, around whose circumference were symbols for the Sun and phases of the Moon; the Sun completed a revolution every 365 days, while the Moon took just over 29 days. Yi-Xing's clock gave the exact time of sunrise and sunset, the dates of the new and full Moons, and marked each hour and quarter of an hour respectively with a chiming bell and a drumbeat. The water-clock was improved upon by the astronomer Zhang Sixun in 906 and the statesman Su Song, who in 1090 erected a five-storey astronomical clock tower operated by 96 automata.

the speed at which the weight dropped was known as the 'escapement'; this consisted of a bar (the foliot), with a weight at each end, which oscillated horizontally around a vertical rod (the verge). The verge was controlled by two teeth (the pallets) set at right angles to one another, which by turns engaged a large vertical cogwheel (the crown-wheel) mounted on the drum, slowing its rotation. Periodically, the crown wheel set in motion a series of gears and levers that would either ring a little bell or tip a container of water over to wake the monk charged with ringing the bell for prayers. The weight-driven clock is generally attributed to the Benedictine monk Gerbert of Aurillac, who was consecrated as Pope Sylvester II in the year 999. Gerbert had access to reference material in the best-stocked libraries in western Europe and was familiar with the escapement mechanisms devised by the Greeks. An influential figure, he would also have had the wherewithal to have such a clock built. Three centuries later the 'verge-and-foliot' escapement was being used by every clockmaker. When Giovanni de'Dondi outlined the workings of

The working day thus varied considerably in length, and it was always the bosses who did the measuring.

Countryside folk went about their lives blissfully unaware of such issues. When they were within earshot, however, the daily lives of peasants were regulated by the bells of their local church. The working day began before sunrise, with the first ring of the bell, and ended as the Sun went down at the third ring marking Vespers. It was bells such as these, rung seven times daily to mark the canonical offices, that inspired the invention of the mechanical clock. Instead of relying on a clepsydra to know when to sound each call to prayer, priests turned to a new system – the weight-driven clock.

Verges, foliots, pallets and crown-wheels

The principle behind weight-driven clocks was simple: movement was caused by a slowly falling weight at the end of a cord wrapped around a drum. The mechanism controlling

The 'Astrarium'
An astronomical clock constructed by the Paduan craftsman Giovanni de'Dondi between 1363 and 1380, and rebuilt in 1985, replicates the movement of the stars within the Solar System.

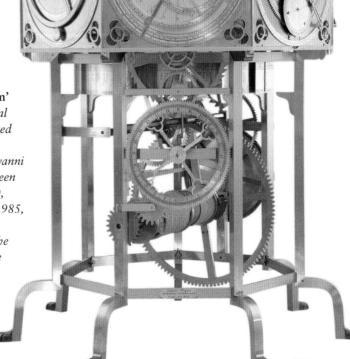

Measure of all things
The huge astronomical clock on the Old Town Hall in Prague features a skeletal personification of Death. Measuring time set the medieval mind brooding on the mortality of living things.

Princely possession
In the 16th century, a personal clock was an extraordinary luxury. This ornate timepiece (right), made of iron with gilded details and dating from 1569, carries the coat of arms of Prince Werdmüller von Elgg.

an astrological clock that he made in *c*1364, he did not describe the verge-and-foliot mechanism 'in the same detail as the other components, since everyone is quite familiar with this already in its many different forms'.

Mainly for show

With the addition of clockfaces, weight-driven clocks could visibly register time. In the 14th century, for example, a dial was added to the clock of the original St Paul's Cathedral in London. But early clockfaces were barely accurate; they rotated around a single fixed hand and mostly had just six numbers marked on them. Very few people at the time were capable of reading Roman numerals; the number 4 was often written as 'IIII' rather than 'IV' to save confusion with the number 6 (VI).

In truth, the clockface was little more than an excuse for ostentatious display. Many clocks had more than one face, plus a whole army of automata to enthrall the onlooker. The clock at Cluny Abbey, for example, made in 1340, featured the mystery of the Resurrection, the spectacle of Death, Saint Hugh, Saint Odilon, the Feasts of the Blessed

Virgin Mary and the Blessed Sacrament, and an animated scene of Christ's Passion. There was also a cock that beat its wings and a cherubim that greeted the Virgin Mary, while the Holy Spirit descended in the form of a dove and the Eternal Father blessed the assembled automata.

Lack of precision

Town clocks caught the public's imagination, and gave rulers and other influential people an opportunity to flaunt their power and wealth. But because mechanical clocks were prone to breaking down, a clockmaker had to be in constant attendance to oil the mechanism, to adjust the time using an hourglass and, above all, to reset the clock by the sundial. Weight-driven clocks could easily lose as much as an hour every day.

The lack of precision only really became a problem two centuries later, and then to mariners rather than town-dwellers. Sailors had long been able to pinpoint their latitude, but they did not yet possess an

One-hand clock
Many old clocks had just a single hand, like this l ate 16th-century drum clock (below), which also marked the phases of the Moon.

AN ILL-DEFINED PROFESSION

There were no dedicated clockmakers in the Middle Ages. When Anthony Bonelli was commissioned in 1356 to erect a clock tower in the southern French town of Perpignan, the notary who oversaw the project described him as: 'typical of that class of multi-skilled technicians who characterise the current age: though strictly speaking a plumber by trade, he is also an engineer, a mechanic, an architect and a builder.' Bonelli's workforce included 'stonemasons, bricklayers, blacksmiths, iron-founders, plasterers, cobblers, carters and sundry other artisans.' It was the 16th century before clockmakers could muster enough members in cities to form guilds: a Paris guild was formed in 1544, followed by Blois in 1597, Geneva in 1601 and London in 1631. By the end of the 17th century, there were over 100 master clockmakers in Geneva, employing around 300 craftsman and making 5,000 timepieces a year.

PORTABLE TIMEPIECES

Filippo Brunelleschi (1377–1446), the famous architect of the dome on Florence Cathedral, was also a certified goldsmith with an interest in timepieces. At the beginning of the 15th century, he began to manufacture 'for his own amusement small clocks and chiming timepieces using various types of spring'. The springs took the place of the driving weight and gear shaft in traditional clocks; to make up for the loss in tension, clockmakers introduced the 'snail' – a conical cylinder cam, shaped like a spiral, around which was wound a cord or chain attached to the spring. From making portable clocks, craftsmen soon went on to produce even smaller versions that were the forerunners of the modern watch. It is not known for certain who produced the very first watch, but in the late 15th or early 16th century Peter Henlein, a lockmaker from Nuremberg in Germany, manufactured 'from a little iron clocks with a lot of wheels, which, however you might turn them, show and strike 40 hours without any weight, even if they are worn on the chest or carried in the purse'. Such devices came to be known as 'watches' from the fact that they were used predominantly by town watchmen. They had just one hand and marked the time only to the nearest half-hour, making them scarcely more accurate than the first public clocks.

Luxury items *An early fob watch (near right) made by the French clockmaker Breguet, founded in 1775 in Paris. Adjusting the timing of a grandfather clock (far right).*

accurate instrument for determining the degree of longitude. In 1604, Philip III of Spain offered a handsome reward to anyone who could solve the problem. Soon afterwards, in 1636, the celebrated Italian astronomer Galileo Galilei offered his services to another seafaring nation, the newly independent Dutch Republic.

Dutch master

A contemporary French engraving shows Dutch scientist Christiaan Huygens demonstrating the principle behind his free-pendulum clock, which revolutionised timekeeping.

Enter the pendulum

As early as 1581 Galileo had noticed that all pendulums, irrespective of their length and amplitude (the arc of their swing), have the same 'period', that is, they take the same time to complete a single oscillation. He had plans to exploit this to make a marine chronometer, when he tragically went blind in 1638. His son Vincenzo sketched a clock based on his father's theories in 1642, but he died before he was

able to build it. The idea was revived several years later by a young Dutch scientist named Christiaan Huygens. Just 13 years old when Galileo died under house arrest, Huygens was already set on pursuing a scientific career. He came from a privileged background and was familiar with all the latest discoveries: the mathematician Marin Mersenne corresponded regularly with Huygens's father and René Descartes was a family friend. Christiaan's early exposure to astronomy stimulated his interest in clockmaking. Like Galileo, he had hit upon the idea of using a pendulum as a timekeeping mechanism in place of the foliot. In 1657, working to his instructions, a clockmaker from The Hague named Salomon Coster built the world's first pendulum clock.

The new timepiece had extraordinary precision, losing or gaining no more than five minutes a day. Yet Huygens soon discovered that a pendulum could not swing freely on board a pitching and tossing ship. The marine chronometer was still some years from being realised, and it was another scientist who would capitalise on Huygens' pioneering work.

Keeping time at sea

Robert Hooke was only 10 years old when he made his first clock. At Oxford University, where he went to study in 1653, Hooke became renowned for building machines to test his fellow students' theories. The natural philosopher Robert Boyle spotted Hooke's potential and took him on as his assistant in 1655. In 1658, Hooke had a remarkable brainwave: to drive a clock's mechanism he conceived of the 'use of springs instead of gravity for making a body vibrate in any posture'. To regulate the movement he used an improved mechanism called the 'anchor escapement', which controlled the amplitude of the pendulum and was probably the invention of the English clockmaker, William Clement.

Alhough Hooke's researches were supported by wealthy patrons, he let slip an opportunity to patent his spring-driven clock. He would come to regret this, as Christaan Huygens continued to hone his clockmaking skills. In 1675, on Huygens' instructions, the Parisian clockmaker Isaac Thuret made the first clock with a spring mechanism. In this, the foliot was replaced by a kind of wheel, or balance, at the centre of which was a coiled spiral spring. Every time this tightened or slackened,

Balance

Spiral spring

Anchor escapement

The spiral spring was a major step forward in the technology of watchmaking. It would remain the standard mechanism driving all watches until the invention of quartz and battery-powered watches in the late 20th century.

Anchor

Pallet

Escape wheel

HARRISON'S LEGACY

Not only seafarers, but also explorers and geographers, owe an immense debt of gratitude to John Harrison, the inventor of the first reliable marine chronometer. Once it came into service in 1764, this instrument enabled travellers to determine their precise degree of longitude at sea at any given time. Provided one knew the time in the ship's home port and the exact time at which the reading was taken at sea, the difference between the two could be expressed in nautical miles, given that one hour represented one 24th of the distance the Earth travels in making one complete revolution, equating to 15 degrees of longitude. For the first time, this made it possible to work out the actual distance from one point to another on the Earth's surface.

Measuring longitude
John Harrison spent 19 years building the third of his marine chronometers (left), a prototype numbered H3 which dates from 1757. It lacked the reliability of his definitive model, the H4, which he completed two years later. Later watchmakers further refined the marine chronometer; the example above, encased in mahogany, was the work of John Arnold (1789).

Stop the clock
An iconic image of Harold Lloyd, funny man of the silent movies, dangling from a clockface in the film Safety Last! *(1923).*

it moved a tiny anchor back and forth, which allowed the escape wheel to tick on one more notch. This ingenious mechanism clinched the matter; Huygens' spring-driven clock represented a huge advance in accuracy, losing no more than two minutes a day. Robert Hooke was devastated, even accusing the Dutchman of stealing his idea and presenting a spring-driven clock of his own to King Charles II in pursuit of his claim.

Huygens' clock set the benchmark for other clockmakers, whose numbers continued to grow, especially in London, Paris and Geneva. But clocks still were not precise enough to solve the problem of longitude: at sea, an inaccuracy of just one minute could send a ship off course by as much as 30 kilometres (20 miles), no small distance. Humidity and fluctuating temperatures on board ship also seriously affected accuracy. The problem was finally solved in 1759, after 50 years of arduous work, by the English clockmaker John Harrison, inventor of the first reliable marine chronometer.

Throughout the 18th and 19th centuries, timekeeping technology continued to improve, as clocks and watches became household items in virtually every home. Today, some 1.5 billion clocks are manufactured worldwide every year.

OIL PAINTING – c1434
A new reflection of the world

From the 15th century onwards, historical events and the culture of the West became glorified in painting. This artistic revolution came about as a result of a technical innovation – the dilution of coloured pigments with linseed oil and the evolution of their application.

Standing in front of an oak panel he had set up in his studio in the Flemish city of Bruges, the artist Jan van Eyck (1390–1441) was working on his painting, *The Arnolfini Portrait*. The various transparent pigments that he had crushed with a pestle to create his colours lay mixed with linseed oil on his stone palette, ready to be transferred to the flat surface before him to portray three-dimensional objects. As he worked, van Eyck varied the thickness of the pigments to capture the volume of the subjects' clothes, or to accentuate the interplay of light and shade. As he applied more layers of paint, the colours grew more iridescent. The remarkable luminosity of the oil paint was even more striking against the lime wash backdrop with which he had prepared the oak panel. When, on 10 October, 1434, the painter put his signature above the mirror that reflects the room and its occupants, he must have been well satisfied with the final result.

The genesis of oil painting

In his *Lives of the Artists* (1568), the Italian painter, architect, writer and biographer Giorgio Vasari (1511–74) credited Jan van Eyck with inventing oil painting, instigating a legend that persisted for many centuries until

Striking realism
The advent of heightened realism, which appears in the convex mirror of Van Eyck's The Arnolfini Portrait *(1434), coincided with the adoption of oil paints in Western art.*

EGG TEMPERA

Prehistoric cave painters would mix, or bind, their mineral pigments with either water or animal fat. In classical antiquity, painters experimented with various different binding agents, including animal-based glues, oil, wax, resin and egg yolk. For paintings on wood panels, egg tempera proved the best and it remained the most common medium from the Middle Ages to the Renaissance.

Working with egg tempera required the painter to build up the picture methodically. To begin with, the wood was given up to eight coats of gesso – plaster of Paris mixed with animal glue. When the final gesso coat was dry, the picture was sketched out in charcoal or black paint; because tempera dried almost instantly, any deviation from this original sketch would be visible. Before commencing the actual painting, the dry, ground pigments were mixed with water; they were then emulsified with egg yolk just before being applied. Pigment colours could not be mixed together, except for lead-white, which could be added to other pigments to obtain lighter shades. Transitions between colours had to be done by applying cross-hatched strokes.

Although egg tempera was supplanted by oil painting well over 500 years ago, it retains an inimitable luminosity from its many transparent layers. As a result the medium is beginning to attract a new following among some modern painters.

only as a base coat, which he covered with layer upon layer of oil paint. The new technique enabled Bellini to infuse his colours with a richness and density never seen before.

Bellini's work formed part of a more general Renaissance trend towards more realistic and sensual paintings. Artists of the period strove for a technique that would allow them to capture reality more closely. Each layer of egg tempera dried quickly as it soaked into the thick gesso layer, but oil paints remained workable for far longer. By manipulating them with a brush, painters could make objects appear more solid, rounded and lifelike. Oil paints also allowed different colours to be

Sumptuous detail
Giovanni Bellini's Martyrdom of St Mark *(detail, left), a painting executed entirely in oils in 1515. Detail of facial expression and in the clothing of the crowd showed a new realism in artistic representation.*

research into art history eventually got to the truth of the matter. In fact, painting in oils was not new when van Eyck created his celebrated portrait. The first known mention of the technique is in 1239, when an artist named Odon apparently used linseed-oil-based paint to create wall paintings for the Queen's chambers at the Palace of Westminster. In the 14th century a follower of Giotto, Cennino Cennini, described how to use oil paints 'to create a fresco, or paint onto a wooden panel, or metal, or whatever surface you wish'. Yet these early experiments in using oil as the sole binding element for pigments were taken no further and their practitioners were forgotten.

So others had used linseed oil to dilute their pigments before Jan van Eyck, but what he and his brother Hubert did that was new was to use the oil-based paint only at a late stage in the painting. The oils were used for the final layers of paint, in effect for the finishing touches, on pictures created initially using the popular medium of the day: paints made with egg yolk known as tempera.

An ideal medium for realism

In 1475 two Venetian masters, Antonello da Messina and Domenico Veneziani, borrowed the Flemish innovation of adding oil touches to a tempera base. But it was another artist from Venice, Giovanni Bellini (1430–1516), who really exploited this combination of new and old media. In his later works, he used tempera

blended directly on the surface of the picture, impossible with tempera. In this way, a base coat of burnt sienna, for example, could be 'warmed up' with vermilion or 'cooled down' with blue or green. Oils brought out the contrast between the opacity of certain materials and the luminosity of features such as the sky or people's skin tones, or the sparkle of eyes or crystal glasses. Lastly, oils enabled the painter to redo sections, not an option in tempera, where the slightest change showed through the transparent layers.

Light and shade
Antonello da Messina, an innovative Renaissance painter, made extensive use of oil in his 'Virgin and Child' (left), painted in 1475 as part of an altarpiece for the church of San Cassiano in Venice. The painting – one of only three fragments of the altarpiece to survive and now in a museum in Vienna – is notable for its pioneering use of deep shadow.

WATTEAU – VICTIM OF HIS ART?

Painting with oils involved a lot of mixing of pigments and some artists, quite unaware of the hazardous chemical properties of certain pigments, often did this with their fingers. It is generally assumed that the French artist Antoine Watteau (1684–1721) died due to lead poisoning caused by ingesting either lead-white or lead oxide in the process of his work.

Coming to life
Tintoretto's 1570 painting The Origin of the Milky Way *is a fine example of how oil paints freed artists from static, two-dimensional compositions, allowing them to indulge in an explosion of colour and form. Below left: a palette used by the French Impressionist painter, Edouard Manet.*

ANIMAL, VEGETABLE AND MINERAL

In Van Eyck's day, painters had around 40 natural pigments at their disposal. To the yellow and red ochres, white (from china clay), black (from charcoal) and brown (from manganese dioxide) used by the prehistoric cave painters of Lascaux, Classical artists had added a variety of colours including different reds obtained by grinding hematite or red mercury sulphide (cinnabar), yellows based on orpiment (arsenic sulphide), 'Egyptian blue' (derived by heating malachite; cold-ground malachite produced green), another blue from lapis lazuli and white from white lead or lead oxide. Medieval apothecaries discovered new plant and animal-based pigments that were ideally suited to mixing with oil, including carmine from the cochineal bug, yellow from buckthorn berries and red from madder root.

Renaissance masters of Venice

The true glory of oil painting was still to be revealed. Titian (*c*1490–1576) and Tintoretto (1518–94) were the first to completely dispense with the tempera base and to use an impasto technique, where thick brush strokes were left clearly visible, catching the light. These two Venetian masters astonished the Western world with canvases whose realism and heroic scale prefigure photography and the cinema. Tintoretto's dazzling masterpieces include the *The Origin of the Milky Way* of 1570 (above). Titian's earlier *Assumption of the Virgin Mary* (1516) was a stunning interpretation of the glories of heaven.

Neither of these magnificent works would have been possible without oil paints.

The law of three layers

Another advantage of painting in oils was that artists could paint directly onto the canvas, provided it was sufficiently durable and had been properly prepared. In the Renaissance, preparation consisted of repeatedly coating the canvas with layers of gesso and lead-white paint to create a base colour (the exact base shade varied according to the individual artist). This was then polished with pumice stone to produce a glossy finish, with none of the texture of the canvas coming through which would have absorbed the oil paint.

Three artistic geniuses – Velasquez (1599–1660), Rubens (1577–1640) and Rembrandt (1606–69) – established a new mode of painting that brought out the impact of oil-based pigments to best advantage. The method is still taught in art schools today, albeit only as an historical technique. It entails working in three stages: first, the picture is roughed out in *grisaille* (a light grey shade), with masses of white where vivid colours are to be applied; next, the composition is created in a monochrome colour scheme of browns and ochres; finally, the colour is applied. As each layer becomes progressively thinner and the oil evaporates, the underlying layer of white shines through, catching reflected light that lends the pigments an added glow. Different colour combinations have different effects – a vermilion base coat, for example, warms up a top layer of black that might otherwise appear heavy or lifeless.

In Britain, before the growth in popularity of watercolours in the early 19th century, oils were unchallenged as a medium for painting. The way that paints were made up also remained unchanged, until standard pre-mixed paints using synthetic dyes became available from 1840 onwards.

Portrait of the artist
One of the many self-portraits by Dutch painter Rembrandt van Rijn (below); this one was painted in 1660.

Assumption of the Virgin
Titian's masterpiece, begun in 1516, is notable for the dynamic poses and high degree of realism of the figures in the imagined scene, as well as the sheer theatricality of the composition.

THE TRIUMPH OF OIL PAINTING

An important social factor helped to promote the rise of painting in oils: the increasing luxury of aristocratic homes. From the 15th century painting began to rival sculpture as a way in which rich patrons could enhance the opulence of their domestic décor and display their artistic taste. Amateur art-lovers turned increasingly to works that they could hang on their walls, display on easels and even take with them, along with furniture and other belongings, when they decamped to their country seats. Tempera paintings had tended to be small; they were also fragile and therefore vulnerable to damage in transit. This was not the case with large oil-painted canvases, which could be detached from their frames, rolled up for ease of transport, and then unrolled and remounted to bring their drama and glamour to their new situation.

In search of realism

The Renaissance originated in Florence in the early 15th century and then spread throughout Europe, setting a new agenda for visual art. The paramount task for painters was to convey their message as clearly as possible through a realistic rendering of the natural and human worlds. The invention of single-point perspective – also called linear or artifical perspective – was central to this new artistic goal.

Geometry and realism
The difference between linear perspective and the Chinese technique of axonometry can be seen in a comparison of the two paintings below. The Fresco of the Masks *from the Villa Augusta in Rome (30 BC; top) has a vanishing point which creates an impression of increasing distance, while the more realistic 10th-century-AD Chinese painting (bottom) does not.*

One day in 1413, a curious scene was played out in the central square of Florence. By the front door of the cathedral, known to all as the Duomo after its celebrated dome, stood a man facing the Baptistery and holding a wooden panel up to his face with his right hand. On the reverse of the panel was a painted scene of the Baptistery. In his left hand, which he extended beyond the panel, the man held a mirror. Looking through a small hole in the centre of the panel, he could see reflected in the mirror an exact replica of what he could see for real directly in front of him, if he peered over the top of the panel: it was a perfect optical illusion. This anecdote is related by Antonio Manetti in his biography of Filippo Brunelleschi (1377–1446). For Brunelleschi, renowned sculptor and architect of the cathedral's dome, was the man in question, and the purpose of his strange behaviour was to demonstrate the principles of single-point perspective, a newly rediscovered technique that enabled artists to depict three-dimensional space on a two-dimensional surface by creating the illusion of depth.

A window on the world

Linear perspective is based on the perception of an object – or of the world around – as if observed through a single eye. It is constructed around the apparent convergence of so-called 'orthogonals', imaginary parallel lines running from the edge of the picture plane to a single 'vanishing-point' on the horizon. Leon Battista Alberti (1404–72), another Florentine architect, was the first to set out ground rules for how artists could use linear perspective. In his 1435 treatise *De pictura* ('On Painting') Alberti called the picture surface an 'open window' on the world; the scene depicted by the artist is what we see through that window. Heeding the call of their poet compatriot Petrarch (1304–74), acclaimed as the father of the Renaissance, Brunelleschi and Alberti set about rediscovering the work of the classical artists of ancient Greece and Rome and investigating the relationship between the arts and sciences. Linear perspective, it emerged, had its origins in classical antiquity.

Learning from the ancients

In the paintings of ancient Egypt, the external world was rendered in a purely conceptual manner. In order to depict in two dimensions the volume of a three-dimensional object such as the human body, Egyptian artists showed the person's head and legs in profile but turned the torso face-on. Thereafter, independently of one another, the Chinese and Greeks developed more realistic ways of projecting space onto a flat picture plane. Chinese painting adopted a technique known as axonometry, or parallel perspective, which retains true geometric values but has no vanishing point and is not based on optical principles. In contrast, the Greeks and later the Romans showed objects distorted in space (foreshortened) by orthogonal lines to make more distant figures appear smaller than those in the foreground.

The fact that linear perpective was only rediscovered ten centuries later is principally due to the rigid requirements of Christian iconography. From the Byzantine period right up to the Italian *Quattrocento* (15th century), art played an essentially devotional role, and it was considered inappropriate, even sacrilegious, to show Christ and the saints in an everyday setting.

PERSPECTIVE MACHINES – FROM THE SPORTELLO TO THE *CAMERA OBSCURA*

To help artists gain a firm grasp of linear perspective and learn to draw in scale, Alberti suggested in his *De pictura* that they use a grid traced onto transparent cloth stretched over a frame – the first 'perspective machine'. The German artist Albrecht Dürer (1471–1528) came up with improvements on this basic design. One such device, the *sportello*, comprised a wooden frame across which were stretched two movable silk threads forming a right-angle, with a line tied at one end to a ring fixed in the wall behind the artist and fitted at the other end with a pointer. Artists positioned the frame between themselves and the objects they wanted to reproduce. The sight-line traversing the frame was pulled taut, the pointer aimed at the object, and the threads on the frame adjusted to meet at the sight-line. The artist lowered a sheet of paper over the frame, and traced on it the point at which the threads intersected. Point by point, the object was faithfully reproduced on the paper.

Leonardo da Vinci's solution was the *camera obscura* (literally 'dark room'), in which the light rays reflected by objects were concentrated in a lens, which cast an upside-down, reduced image on a frame covered with a sheet of paper. A mirror was then used to turn the image the right way up. The principle was the same as that used later by the photographic camera. In the 17th century, the Dutch artist Vermeer used such devices to great effect.

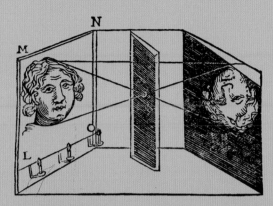

Forerunner of the photo
The principle of the camera obscura, *the precursor of the photographic camera, is illustrated in this diagram (left). In the 17th century, portable examples of such devices (below left) already existed.*

Dürer's perspective devices
The sportello *('window') devised by Albrecht Dürer allowed the artist to transfer the exact proportions of his model onto paper (below). A plate from Dürer's* Instructions on Measuring *(1525, above) shows his apparatus being used to foreshorten objects (in this case, a lute). A pointer is attached to a thread running through a pulley on the wall. The thread represents a ray of light passing through the picture plane to the theoretical eye-point denoted by the pulley.*

Near and far

According to the laws of perspective, people further away from the viewer are shown smaller than close-up figures, as in St Stephen Preaching at Jerusalem *(1514, right) by Vittore Carpaccio, or the detail from the* Coronation of the Virgin *(c1434, below) by Fra Angelico.*

Refreshing realism

Starting with painters like Giotto (c1266–1337), Fra Angelico (1387–1455), Uccello (1397–1475) and Mantegna (1431–1506), realism began to triumph over ideology. In Giotto's *Feast of Herod* (1320), for example, the artist instinctively rediscovered the principles of linear perspective, while in *Coronation of the Virgin* Fra Angelico gave the angels in the background markedly smaller faces than the figures in the foreground.

The basic principle was simple: the appearance and size of bodies in space were modified in strict accordance with their position within the receding orthogonal lines. The new, more realistic painting found a ready market both among powerful princes and the ordinary citizens of Tuscan towns like Florence and Siena.

Understanding the world

A prime mover behind the rediscovery of linear perspective was the fundamental urge of Renaissance artists and scientists to comprehend the world around them. The period saw the growth of Europe's first universities, a proliferation of commentaries on ancient texts, the beginnings of astronomy, the rise of anatomy and adventurous expeditions of discovery such as Marco Polo's journey to China and Columbus's voyage across the Atlantic. These all helped to bring about a new conception of space. In the same way that astronomy began to reveal to people their place in the Cosmos, so perspective was giving them a sense of their place on Earth. In this context, the rebirth of single-point perspective took on a psychological, even philosophical, dimension.

Drawing in the viewer

Paradoxically, the highly ordered framework of linear perspective freed artists to unfold their narrative more clearly, leading the viewer-reader through the pictorial space. Just as Brunelleschi had done by placing the hole in his Baptistery *tavoletta* precisely at the vanishing-point, so later painters would direct the viewer's gaze by choosing a particular viewpoint, or by making the

FROM ARTISAN TO ARTIST

In his *Lives of the Artists*, the Italian painter and architect Giorgio Vasari relates how Paolo Uccello (1397–1475) was so enthralled by perspective that he gave up sleeping to spend his nights trying to find new vanishing-points. The same obsession led his close contemporary Piero della Francesca (1416–92) to renounce painting and devote himself instead to mathematics. Vasari's stories bear witness to the commitment of this generation of artists to capturing reality, and also to a conscious desire to raise the profile of the painter. Until the Renaissance, painters were regarded as artisans, craftsmen with a degree of technical ability who worked within guilds or corporations. But Uccello, della Francesca and other leading figures of the Renaissance began to think of themselves as artists by virtue of both their physical skill and their wide-ranging erudition, notably in the field of mathematics. All their finished works testify to the depth and breadth of their learning as true 'Renaissance men'.

orthogonal vanishing lines converge on a particular person or scene. With time, they manipulated the laws of perspective to drive their message home. An extreme example of this is the anamorphic (deformed perspective) skull in the foreground of *The Ambassadors* (1515), a celebrated painting by Hans Holbein the Younger; the skull is placed in a scene of worldly opulence as a *memento mori*, to remind the viewer that human life is transient.

New ways of seeing

Renaissance art had a profound and lasting impact on painting. From the Mannerism of the later 16th century, with its stress on artificial beauty and sophistication, through to Romanticism, which flourished in the late 18th century, art continued to pay homage to that earlier fertile period of creativity. Painterly composition and expression were guided by the rules of linear perspective and the interplay of light and shade (*chiaroscuro*), while the human body, inanimate objects and landscapes were all shown in proportion.

In the latter half of the 19th century, the solidity of portrayed objects began to dissolve in the works of the Impressionists who, inspired by the paintings of JMW Turner (1775–1851), discovered that reality changed constantly under the influence of light. They stressed the primacy of the beholder when confronted with a welter of colours, which redefined and reinterpreted objects in space. Gradually, as the idea took hold that objective reality and its depiction shifts according to the individual's subjective perception, perspective and proportion ceased to be regarded as immutable elements of visual space. From the early 20th century onwards, this opened the floodgates for abstract artists to deconstruct reality and explore instead the dizzying heights and depths of the human psyche.

Trompe l'oeil
In 1471–4, the artist Andrea Mantegna painted this 'oculus' in the ceiling of the Camera degli Sposi at the Palazzo Ducale in Mantua, Italy, creating an optical illusion of height.

AERIAL PERSPECTIVE

Long after painters had taken on board the rules of linear perspective, they still ignored an essential corollary to the basic principle: aerial perspective. This dictated that far objects should appear not only smaller but also less distinct than near ones. In Carpaccio's *St Stephen Preaching at Jerusalem* (above left), the buildings in the distance are just as bright and sharp as those in the foreground. Then, following Leonardo da Vinci's observation that the further away mountains were, the closer they were in colour to the sky, painters began indiscriminately to apply a blue haze to their backgrounds. Eventually, they learned to use aerial perspective more subtly.

Revolutionising the written word

The year 1456 saw the appearance of the world's first printed book, a Bible produced in the German city of Mainz. It was the work of the inventor Johannes Gutenberg, who teamed movable metal type (which he had been experimenting with since the 1440s) with a printing press. In a Europe caught up in the intellectual ferment of Humanism and eager for knowledge, the advent of printing was far more than just a technological revolution.

On 12 March, 1455, Bishop Enea Silvio Piccolomini, the future Pope Pius II, wrote to his friend Cardinal Juan de Carvajal. Piccolomini had just seen the unbound folios of a printed Bible, which he described as having 'beautiful lettering, not faulty in any way, and so neat that Your Grace' – and this next passage the Bishop underlined – 'would easily be able to read it without your glasses'. He goes on to promise that he will try to obtain a copy for the Cardinal.

The first printed Bible

The work in question was the so-called '42-line Bible' (named from the number of lines printed on each page), illuminated and bound by Heinrich Cremer of St Stephen's Church in Mainz, a task he completed on 24 August, 1456. The paper used for the printing was 'double-folio', with two pages printed on each side (making four pages per sheet); after printing the paper was folded once to the size of a single page.

This monumental work, spanning 1,465 pages, was eloquent testament to the capabilities of the new printing press: it contained no fewer than 350,000 separate characters, printed in a Gothic script called 'textra quadrata', which was widely used for Bibles and liturgies at the time. The pages had been produced at least a year beforehand in the studio established in Mainz by Johannes Gutenberg and his associates Peter Schöffer and Johann Fust. The first print run of the Bible probably comprised 160 copies, all identical.

The Gutenberg Bible contains no imprint information to identify the precise date of publication or even the printer. But it is inconceivable that anyone else in the mid 15th century had the capability of producing such an object. Gutenberg had laboured long and hard to realise his dream of perfecting a device that would free people from the need to have texts copied by hand. For centuries, hand-written texts were the only way to disseminate the written word in the West. For at least 15 years, maybe 20, Gutenberg had tried to devise a system for mass-producing script.

There was certainly a ready market: from the 12th century onwards, the growth of the universities and the rise of a new educated urban middle class had created a substantial demand for books. The cottage industry of monk copyists in the scriptoria of their abbeys, or of students employed by secular libraries working in backrooms, could not meet the demand,

Wooden type
Characters carved in the Central Asian Uigur language in the 13th or 14th century.

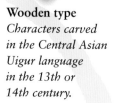

Luxury edition
A Book of Hours printed on vellum in 1498 by the Parisian printer Philippe Pigouchet. The pages shown here depict the death of the Virgin Mary.

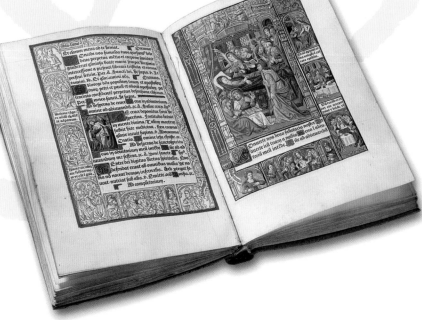

The Good Book
*The 42-line Latin Bible printed by Gutenberg,
Schöffer and Fust first appeared in Mainz in 1456.*

and texts remained both rare and expensive.
Not only that but, to use Bishop Piccolomini's
phrase, they were often 'faulty' because of
errors made in the copying.

Three centuries in the making

The legend of Gutenberg single-handedly
devising movable characters, solving the
problem of how to manufacture them and
inventing the printing press to apply them has
not withstood historical scrutiny. The concept
of movable type is thought to have originated
in Korea, but its use can be traced back to
China, where in 1041–8 an obscure commoner
named Bi Sheng baked ideographs of clay and
arranged them in a frame (held in place with
resin and slivers of bamboo) for printing. The
first wooden movable type was invented in
China during the Yuan Dynasty (1271–1378);
an official, Wang Zhen, used over 50,000 type
characters to print his treatise *Nong Shu* (the
'Book of Agriculture') in 1313.

Movable type probably arrived in the West
with the Mongol invasions of Russia (1240),
Poland (1259) and Hungary (1283). Around
the same time, Chinese merchants may well
have introduced the technology to the great
commercial and cultural hub of Byzantium
(Constantinople). By then, European paper
mills were already turning out high-quality
paper, an ideal medium on which to both write
and print. All the conditions were converging
for the development of printing in Europe.

Between 1423 and 1437 the Dutch printer
Laurens Janszoon Coster of Haarlem was the
first to apply the principle of movable wooden

Spreading the word
*A 15th-century
printer's studio
in Florence,
as imagined by
the Italian painter
Tito Lessi
(1858–1917).*

83

The art of printing
A decorative capital 'P' created by renowned French printer, typesetter and publisher Pierre Didot (1761–1853, left), alongside a modern reconstruction of Gutenberg's printing press.

printing blocks to Latin script; the printed work *Speculum humanae salutis* ('Mirror of Human Salvation') is attributed to him. Soon after, in *c*1444, Prokop Waldvogel, a goldsmith originally from Prague but resident in Avignon, is believed to have practised so-called 'artistic writing', though no works of his survive.

Printing with metal type

Meanwhile, printers in Holland and the Rhineland had abandoned wooden type in favour of cast copper or brass characters. Their working method was to press the made-up page down onto a soft base, such as clay or lead, to produce a die. Once this had hardened, molten lead was poured into it to make the printing plate. The technique, the forerunner of hot-metal typesetting, had disadvantages: the characters

EVOLUTION OF THE BOOK

While printing technology saw hardly any major advances until the 19th century, books underwent radical changes from the early 16th century onwards. To make type more legible and to move away from manuscript conventions, Humanist printers introduced Roman typefaces – upright, rounded, graceful – in place of the slanted Italics which had originally been adopted to mimic manuscript writing. The design of individual characters, known as the 'font', were varied to create hierarchies of headings and improve the spacing on a page. Punctuation was standardised. Information such as the title of the book and the name of the author and printer – originally gathered together in the colophon at the end of a book – was moved to the front, creating the title page. In the second half of the 16th century pages began to be numbered in Arabic numerals and indexes made their first appearance, allowing readers to look up specific passages.

Print shop
A late 16th-century printer's workshop (left). Printing technology gave rise to several new occupations in addition to printers: compositors, who made up the type; proofreaders who read pages for errors; and printers' apprentices, who inked up the blocks. Print shops remained much the same for centuries.

quickly wore down and their alignment also went out of true. Even so, it's use survived for many years, notably in Strasbourg.

This is the point at which Gutenberg appeared on the scene. He reverted to the Chinese method of printing directly with movable characters fitted into a frame, but cast from a more resilient metal – a low-melting alloy of lead, tin, and antimony – which was poured into copper moulds that had been stamped out with a steel die. The financial difficulties that Gutenberg got into indicate that the enterprise was more tricky and costly than he had anticipated. Composing a double page, for example, entailed casting over 100 separate characters.

Gutenberg's truly pioneering innovation came in adapting the screw press, traditionally used for crushing grapes or olives, to his new purpose. The apparatus exerted sufficient pressure to ensure that the special ink concocted for the task left behind a clear impression on the paper. Developed from the ink used by wood engravers, printer's ink was actually more like a varnish, a viscous blend of black antimony and carbon thinned with linseed oil. The oil base helped the ink to adhere to the metal type.

Gutenberg's imitators

Playing cards printed in several colours and dating from the 9th century indicate that colour printing also originated in China. The technique was revived in the 36-line Gutenberg Bible of 1458–9; in contrast to Cremer's 1455 work, in which the illuminated letters were added in traditional manner by hand, the Gutenberg Bible was decorated with printed red initial capitals. The effect was achieved by coating selected characters with red ink before printing. At the beginning of the 16th century, the method was further refined by the technique of *chiaroscuro* printing, where lines of black ink partitioned the fields of colour off from one another (this also had the benefit of masking any smudging that might occur). Stencilling was widely used to produce playing cards.

In 1457 Fust and Schöffer, who had in the interim split from Gutenberg, produced the *Mainz Psalter*, which was printed in red, blue and black and included for the first time a colophon – an inscription at the end of the book giving the names of the printers and date

PRINTMAKING TECHNIQUES

The earliest printed works relied upon illuminators to create ornate capital letters by hand and add colour to illustrations (printed from woodcuts). Soon, the great engravers of the day, like Albrecht Dürer, started to take an interest in book illustration. Copperplate or line engraving became widespread from the early 1500s; its unmatched level of detail made it ideal for illustrating the new scientific and technological treatises that now began to appear. Line engraving uses a special press, comprising two large wooden rollers that press the paper onto a copper plate engraved in intaglio (that is, the image is hollowed out from the plate's surface). In 1798 the German Aloys Senefelder invented lithography. This process involved drawing a negative of the image on a polished limestone plate with a grease-receptive wax crayon; greasy ink was then applied to the plate, where it adhered only to the grease-receptive areas (the rest of the plate was made grease-repellent with water); finally, the ink was transferred to the paper. Lithography later evolved into offset printing (which uses an intermediate rubber-coated cylinder to transfer ink from the plate to the paper), first introduced in 1875.

Copperplate masterpiece
An engraving by Dürer entitled Knight, Death, and the Devil *(1513).*

Mark of an educated man
Beautifully bound in leather and with titles embossed in gold leaf, books became prized possessions. A well-stocked library proclaimed the learning and good taste of its owner.

BIRTH OF THE PAPERBACK

The great Italian humanist publisher Alde Manucce was the first to produce small paper-bound books that were cheaper and easier to carry than standard editions. Manucce was based in Venice, where he published 150 works from 1494 to 1515. His paperbacks were in octavo format, with a page size one-eighth of the original printed sheet.

of publication. Fust and Schöffer published around 30 works up to 1466. In around 1460 Johann Neumeister, a former apprentice of Gutenberg, set off for Italy at the invitation of leading churchmen and prominent lay people there. He went first to Rome, then on to Foligno in Umbria, where he printed the first book in Italian, an edition of the works of Dante. Before long, there were printing presses in more than 100 European cities. By 1470 the university in Paris had its own press. William Caxton, who printed the first book in English in 1474, while living in Bruges, set up a press in London in 1476.

Disseminating new ideas

Prior to 1501, the date up to which convention dictates that printed works are referred to as 'incunabula', book historians have counted around 27,000 separate editions printed in more than 210 cities, totalling some 10–15 million individual copies. Major early centres of printing included Venice, Paris, London and Lyons. There were also large book fairs, notably in Leipzig and Frankfurt. From their city

Purveyor of knowledge
Outside Europe's cities, books were sold by travelling hawkers like this one engraved by Albrecht Dürer (left).

workshops, master printers – well-educated men for the most part – were instrumental in spreading the humanist ideas of scholars like Erasmus and Thomas More. They worked alongside academics to revive the great texts of classical antiquity. Books began to circulate widely; from the 16th century printed material was distributed outside the major cities by hawkers, both men and women, who sold pamphlets recounting the major events of the day, a range of religious tracts, and practical tomes and almanacs.

Promoting the vernacular

But although reader numbers continued to grow, they were still a distinct minority. Major publishing houses dared not risk print runs of more than a few hundred for scholarly works, running to 2,000 or 3,000 for surefire sellers like books of hours or missals. Before long, the book became a powerful conduit for critical, dissenting ideas. The printed word played a powerful role in advancing the Protestant Reformation; in 1520, for example, 4,000 copies of Luther's polemical pamphlet *To the Christian Nobility of the German Nation* sold out in a few days. Luther's translation of the Bible, which played a crucial role in the standardisation of the German language, appeared in 430 editions between 1522 and 1546. Nor was this an isolated case. Throughout Europe, printing promoted the rise of 'vulgar' languages over Latin, and in so doing generated an ever greater readership.

The infinitely adaptable book

The authorities quickly grasped the subversive impact that the printed word could have. Their first reaction was to censor and persecute printers, but they soon saw that books could promote an orthodox viewpoint. Likewise, it was not long before enterprising spirits realised that books could be used for entertainment and escapism as well as for learning.

Print technology largely atrophied until a spurt of progress in the 19th century, when steam was used to power printing machinery. The introduction of rotary presses (from 1843) reduced costs and made longer print runs possible. A key step was the invention, in 1884, of the Linotype machine by the German émigré Ottmar Mergenthaler for the *New York Tribune* newspaper. Whether producing books or newspapers, the printing press played a decisive contribution to the growth of democracy around the world – a fitting tribute to Gutenberg, the visionary who, almost 450 years before, pulled the elements together that set the communications revolution in motion.

A proud profession
Printers have long been aware of the great social role that their trade has played in disseminating knowledge. This cover of a French print trade-union bulletin harks back to the origins of the profession.

Hot metal
A typesetter composing lines of type from a set of compositors' trays; the technology is now only used for short print runs of specialist publications produced by the letterpress method.

Eclipsed by his own invention

Surprisingly little is known about the inventor of modern printing. In fact, the details of his life are so sketchy that some far-fetched ideas have been put forward to fill the gaps. What emerges from a careful study of the historical record is a portrait of a man more interested in the technology of his craft than in business.

The birth date of Johannes Gensfleisch, better known as Gutenberg, is uncertain: it fell somewhere between 1394 and 1399. He was a native of the German city of Mainz on the River Rhine, where his father was a goldsmith attached to the ecclesiastic mint of the city's archbishop. This biographical detail is important: it was during his apprenticeship as a goldsmith that the young Johannes came into contact with metal founders who, over the course of the preceding two centuries, had revived the art of die-casting coins by pouring molten metal into moulds.

The Strasbourg years

Gutenberg became involved in an uprising by the guilds of Mainz against the patricians and was forced to leave the city. He moved to Strasbourg, where he lived and worked for at least a decade (1434–44). While there, he demonstrated his budding entrepreneurial spirit by mass-producing small metal hand-mirrors for pilgrims to Aix-la-Chapelle (they were thought to capture the 'holy light' from religious relics). His lack of business acumen became apparent when the plan misfired; he had got the date of the pilgrimage wrong, so the mirrors went unsold.

In 1439 Gutenberg became embroiled in a lawsuit against his investors. Documents from the case reveal that he was engaged at the time in investigating a 'new art' relating to printing. In an attempt to develop typographic characters made of lead alloy and a hand-cranked printing press, he had engaged the services of a goldsmith, Hans Dünne, and a joiner, Conrad Sahspach, whose task in all

Genius at work
Johannes Gutenberg in his workshop, depicted in a coloured woodcut inspired by the bas-relief on a monument erected in his honour in his home town of Mainz.

Printing paraphernalia
The tools of letterpress printing, including lead-alloy plates and compositors' trays, are now most likely bought and sold as curios.

likelihood was to build the press. Almost nothing of this venture had leaked out, thanks to Gutenberg's obsession with secrecy, but no sooner had the lawsuit been filed than he immediately ordered the apparatus to be dismantled. It is inconceivable that Gutenberg could have been solely responsible for devising the printing press. Such an ambitious project would have involved a team of highly skilled experts in their different fields, and above all raising substantial funds.

Return to Mainz, the cradle of printing

Like so many aspects of Gutenberg's life, we have no idea what originally sparked his interest in printing – perhaps it was the prospect of future profit. At the time, beginning in Holland and spreading to Gutenberg's Rhine homeland, several inventors were experimenting with replacing the woodcut block with a moulded metal plate that had letter characters already stamped into it in intaglio relief.

Gutenberg's genius was to realise that proper alignment of the letters could only be achieved with individual movable characters. To cast this 'type', he would need to devise a special mould that could make the tiny letters and be adjusted for different characters. The device may have been the brainchild of the technician Peter Schöffer, who joined Gutenberg in 1452, four years or

The printed page
A page printed by Gutenberg dating from 1460 (above); the large initial capitals and margin illuminations were added by hand.

more after the latter returned to Mainz. Meanwhile, Gutenberg had also secured the backing of the financier Johann Fust.

Spurned by posterity

The first publications to emerge from Gutenberg's press were Latin grammars and calendars. Then came a far more ambitious undertaking – the Bible. Its publication was conclusive proof of the success of the printing press, but it also marked the start of Gutenberg's tribulations. In late 1455 a fresh lawsuit pitted him against his former partners. Gutenberg, an inventor of genius but a less-than-inspired businessman, could not repay Fust's investment. The settlement forced him to hand over the operation lock, stock and barrel to Fust, including several valuable sets of movable type. In partnership, Fust and Schöffer, who by this time had mastered composition and printing, went on to enjoy enormous success as publishers.

After his bankruptcy, Gutenberg bounced back and raised new finance to open another printing shop. There, between 1457 and 1460, he printed another Bible, known as the '36-line', as well as other religious texts and a small encyclopaedia called the *Catholicon*. In 1462 his workshop was destroyed during the sack of Mainz by Archbishop Adolph von Nassau. Yet in 1465, in recognition of his achievements, Adolph granted the ageing Gutenberg an annual stipend to ensure that he did not spend his last days in penury. The inventor of modern printing died three years later, taking the secret of his inspiration to the grave with him. His enormous contribution to the rise of the printed word was only properly recognised in the 19th century.

PERENNIAL BESTSELLER

From the very first Bible that was printed in Gutenberg's workshop, the sacred text of Christianity has been a runaway success, topping the bestseller lists every year. Since the beginning of the 19th century, some 7 billion copies of the Bible have been produced worldwide; in 2008 alone, it is estimated that around 25 million Bibles were sold in the USA.

The world in miniature

In 1492 the German navigator and geographer Martin Behaim made the earliest-known terrestrial globe, showing the Earth in three dimensions for the first time. Behaim was trying to go beyond earlier, symbolic depictions of the world and show it as it really was. Yet even as he was completing his globe, western Europe stood on the verge of an Age of Discovery that was to render it instantly obsolete.

Tabernacle Earth

In the 6th century AD, the monk Cosmas Indopleustes put forward a conception of the Earth's shape that he had gleaned from his reading of the Bible: he imagined a mountain surrounded by four seas, around which the Sun revolved. The heavens were represented as a cover like that of the ancient Hebrew Tabernacle (right).

Practically everyone, at some point in childhood, must have stood fascinated before a globe, lost in wonder. Globes put the Earth quite literally at our fingertips, giving us an instant grasp of its shape and dimensions. Spinning a globe round, it is possible to trace the outlines of distant, exotic continents, pinpoint islands in vast, empty expanses of ocean, and dream of travel and discoveries to be made. As we contemplate this world in miniature and consider the reality it represents, the huge distances involved can make the head spin as well as the globe itself. When Nuremberg cartographer Martin Behaim first introduced his globe of the Earth to his peers in 1492, he must have produced just such a sense of childlike wonderment.

The 'Earth-apple'

Behaim's globe was like nothing anyone had ever seen before. Made from papier-mâché and plaster, with a parchment skin painted with the outlines of all the known continents, it miniaturised the Earth in a 51cm-diameter sphere. The shape explained its contemporary nickname *Erdapfel*, literally 'Earth-apple'. But what gave Behaim the idea of showing the Earth in this way in the first place?

In the 6th century BC, the Greek mathematician Pythagoras was the first to suggest that the Earth might be shaped like a ball, an idea later taken up by both Aristotle and Euclid. It may even be the case that the ancient Greeks, who we know made celestial globes, also made terrestrial ones. Once the geographer Eratosthenes had worked out the circumference of the Earth, in the

3rd century BC, it would have been a simple step for people to calculate the planet's diameter, surface area and volume, and to make a scale model. But no example of a globe survives from this time, or even any written account of one. Martin Behaim's globe is incontestably the oldest globe we have.

A well-founded fact

Contrary to a persistent myth peddled for many decades in schoolbooks, the great majority of educated people in the Middle Ages, including ecclesiastical scholars, accepted that the Earth was round. A monk named Cosmas Indicopleustes had, in *c*550, written the *Christian Topography* rejecting the idea of a spherical world and claiming, on the basis of Biblical evidence, that it was modelled on a tabernacle with the heavens shaped like a curved box lid. But his Greek text – which is cited as a key piece of evidence by those who claim that medieval people believed the Earth

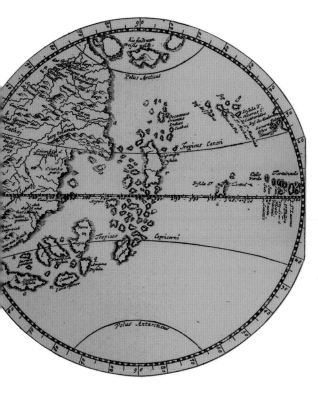

Martin Behaim's planisphere
Behaim's map of 1492 portrays the Earth as two hemispheres; the Americas are missing altogether. For many years, this German cartographer and probable inventor of the globe was employed as official geographer to King John II of Portugal.

Tresor, Bruno Latini put forward new arguments to prove that our planet was spherical. Yet such scholarly musings would have been beyond the ken of illiterate peasants and labourers in the Middle Ages, and it is highly likely that the general public did indeed imagine the world as flat before they first set eyes on a terrestrial globe.

Biblical geography

Even so, medieval scholars' conception of the Earth would have had little in common with the one we know. The geographical studies of Erastosthenes, Hipparchus and Ptolemy – together with their adjunct, Greek scientific cartography – were entirely neglected or ignored in the Middle Ages. The only reference that counted was the Bible. Right up to the

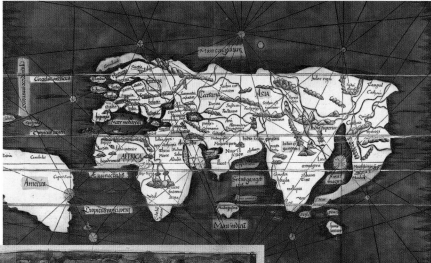

was flat – remained largely unknown outside Byzantium. Recent researches have shown that whenever the question of the shape of the Earth crops up in medieval texts (which is not very often), the sphere is invariably mentioned. This emerges even more clearly in texts from the 12th and 13th centuries: in 1120, for example, the French encyclopaedist Lambert de Saint-Omer included an illustration in his *Liber Floridus* of the Earth as the world's ninth and final sphere. In around 1265, in the first French-language encyclopaedia *Li Livres dou*

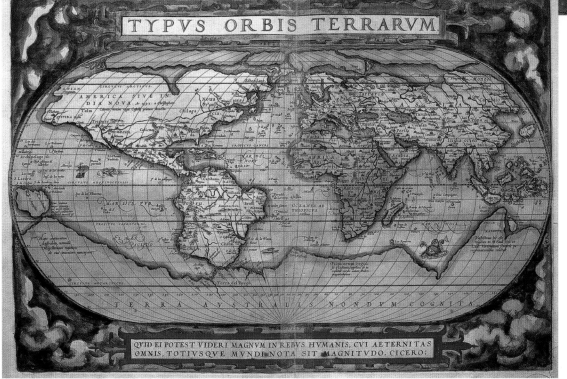

A new world
The rapid advances in geographical knowledge during this period can be gauged by comparing the map of 1541 (above), based on Ptolemy's world map of cAD 150, with its counterpart from the Atlas produced by Abraham Ortelius in 1570 (left). Although on the later map, the outline of the Americas is still notional, Europe, Africa, and Asia are instantly recognisable. This new accuracy was the fruit of 30 years of intensive maritime exploration.

THE FLAT-EARTH FALLACY

From the Renaissance onwards, scholars put about the idea that their medieval counterparts, unaware of the work of ancient Greek geographers, had thought the Earth was flat. To support the assertion, they pointed to medieval *mappae mundi*, which traditionally represented the world as a flat disc instead of showing it in three dimensions. But it was in the 19th century that the myth really took root. In 1828, the American author Washington Irving, writer of popular historical novels, published *The Life and Voyages of Christopher Columbus* in which he claimed that, in order to justify his plan to sail west across the Atlantic, the Genoese seafarer had first to convince his backers that the Earth was round. Then, in 1834, the fiercely anti-clerical French geographer Antoine-Jean Letronne published in the *Revue des Deux Mondes* an article entitled 'The cosmographic views of the Church Fathers', stating that they and their successors believed that the Earth was flat. The myth was a powerful piece of propaganda for advocates of the French republican ideal and secular schools, who were convinced that the Church had a vested interest in keeping people ignorant. The myth still clings on in some school textbooks and the popular imagination, despite many recent works by medievalists showing it to be untrue.

14th century, medieval *mappae mundi* were all in the same vein as that created by Isidore of Seville back in the 7th century, showing Jerusalem at the centre of a terrestrial world divided into three continents – Europe, Africa and Asia. The celestial sphere, or paradise, was believed to lie in the east, immediately above the Holy Land. As a result, maps were always oriented with East at the top. In short, the sole purpose of maps at this time was to corroborate a religious view of the world.

Cresques' *Catalan Atlas*

Anyone – be they rulers, merchants or seafarers – who wanted a more practical overview of trade routes and lands that had already been discovered, or regions that had yet to to be explored, had to get their information from other sources. In the 14th century, for instance, when Charles V of France wanted an accurate map of the world, he turned to scholars in Spain, which at the time was still steeped in Moorish culture, and specifically Islamic science, which had preserved and enriched the legacy of ancient Greek geography.

The *Catalan Atlas* commissioned by Charles was produced in 1375 by Abraham Cresques, a Jewish master cartographer from the island of Majorca. The work comprised a series of maps depicting the known world; never before had the subject been treated so fully or meticulously, purged of all Biblical references. Cresques created a truly scientific work, well-researched and supported by first-hand accounts from both European and Arab seafarers and explorers. The coastline of the Far East was still sketchy, but his map of the Near East and South Asia, clearly showing the Persian Gulf and India, was remarkably accurate. The map of Europe corresponded closely, give or take a few details, with portolan charts of the time – nautical charts used by European sailors to plot coastal routes from at least 1290, the date of the *Carte Pisane*, the earliest known nautical chart.

The world in the round

Behaim's globe was made in much the same spirit as Cresques' atlas, being a representation of the real world and a compendium of all current geographical knowledge. He took as

Seas of Europe
The Mediterranean, as represented by Abraham Cresques in the Catalan Atlas *of 1375. The Black Sea above it is disproportionately large.*

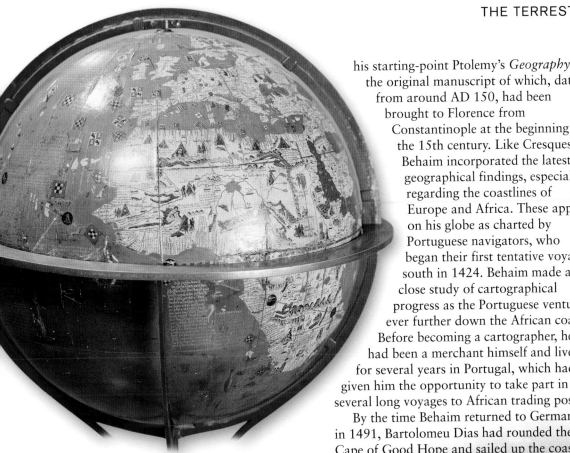

his starting-point Ptolemy's *Geography*, the original manuscript of which, dating from around AD 150, had been brought to Florence from Constantinople at the beginning of the 15th century. Like Cresques, Behaim incorporated the latest geographical findings, especially regarding the coastlines of Europe and Africa. These appear on his globe as charted by Portuguese navigators, who began their first tentative voyages south in 1424. Behaim made a close study of cartographical progress as the Portuguese ventured ever further down the African coast. Before becoming a cartographer, he had been a merchant himself and lived for several years in Portugal, which had given him the opportunity to take part in several long voyages to African trading posts. By the time Behaim returned to Germany in 1491, Bartolomeu Dias had rounded the Cape of Good Hope and sailed up the coast of

Contemporary of Columbus

Martin Behaim made his terrestrial globe (left) in 1492, the year that Christopher Columbus made his first exploratory voyage west and discovered Cuba and Hispaniola.

Contemplating the stars

Painted in 1668, The Astronomer by Jan Vermeer (below) captures some of the sheer wonderment felt by 17th-century Europeans during the great Age of Discovery.

CELESTIAL GLOBES

Since classical antiquity, the heavens had commonly been portrayed as a sphere. From the 2nd century AD onwards, all Greek, Roman and Arab celestial globes were based on Ptolemy's *Almagest*, which contained a catalogue of 1,022 stars in 48 constellations, representing them as figures from mythology. From the beginning of the Middle Ages, monks in the West made similar celestial globes in order to fix the calendar of religious festivals from the position of the stars. Celestial globes reached a height of sophistication in the 16th and 17th centuries; the axis of inclination was made adjustable to ensure that the part of the globe situated above the broad horizontal band around its centre (known as the 'horizon') always showed the sector of the sky visible from the user's location. The sector would shift according to latitude and time of year. The ring corresponding to the equinoctial meridian was fitted at the North Pole with a printed hour circle and a brass pointer that formed an extension of the axis of rotation. As users turned the globe, they could read off from the pointer the time at which any particular part of the sky and its constellations would come into view.

FROM TWO TO THREE DIMENSIONS

Wood, gold, copper, ivory, glass – all kinds of materials were used in the manufacture of luxury globes, which right from the outset were made for the collectors' market. Globes for everyday use were generally made from a thin skin of papier-mâché covered with a smooth coat of plaster. The map of the world was first painted onto a piece of parchment and then printed onto paper to form the globe's outer cover. This meant adapting a two-dimensional map to the spherical form of the globe. The monk Martin Waldseemüller devised a technique whereby the world was divided into segments (usually 12), each running from the North to the South Pole. This segmented map was engraved back-to-front onto a wood block or copper plate ready for printing. Cut to shape, the paper segments aligned perfectly when they were stuck down onto the globe's surface. The globe was then mounted on an axle set at the same angle as the Earth's rotational axis (23.5° from the vertical). Finally, the whole assembly was fitted onto a frame comprising a tilted equinoctial meridian and a fixed horizontal band – the horizon.

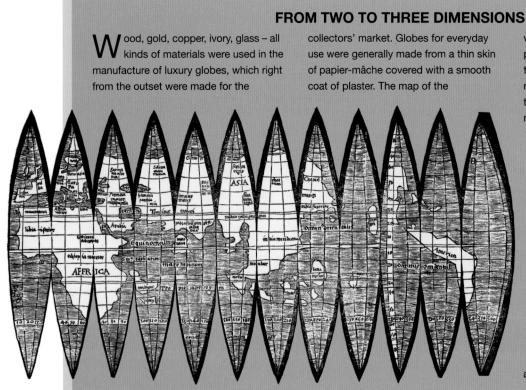

Master cartographer
Martin Waldseemüller's celebrated 12-panel map of the world (above) was made in 1507. It was the first map to use the name 'America' to designate an outline of the New World.

East Africa, confirming in the process that the Indian Ocean could be reached from the Atlantic. The treasures of the East beckoned. Behaim was utterly convinced of the commercial worth of these expeditions, and it seems likely that one of his main motives in making a terrestrial globe was to persuade his compatriots of the benefits that would flow from financing future voyages of discovery.

The Americas do not feature on Behaim's globe; when it was created Christopher Columbus had not yet made history by landing in the West Indies. There is nothing to indicate that Columbus, who embarked on his first voyage that same year, 1492, knew of the existence of the *Erdapfel*.

Like Ptolemy, Behaim overestimated the surface area of the continents compared to the oceans. On his globe, which is divided into

MAJOR MISCALCULATIONS

Christopher Columbus's tribulations on his first voyage west – to the East Indies, as he thought – were not just caused by Ptolemy's huge underestimate of the distance between western Europe and East Asia. Many of Columbus's maps were based on Arab documents, which gave distances in nautical miles, and he failed to take into account that an Arab nautical mile was a third longer than the mile measurement used in his native Genoa in Italy. As a result, his ships took far longer than anticipated to cross the Atlantic.

360 degrees of longitude (by then common currency among all scientific cartographers), the Eurasian landmass covers fully 234 degrees (the actual span is 131 degrees). As a result of the error, the single expanse of ocean separating Europe from East Asia on the globe was greatly shrunken. Relying on this information, a European seafarer heading due west might expect to reach the coast of Asia in just a few weeks. Whether Columbus knew of Behaim's work or not, he certainly had a copy of Ptolemy's *Geography* in his library, and it was this commonplace misconception of a narrow western sea with no intervening landmass that lay behind his famous plan to reach the East Indies by crossing the Atlantic.

A new continent

After Behaim, globes and maps continued to reflect contemporary advances in geographical knowledge. Cartographers were able to supply a public eager to keep abreast of the latest discoveries with up-to-date maps of the world, largely thanks to the new invention of printing.

In around 1507 Martin Waldseemüller, a monk from Lorraine, published a wall map of the world and a small globe. Both featured the new continent, which Waldseemüller dubbed 'America'; according to one theory he named it after the Italian explorer Amerigo Vespucci, who was the first to realise that the lands of the New World constituted a fourth continent. There was another, technical, novelty about Waldseemüller's globe; unlike previous globes it was not covered with painted parchment, but with a map printed on paper from a woodcut. To achieve this, he had divided his world map into 12 segments, an innovation subsequently adopted by all globemakers.

Starting a trend

Within the space of 50 years, Behaim's invention became not only an important adjunct to cartography but also a symbol of a certain cultural and social status. Ownership of a globe hinted at good taste and refinement. In the 16th and 17th centuries, Flemish and Dutch cartographers exploited this by marketing, from 1515 onwards, matching pairs of terrestrial and celestial globes. One of the most famous globemakers of the age was Gerardus Mercator, who as the father of the modern science of cartography opened up a whole new chapter in the history of how people looked at the world.

Combining art and science
Like Leonardo da Vinci, the painter and engraver Albrecht Dürer had a keen interest in contemporary science. In 1515, he produced this exquisite world map (left), which reflected the most up-to-date scholarship of the time.

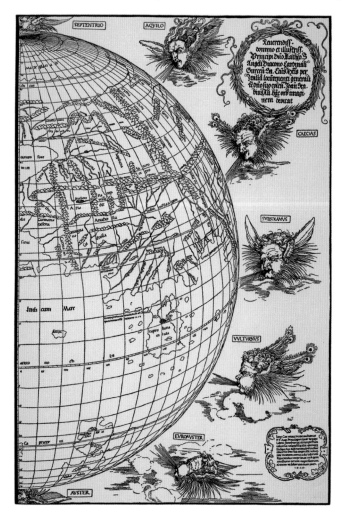

Apogee of the globemaker's art
Johannes Praetorius of Nuremberg cast this magnificent brass terrestrial globe in 1568. It has a scale of 1:45,000,000.

A QUESTION OF SCALE

A globe – a three-dimensional representation of the Earth – does not suffer from the deformation that a projection of the world onto a flat piece of paper entails. On the other hand, globes cannot do full justice to the mapmaker's art. Any attempt to impose a larger scale to make room for more detail increases the diameter of the globe and its weight. With a diameter of 51cm, Behaim's globe shows the world at a scale of 1:20,000,000 – that is, 1 centimetre on the map represents 200km on the ground. Nowadays, the most common diameter for globes is 31cm, or 1:40,000,000. At such a small scale, they are of very little use to navigators.

Europeans discover the world

From the early 15th century onwards, a number of different factors – the lure of gold and spices, the urge to spread Christianity, and sheer curiosity – drove European navigators to set sail in search of new lands and sea routes. Expanding their horizon on the world meant overcoming both their own fear of the unknown and the technical limitations of medieval navigation.

The year is 1434. A small, converted fishing boat approaches Cape Bojador, just south of Cape Juby in present-day Western Sahara. Beyond this headland, so the story goes, lies a 'Sea of Darkness', inhabited by monsters. On board, the terrified crew pray fervently for their salvation. Even the ship's Portuguese captain, Gil Eannes, is struggling to contain his sense of doom. Yet Prince Henry, son of King John I of Portugal, had appealed to him as a gentleman to pursue this mission and Eannes is determined not to let his Prince down. After 10 years of failed attempts to round Cape Bojador, a Portuguese navigator will finally go where no European had sailed before.

To steer clear of the formidable barrier of reefs and the perilous currents off this stretch of the African coast, Eannes orders his helmsman to head west. Offshore winds blow the ship along at a rate of knots but, alone on this vast expanse of ocean, time seems to stand still. After what seems an eternity, the captain issues a new order: bear south and pick up the coast once more. Presently, the shoreline comes into view again. It is a hostile landscape of low, desert dunes – but no sign of monsters. The headland that long inspired the terror of the unknown is behind them. They duly return in triumph to Portugal, mission accomplished.

For gold and glory

Eannes's voyage was vital in overcoming a major psychological barrier. Now there was nothing to prevent the systematic exploration of the African coast and the Portuguese ventured ever further south. Their aim was to open up a new sea route to give them direct access to gold from the kingdoms of Africa. Since the mid-14th century,

Cradle of navigation
In 1420 Prince Henry the Navigator established the world's first naval academy at Sagres on Cape St Vincent in the far southeast of Portugal (above). Statues of Henry (left), Vasco da Gama, Magellan and other Portuguese explorers line the banks of the River Tagus at Belem in Lisbon.

the traditional flow of gold by camel caravans across the Sahara to the ports of North Africa had dwindled to a trickle.

Henry the Navigator prepared his ambitious campaign of exploration with great care. He gathered together the leading cartographers, astronomers and shipbuilders of the age at his new school of navigation at Sagres. The extensive library there contained all the latest maps and nautical charts, plus a vast array of manuscripts from past explorers and geographers. Henry also ordered all current Portuguese merchants and seafarers to divulge to him any new information they came by.

Age of the caravel

Even the best documents of Henry's day could only give a sketchy idea of the size and shape of Africa. Sailors in the Mediterranean had been aided by portolan charts since at least the end of the 13th century, but none existed for the region Henry intended to explore. Portolan charts contained valuable detailed information on coastlines, reefs, anchorages and distances, and were constantly updated. Sailors navigated quite literally by eye, trying whenever possible to keep the coastline constantly in view.

Over several decades the shipyards of Lagos, near Sagres, developed and perfected an ideal ocean-going type of ship: the caravel. It is not know when or where the very first caravel was built. It was a perfect synthesis of boatbuilding techniques from the Mediterranean and Atlantic Europe, combining the sleek lines of Viking longships, the high sterncastle of the Hanseatic cog and the lateen sails used on Mediterranean galleys. Caravels were also equipped with sternpost rudders, which had become standard equipment on both northern and southern European vessels by the late 14th century. But the caravel's chief assets were its spry handling and its ability to sail into a headwind, which instilled sailors with the confidence that they could and would return safely home.

Portuguese caravel
Not all ships making voyages of discovery were the high-sided carracks later made famous by images of Christopher Columbus's flagship, the Santa Maria. Caravels were smaller, lateen-rigged and with a lower freeboard, as shown by this illustration of a three-master (above). The ship formed part of the fleet under the command of Vasco da Gama, one of the great seafaring heroes of Portugal's age of discovery.

Driving spirit
Prince Henry the Navigator (seated, holding a model ship) surrounded by his cartographers and admirals, key players in his campaign of discovery and conquest of unknown lands.

The stars and the winds

In 1471 Portuguese seafarers crossed the Equator for the first time, reaching the mouth of the Congo River and the Skeleton Coast of the Namib Desert between 1480 and 1485. Although Henry the Navigator had died in 1460, his brother King John II continued with the programme of exploration, encouraged by the positive results of the African venture. Valuable commodities such as slaves, gold and Guinea pepper poured in from Portugal's African trading posts.

The further south the Portuguese went, the more sophisticated their methods of navigation became. The astronomers and mathematicians of Sagres devised the quadrant, which enabled sailors to take accurate star sightings and work out their elevation above the horizon. Beyond the Equator the Pole Star disappeared from view, and so the only way to determine latitude was to observe the position of the Sun. But only the most skilled sailors were versed in astronomical navigation, which was still in its infancy. Sea captains relied on the tradewinds, which blew in different directions on either side of the Equator. In order to travel south to Africa, a

Circumnavigating Africa
A 16th-century German map (below), with a title that translates as 'Africa, Libya, Mauritania and all the known kingdoms of the continent', shows a fairly accurate depiction of Africa's coastline. The astrolabe is from the same period. The portrait (right) shows Vasco da Gama, the first European navigator to sail to India.

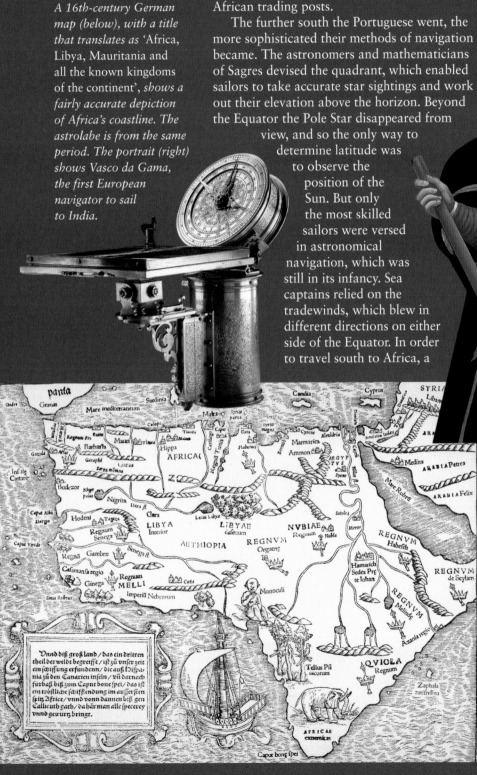

ship would first head west and be carried by prevailing northeasterlies far out into the Atlantic. After passing the doldrums around the Equator the ship would turn back east in a wide arc, sailing into southeasterlies, to pick up the African coast once more.

A route to the east

Bartolomeu Dias sailed from Lisbon in the summer of 1487 and performed precisely this manoeuvre to reach the coast of southern Africa. The aim of his expedition was to find out whether the Atlantic connected with the Indian Ocean, as some accounts had claimed. He would be flying in the face of ancient cartography, but if it were true, it would open up a sea route to the east and to India.

On 3 February, 1488, after weathering a storm off the Cape of Good Hope, Dias

EARLY NAVIGATIONAL AIDS

In the 1500s, determining latitude became more precise thanks to the nautical astrolabe and the Jacob's staff, a device for measuring the altitude of the Sun and Pole Star. The Mercator map projection made navigation by magnetic compass more reliable, but it was John Harrison's marine chronometer (1759) that made navigation a truly scientific discipline. At the same time the chip log – a simple wooden panel with a knotted piece of rope – provided a reasonably accurate estimate of a ship's speed (hence the term 'knots').

dropped anchor on the east coast of Africa, some 250 miles (400km) east of the southernmost point of the continent. He had rounded Africa's southern tip and reached the Indian Ocean, but soon the ravages of scurvy on his crew and the damage that his fleet had sustained forced him to turn back. A decade later, it fell to Vasco da Gama to retrace Dias's steps. He left Lisbon on 4 July, 1497, and arrived at the port of Calicut (modern Kozhikode in the Indian state of Kerala) on 22 May, 1498 – a voyage of some 10,000 miles (16,000km). It had taken him 27 days to cross the Indian Ocean after leaving the Mozambique Channel, having engaged the services of an Arab pilot who was familiar with navigation in this part of the world.

Columbus and the route west

Meanwhile, Portugal's neighbour and great rival Spain also became involved in maritime exploration. In 1492 Christopher Columbus, a Genoese seafarer in the service of Ferdinand of Aragón and Isabella of Castile, set sail due west. Drawing on Portuguese knowledge of prevailing winds, it took him three months to cross the Atlantic and make land in what he thought was the East Indies. Of course, we now know that he landed on the Greater Antilles. His mistake, which he failed to acknowledge despite three further voyages to the Americas, arose from his reliance on charts based largely on Ptolemy's map of AD 150, and on the journals of Marco Polo.

Columbus commanded a fleet of three ships. The *Pinta* and the *Niña* were caravels of around 50 tonnes apiece. His flagship the

Santa Maria was a carrack (or *nao*) about 25 metres long and 7 or 8 metres in the beam, with fore and aftcastles. She had three masts, two rigged with squaresails, which were better suited to sailing the high seas. During a stopover at the Canaries, the lateen sails of the *Niña* were also replaced with squaresails. After Columbus' first voyage, the construction and rigging of the *Santa Maria* became the model for ships used on voyages of exploration.

The only things Columbus could rely upon in navigating these unknown waters were the basic soundness of his ships and his considerable experience of the sea. He maintained his heading with a magnetic compass and gauged his rate of progress using a time-honoured method employed by generations of seamen: standing on the aftcastle, a sailor threw a light piece of wood into the wind towards the prow of the ship

Conquering the high seas
The panoramic painting of ships under Vasco da Gama's command (left) shows that different sails were used even within the same fleet. Christopher Columbus's flagship Santa Maria *(below) became the model for ships built for long-distance exploration. The map of Columbus's fourth voyage (bottom), drawn by his brother Bartolomeu, clearly indicates that the explorer thought he had reached the coast of Asia.*

TRADING TOMATOES FOR HORSES

The conquest and colonisation of the Americas got underway from Columbus' second voyage (1493) onwards. This enterprise witnessed not only great movements of people but also a large-scale intermingling of species hitherto confined to one part of the globe (including pathogenic microbes). Imports from the New World to Europe included maize, tobacco, tomatoes, squashes, potatoes, sunflowers and the turkey. Many plants native to the Americas – such as sweet potatoes, cocoa, groundnuts, rubber and cotton – would later be successfully transplanted to Africa and Asia when they were colonised in their turn. In exchange, species introduced to the Americas from Europe, Asia or Africa included horses, sheep, pigs, cows and chickens, as well as wheat, oats and rice.

Divine discovery
A Mexican woman preparing xocoatl. *Europeans instantly took to this sweet confection, importing it under an adaptation of its native name – chocolate.*

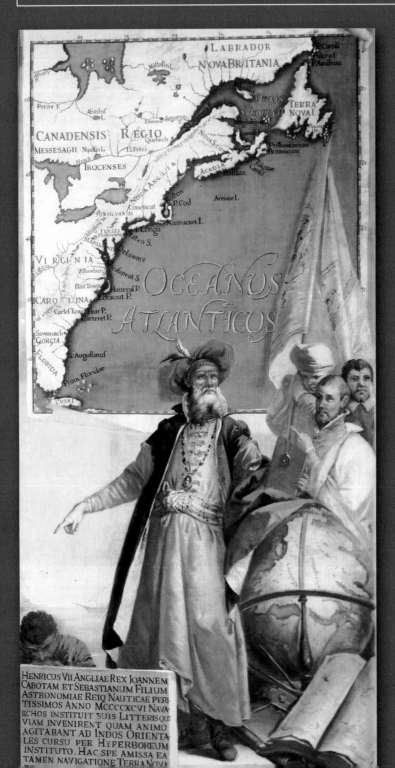

and measured with an hourglass the time it took to drift back to the stern. Yet even with such rudimentary techniques and no accurate nautical charts, Columbus managed to select the best possible route to the Americas.

From America to the Pacific

Before long, other navigators were pioneering routes to the west. On his second voyage, in 1497, John Cabot reached the continental landmass of North America on a route that ultimately led to the discovery of the rich fishing grounds off Newfoundland. Soon after, in 1500, Pedro Cabral was sailing to India via south Africa when he was blown off course; as a result he discovered the coast of Brazil and claimed this vast territory for Portugal. After Amerigo Vespucci had crossed the Atlantic and ventured far down the coast of South America in 1501–2, Europeans began to realise that the Americas were one vast 'New World', showing it on maps as two continental landmasses separated by a narrow isthmus. In the wake of the explorers, came fleets of galleons and carracks, as the conquest and exploitation of these 'virgin' lands gathered pace.

Even so, the riches of the Americas could not dispel the dream of lucrative trade routes to the East. After Cabot, many explorers perished trying to find a Northwest Passage to the East sailing north of Canada. Meanwhile, Ferdinand Magellan, a Portuguese sailor in the service of Spain, tried to find a passage to the south of Brazil. Like Columbus, Magellan relied on an inaccurate map, as well as on false reports by Portuguese sailors who claimed to have found a passage from the Atlantic to the expanse of ocean that the conquistador Nuñez de Balboa had spotted on the far side of the

Exploring northern climes
The Venetian Giovanni Caboto, whose name was Anglicised as John Cabot, in an 18th-century engraving (left). Sailing on behalf of the English crown, he was the first European to set foot on the North American mainland, in 1497.

PRECOLUMBIAN AMERICA

Various pieces of archaeological and historical evidence suggest that the first contact between the Old and the New Worlds took place much earlier than Columbus's 'discovery' of America in 1492. For example, 12 of the famous colossal heads made by the Mesoamerican Olmec people, found in the Veracruz region and dating from the 6th century AD, have markedly African features, while many similar black figures appear on murals throughout pre-Columbian Mexico. Nobody knows their origins.

The Dominican friar Gregorio Garcia, who spent nine years in Peru in the early 1500s, wrote of an island off the port of Cartagena in Colombia where the Spanish first set eyes on black people in South America – three decades before the shipping of African slaves to the Americas began.

Other, admittedly sketchy, evidence of early exploration comes from the *Navigatio Sancti Brendani Abbatis*, an 8th-century account of the voyage that the Irish monk St Brendan supposedly undertook two centuries before. In a large boat made of stitched leather and with two square sails, Brendan is said to have set sail from County Kerry and crossed the Atlantic to Newfoundland, fully four centuries before the Viking Erik the Red set foot there.

Advances in shipbuilding may have ensured Europeans mastery of the sea from the 16th century onwards, but it is possible that African peoples learned long before how to exploit ocean currents (notably the Canary Current in the northern hemisphere and the South Equatorial Current in the southern) in order to explore new lands in less sophisticated craft. Certainly, early Portuguese explorers in Brazil discovered large dugout canoes on the Orinoco River very similar to those made in Africa.

Of African descent?
One of the colossal Olmec heads found in the region of Veracruz in Mexico.

Panama Isthmus in 1513. A combination of Magellan's sheer obstinacy and the ambitions of the rulers of Spain led to one of the most incredible voyages ever undertaken.

Proof that the Earth is round

The fleet commanded by Magellan left the port of Sanlucar on 20 September, 1519. After sailing further south than any existing charts recorded, he found a passage around the tip of South America at the strait that now bears his name. On 28 November, 1520, he began the crossing of the Pacific. His crew, racked with thirst and hunger, were tested to the limits of endurance. Finally, on 6 March, 1521, they sighted land – the Marianas Islands.

Magellan was killed in a skirmish with natives on the Philippines, but his surviving crew, led by Juan Elcano, went on to visit the Moluccas – the Spice islands long fabled in the West as the source of nutmeg and cloves – before returning home to complete the first circumnavigation of the globe on 6 September, 1522. Here, then, was conclusive proof that the Earth was round and that the oceans covered far more of its surface than landmasses. Only one of the five galleons that had set out made it back, carrying just 18 men from an original crew of 265.

A changed world

For better or worse, the face of the known world had changed for ever. Cartographers consigned the geography of classical antiquity to the dustbin of history. As the vastness of the Earth unfolded, it lent impetus to new voyages of exploration. Over the course of the 18th and 19th centuries Captain James Cook and his successors fleshed out the map of the Pacific and discovered the Antarctic, while adventurers, missionaries and conquerors pushed deep into distant continents. As white explorers opened up unknown parts of the world, so European civilisation came into contact with new peoples. The profound culture shock of the first encounter between the Old World and the New continued to reverberate down the ages.

Charting the Americas
Sixty years after Columbus, Europeans realised that the western route to Asia entailed rounding the southern tip of the Americas and crossing the vast Pacific. This detail from an atlas of 1571 shows a simplified Strait of Magellan.

Whisky 1494

The Scots and Irish vie for the distinction of having invented whisky (or 'whiskey', in the Irish spelling). The word derives from the Gaelic *uisge beatha*, or 'water of life'. Irish tradition maintains that Saint Patrick introduced the technique of distillation to Ireland in the 5th century. For a long time, *uisge beatha* was used for medicinal purposes.

During the Middle Ages the Scots made it their national drink. A document of 1494 mentions the delivery of 'eight sheaves of barley ... for the manufacture of aqua vitae'. Malt, which is derived from the forced germination of barley, is dried over peat fires to 'smoke' the grain; the malted barley is then steeped in hot water to produce a 'mash', a kind of beer, which is distilled through a still, then aged in oak barrels. This method of making malt whisky has barely changed over the centuries.

Old-style still
The first commercial whiskies were probably made using pieces of apparatus like this (left).

Whisky galore
When the mass production of whisky began in the 19th century, the first bottles were flat (inset, above left), to slip easily into a pocket.

BLENDED WHISKY

For a long time, the spread of whisky was hampered by heavy taxes on its manufacture and export. In the 19th century, the introduction of a new type of still allowing continuous distillation paved the way for the large-scale production of blended whisky, which is grain-based. Together with American Bourbon whiskey, which is made from maize, blended whiskies account for most of the whisky produced worldwide.

Double-entry bookkeeping 1494

The world's first accounts were written on clay tablets, such as those found in the Sumerian city of Ur (*c*2000 BC), or were tokens indicating a commodity, on which marks were made to record transactions. In the Middle Ages, with the introduction of credit, the necessity arose for sets of figures that would track all income and outgoings. The result was double-entry bookkeeping, which involves recording each transaction in two accounts: every expense is debited from one account and every asset is credited to another; an imbalance between the two indicates an error. This method of accounting gave a clear overview of a company's financial situation and introduced the concept of the balance sheet.

INVENTED BY THE TEMPLARS

Double-entry boo-keeping was introduced by the Knights Templar and used extensively from the end of the 13th century in the mercantile cities of Italy. Following the invention of the printing press, the accounting method quickly gained widespread acceptance, thanks in large part to the Venetian mathematician Luca Pacioli (1445–1510), who codified its principles in a 1494 work entitled *Summa de arithmetica, geometria, proporzioni et proporzionalita*.

Counting the beans *Two 15th-century Spanish bookkeepers counting on their fingers (above), almost certainly a satirical jibe by the artist. The background shows an extract from the accounts of Impressionist artist Claude Monet, detailing the sale of his paintings.*

The toothbrush *c*1500

The first toothbrushes were used in China around the end of the 15th century. They consisted of a few bristles from the coat of a Siberian wild boar stuck into a piece of bamboo or bone; crude though the implement was, it had all the essential elements of a toothbrush. But the Chinese were not the first people concerned about dental hygiene. In ancient Egyptian tombs dating from around 5,000 years ago, twigs with frayed ends have been found that may have served as toothpicks or rudimentary brushes. An Indian document from the 6th century BC recommends that to maintain oral health people should chew a twig to soften the end, which must have produced something approximating to a toothbrush.

The modern toothbrush is almost certainly a Chinese invention. European explorers were quite taken by this simple implement and it grew steadily in popularity throughout the 16th century. At first, it was regarded as a luxury, and many were crafted in precious metals or studded with gemstones. Toothbrushes enjoyed something of a vogue at the court of Henry III of France, but faced an uphill struggle to gain acceptance by doctors, who by and large preferred mouthwashes for oral hygiene. If people used anything at all, they were likely to pick their teeth with the quill of a goose feather rather than brushing them.

Imperial accoutrements
Toiletries owned by Napoleon's consort, the Empress Josephine, included this pig-bristle toothbrush and case (above).

BY ROYAL APPOINTMENT

In around 1780, the Clerkenwell stationer and bookbinder William Addis was serving a short sentence in Newgate Prison in London. To help while away the time he made a toothbrush, using a bone and some hairs from a cowhide. No sooner had Addis been released than he decided to mass-produce his invention, just as toothbrushes were coming into fashion. He even won the approval of George IV – an invaluable endorsement. The toothbrush enterprise started by Addis has survived right up to the present-day, under the name of Wisdom.

Pig bristles, or hairs from other animals, continued to be used right up to the Second World War, when the conflict disrupted deliveries from traditional suppliers like China and Yugoslavia. As a result, artificial bristles replaced natural ones. The first synthetic brushes were so stiff that they damaged people's gums, but by 1950 toothbrushes were being made with flexible new nylon fibres.

Personal hygiene
In countries where manufactured goods are not generally widespread, many people use makeshift items as toothbrushes. This Ethiopian man is using a reed to clean his teeth.

LEONARDO DA VINCI – 1452 TO 1519

A life seeking knowledge

Leonardo the painter has long eclipsed Leonardo the engineer and thinker, but as his notebooks amply demonstrate, Leonardo's curiosity ranged far and wide across all realms of theoretical and practical knowledge. Many of his ideas prefigured later discoveries and inventions, often by centuries. Leonardo's extraordinary mind, as reflected in his life and work, makes him the quintessential Renaissance Man.

In around 1481, Leonardo da Vinci wrote a letter of introduction to Ludovico Sforza, Duke of Milan, offering his services to his 'most illustrious Lord'. He expounded at some length upon his skills as a military engineer (Sforza was almost constantly at war), concluding by stressing how useful he could also be to the Duke in peacetime: 'I believe I can give perfect satisfaction and be the equal of any man in architecture, in the design of buildings public and private, or to conduct water from one place to another. I can also execute sculpture in marble, bronze and clay; and in painting can do any kind of work as well as any man, whoever he may be.'

Leonardo was by then almost 30 years old and his aim in writing to the duke was to gain the patronage of a powerful ruler, which would give him the funding that would allow him to pursue his art and studies. He was also keen to gain the recognition and social status that had been denied him in Florence.

A precocious talent

In 1468, when Leonardo was just 16 years old, his father, the notary Piero da Vinci, showed some of his son's drawings to a friend, Andrea del Verrocchio. This great painter professed himself 'amazed at such promising beginnings'. Giorgio Vasari, who tells this story in *Lives of the Artists* (1550), also noted that Leonardo could have had a brilliant academic career if he had applied himself to the grammar and maths lessons given by a local cleric, instead of wandering the streets of Florence on his own and taking off into the Tuscan hills around the town of Vinci. On his wanderings, Leonardo sketched everything he saw, displaying amazing insights in his depictions of nature and people.

Pioneering landscape artist
In this early drawing, from 1473, Leonardo broke with long tradition by allowing the landscape to take centre stage. Earlier painters had always treated the landscape as merely a decorative, or at most allegorical, element in their work.

Foreseeing the future
From the aeroplane to the diving suit, Leonardo da Vinci anticipated many modern inventions. These two pages from his famous Notebooks (above) set out descriptions and diagrams of a propulsion system for a flying machine. He used mirror-writing – no-one is entirely sure why, but one theory is that it was to prevent his ideas being easily read by others. His sketches included the cartoon (top right) of an 'artificial lung' for divers.

Verrocchio's studio in Florence was a hotbed of artistic talent. Leonardo's peers there included Botticelli and Perugino. As was the custom in those days, the apprentices worked on paintings commissioned from the master. Between 1471 and 1476, he painted a superb angel for *The Baptism of Christ*; Vasari claims that Verrocchio, who signed the picture, was so humiliated at being outshone by his pupil that he gave up painting for good.

Art and technology

Before long, Leonardo was signing his own paintings, including portraits such as that of Ginevra da Benci and religious paintings such as the *Annunciation* for the Church of San Bartolomeo. Even so, it was 1481 before he received his first major commission, for an altarpiece for the San Donato convent in Scopeto. Yet the altarpiece – titled the *Adoration of the Magi* and already displaying the characteristic features of Leonardo's art – remained unfinished. By then, Leonardo was champing at the bit to get away from Florence, where he found himself marginalised from the circle of artists cultivated by the city's ruler, Lorenzo de' Medici.

The notebooks that Leonardo produced during his first Florentine period already contained mechanical designs. In 1471, his master Verrocchio completed a lantern and bronze ball to sit atop the magnificent dome of the Cathedral of Santa Maria del Fiore in the city. Filippo Brunelleschi, the architect who had designed the dome, also devised various ingenious machines for lifting the materials for Verrocchio's lantern up to its final location.

Leonardo reproduced Brunelleschi's devices in meticulous detail, dismantling them in his mind and drawing every component separately in order to understand the mechanism better. Combining his own observations which what he had gleaned from others, he was able to give free rein to his imagination and come up with new machines of his own. From the end of the 1470s, on pages that he covered feverishly with sketches and annotations, studies of the Madonna jostle for space with designs for automatic weaving looms, underwater breathing apparatuses ... even self-propelled vehicles.

Leonardo's prototype 'car'

The self-propelled vehicle conceived by Leonardo was a strange contraption consisting of a platform mounted on three wheels and steered by a smaller fourth wheel in front. To set the vehicle in motion, the driver would have had to alternately release and rewind leaf springs that engaged a gearing system. The

The Virgin of the Rocks *This atmospheric painting, begun by Leonardo in 1483, is notable for the skilful use of light and shade* (chiaroscuro) *that enhances the spirituality of the scene.*

CREATING A SENSE OF MYSTERY

Arguably, Leonardo's greatest contribution to painting was to imbue it with a sense of mystery. Paradoxically, he was a stickler for precision and realism in his studies of nature and human anatomy, but he gave many of his paintings – including the *Mona Lisa* (1503–07) the *Virgin of the Rocks* (1483–86) and *St John the Baptist* (1513–16) – an enigmatic atmosphere reminiscent of dreamscapes. He achieved this effect through subtle use of *chiaroscuro* and *sfumato* (overlaying translucent areas of colour to give an illusion of depth). The effect is to suffuse the scene with a half-light, while outlines appear blurred; the technique was enhanced by the use of new oil paints. While his conservative patrons preferred clear, vibrant colours, Leonardo mostly rejected these in favour of large areas of dark paint of an indeterminate colour. As a result, the beauty, spirituality and mystery of his figures shines out all the more strongly. Leonardo's technique started a trend that lasted for almost a century, culminating in the dramatic light effects that characterise the work of Caravaggio.

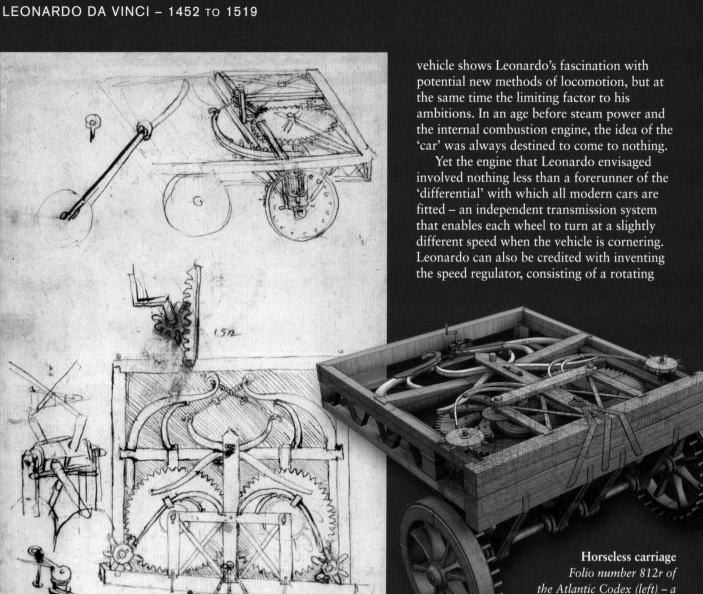

vehicle shows Leonardo's fascination with potential new methods of locomotion, but at the same time the limiting factor to his ambitions. In an age before steam power and the internal combustion engine, the idea of the 'car' was always destined to come to nothing.

Yet the engine that Leonardo envisaged involved nothing less than a forerunner of the 'differential' with which all modern cars are fitted – an independent transmission system that enables each wheel to turn at a slightly different speed when the vehicle is cornering. Leonardo can also be credited with inventing the speed regulator, consisting of a rotating

Horseless carriage
Folio number 812r of the Atlantic Codex (left) – a collection of Leonardo's sketches – shows the self-propelled carriage, including detailed drawings of his proposed cogwheel-and-spring system. Above and below: drawings of a modern, clockwork reconstruction of the vehicle, on display at the Museum of the History of Science in Florence.

FAR FROM UNWORLDLY

Certain commentators have attempted to portray Leonardo as some sort of mystic or visionary. But his writings clearly show that disdained such people. If any further proof of his practical and worldly side were needed, the military hardware he devised should serve to dispel the mystic myth. He drew up designs for a machine gun, an exploding cannonball and even bacteriological warfare in the form of a cannonball filled with excrement and a powerful poison called *acqua toffana*, a mixture of arsenic and lead.

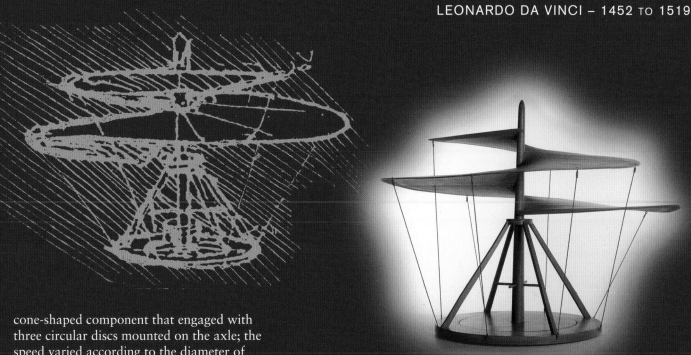

cone-shaped component that engaged with three circular discs mounted on the axle; the speed varied according to the diameter of the disc engaged. In modern parlance, such a device is called continuously variable transmission (CVT).

Serving under Sforza

When Leonardo introduced himself to Duke Ludovico Sforza as an engineer and architect, this was more than simple opportunism on his part. Renaissance princes liked to surround themselves with artists who could build palaces, bridges or canals, and their particular preoccupations dictated in large part the activities of their protégés. Leonardo had a genuine passion for technology, and throughout his life this interest remained intimately linked to his artistic endeavours.

Sforza's ambition was to make Milan a major centre of the Italian Renaissance, and so he invited Leonardo to the duchy in 1482. The great polymath would remain there for 18 years, during which time his reputation grew steadily. In his capacity as official court artist, Leonardo designed and orchestrated the lavish festivities hosted by the duke. He worked on a monumental equestrian statue in honour of Ludovico's father, Francesco Sforza; he created a wooden mock-up of a lantern for the dome of Milan Cathedral; and he painted his famous *Last Supper* mural at the Dominican monastery of Santa Maria delle Grazie. Inspired by the presence in Milan of the architect Donato Bramante, he drew up plans for the construction of an ideal city, while at the same time working on the canalisation of the River Adda.

Leonardo's flying machines

Leonardo's *Notebooks* contain several sketches for a machine on which he intended to fly over and survey the lakes of Lombardy. Before committing a first draft of his flying machine to paper, he had made a careful study of the anatomy of birds' wings and precisely how birds flap them (an action he broke down into its various elements while sketching out his idea). He also investigated air currents and wind resistance, and studied the effects of gravity. The end result was the 'ornithopter', a kind of glider with two pairs of flapping wings controlled by a system of cords and pulleys. The pilot lay in a prone position and used two pedals to power the craft. Leonardo sketched a number of different designs for flying machines, including a pyramid-shaped parachute and an 'aerial helical screw', which he claimed would 'spiral in the air and rise up high', anticipating the principle behind the helicopter.

An original line of thought

In 1496, the arrival of the mathematician Luca Pacioli in Milan opened new horizons for Leonardo. He instantly shelved his other projects and immersed himself in mathematics,

Leonardo's 'helicopter'
The inspiration for Leonardo's 'aerial screw', which he planned to build from wood and linen, was a child's toy. His original sketch of the machine in his Notebooks (above left) formed the basis for a model reconstruction by the Museum of the History of Science in Florence (above right).

OFF THE DRAWING BOARD

The vast majority of Leonardo's ingenious designs never progressed beyond the drawing board, and his ideas only became a reality after his technical drawings were rediscovered in the 19th century. This was the case, for example, with his ornithopter and his pyramidal 'parachute', which was constructed and successfully tested with just one design change: a hole was cut at the top of the canvas envelope to ensure that it remained stable in flight.

a discipline without which, he confided to his *Notebooks*, 'there could be no real science'. He later illustrated Pacioli's treatise *De Divina proportione* (1509) with complex drawings of polyhedra.

With all his diverse interests, Leonardo might appear to have spread his talent too thinly, but in fact he was pursuing a coherent and highly ambitious goal. He was determined to get to grips with as wide a spectrum of phenomena as possible, primarily in order to gain insight into the workings of the universe in its entirety. For example, in order to render human expression and posture accurately, Leonardo pursued an understanding of human anatomy by dissecting corpses. In the process, his mind went off on other fruitful tangents – registering, for instance, the analogy between the circulation of blood and that of water in canals and streams, or likening respiration to the way that winds behave in nature, or comparing human movement with that of machines.

THE DA VINCI CODICES

Leonardo bequeathed some 13,000 pages of sketches and notes – many of them bound up as codices – to Francisco Melzi, a disciple who was with him from his second stay in Milan up to his final years in France. Melzi set himself the task of completing a treatise on painting, the *Codex Urbinas Latinus 1270*, that he had begun with his master; it was eventually published in Paris, in abridged form, in 1651. After Melzi's death in 1570, Leonardo's papers were dispersed and almost half were lost for ever. The study and reconstruction of the surviving manuscripts, either in the order dictated by da Vinci or in many cases more haphazardly, began in the late 19th century. The popular image of Leonardo as a polymath and universal figure of genius dates from this period.

As early as 1473, Leonardo created one of the first true landscape paintings in Western art – a pen-and-ink study of his native Tuscany. Here, landscape is no longer treated as a decorative, secondary element of the composition, as was been customary up till then, but instead forms the main subject of the work. Throughout his life, Leonardo was fascinated by geological formations, meteorology and countless other natural phenomena. During his time in Milan, he took the opportunity to visit the Alps, jotting down remarkably perceptive insights into fold mountains and sedimentation, the origin of fossils and the water cycle. Likewise, for this master of perspective, light and shade, it was only logical that he should make a thorough study of optics.

In search of new patrons

When the French invaded Milan in 1499, temporarily ousting Ludovico Sforza, Leonardo was forced to seek patronage elsewhere. After a brief spell at the court of Marquess Isabella d'Este of Mantua, he entered the service of Cesare Borgia, Duke of Romagna, for whom he drew up maps and architectural plans, and constructed defences. In 1503 he returned to Florence, but left in 1506, having lost the confidence of the city's rulers over the failure of a project to divert the River Arno away from Pisa, Florence's deadly rival. He left a great mural, *The Battle of Anghiari*, at the Palazzo Vecchio, since lost.

Master draughtsman
Left to right: Leonardo's self-portrait of 1515; a study of a foetus in the womb (1510); and a preparatory sketch for the lost painting The Battle of Anghiari *(1506). The background shows a drawing of an icosahedron, a Platonic solid illustrated by Leonardo for Luca Pacioli's* De Divina proportione *(1509).*

Leonardo's sole raison d'etre was his freedom to work unimpeded. Accordingly, on returning to Milan in 1506, he had no qualms about designing a villa for the French military governor of the city, Charles II d'Amboise. In 1512 Leonardo met Giuliano de'Medici, younger brother of the new Pope Leo X, who persuaded him to settle in Rome. While Bramante, Raphael and Michelangelo created art and architecture for the Vatican, Leonardo turned his energies to the city's defensive works and to civil engineering projects, such as rebuilding the port of Civitavecchia and draining the Pontine Marshes.

Fêted in France

When Giuliano died in 1516, Leonardo was invited to work in France under the patronage of Francis I, as 'first painter, architect and engineer to the king'. He was allowed a completely free hand and finished several paintings – including the *Mona Lisa* – which he had carried around with him from place to place for years. He also embarked upon new studies in geometry and mechanics, as well as various architectural projects. Though none of these buildings saw the light of day in his lifetime, one of his designs strongly influenced the builders of the magnificent Loire Château de Chambord (1519–47).

On 2 May, 1519, Leonardo da Vinci died at the Clos Lucé manor house in Amboise. He was renowned as one of the foremost painters of the age and his reputation continued to grow steadily thereafter. His technical and scientific work, on the other hand, languished forgotten for almost four centuries.

A practical bent
For all his flights of technological fancy, Leonardo kept his feet firmly on the ground for many of his inventions, such as this olive-oil press (below), exhibited at the Leonardo da Vinci Museum in his home town.

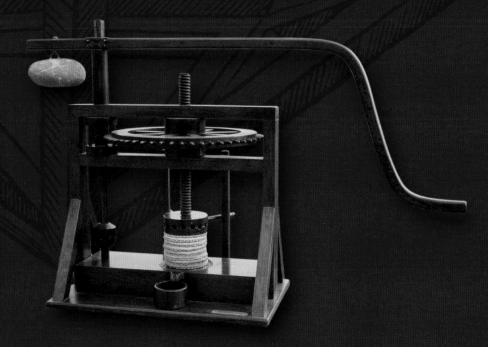

Wallpaper 1509

The oldest known fragment of wallpaper comes from the Master's Lodge in Christ's College, Cambridge, and dates from 1509. Possibly invented in England, wallpaper quickly caught on throughout western Europe from the mid-16th century onwards; a guild of paperhangers was established in France in 1599. In its early days, making wallpaper was a secondary activity for manufacturers of coloured papers, whose main line was playing cards. The first wallpapers were printed in a single colour, occasionally with a raised, stencilled design, and used for lining chests or dressers, or as a substitute for fabric wall-hangings. They were produced in small rectangular sheets, making them unsuitable for covering large expanses of wall.

By the end of the 17th century, advances in paper manufacture saw the advent of long sheets of paper with block-printed designs in matching repeated patterns that made them suitable for hanging; this innovation was the work of Jean-Michel Papillon, a French engraver. The same period saw the arrival of wallpapers from the Far East. Wallpaper hand-painted in gouache or distemper was much in vogue in the 18th century, while the range of motifs, hitherto restricted to flowers or arabesques, kept expanding.

Opulent wallcovering
An expensive hand-painted French wallpaper from the 19th century features a design that harks back to the days of Louis XIV.

THE EVOLUTION OF WALLPAPER

In the 19th century, the increased size of print rollers and the introduction of continuous rotary presses saw wallpaper manufacture enter the age of industrial mass-production. More recently, the most significant advances have been in paper technology, with the invention of washable wallpapers, and printing processes: most modern wallpaper manufacturers use screenprinting.

Meeting the demand
A coloured engraving of a 19th-century wallpaper factory shows the various stages of the manufacturing process, such as printing and applying a stain finish.

Lotteries 1520

The first lottery may have been in China, where Emperor Cheung Leung is said to have invented the lottery game of Keno to raise money for building the Great Wall. Lotteries also existed in ancient Rome, where noblemen used them to distribute gifts to guests; everyone got a prize. Lotteries developed in the Low Countries during the late Middle Ages, with towns selling tickets to raise money for charitable work among the poor. The first to give cash prizes was the Florence lottery of 1530. England's first lottery was established in 1566 by Elizabeth I to pay for harbour repairs. The richest lottery today is Spain's *El Gordo* ('the Fat One'), which had prize money of over £2 billion in 2008.

Drawing lots *The 18th-century French game of Lotto was similar to Bingo, played with numbered wooden tokens and a 90-square board (left).*

Bottle corks 1530

The cork is first mentioned in 1530 in a work by the English lexicographer John Palsgrave entitled *L'esclarcissment de la langue françoyse* ('Elucidation of the French language'). Strictly speaking, the cork appears to have been rediscovered rather than invented in this period. From ancient times, Mediterranean peoples had exploited this natural product, harvested from the cork-oak tree (*Quercus suber*) which grows throughout the region. Flexible, waterproof and airtight, cork was used by ancient Egyptians to seal amphorae and by the Gauls to plug barrels of wine, alongside seals made from clay, wax or even plaster of Paris. The cork went into decline as amphorae gave way to wooden barrels for storing wine, which were sealed with wooden dowels wrapped in oiled hemp. The first glass bottles had fragile necks that were prone to break under pressure from an expanding cork.

Making a comeback

Even though out of favour elsewhere, cork continued in use throughout the Mediterranean region. Though possibly apocryphal, the story goes that the French Benedictine monk Dom Perignon, inventor of champagne, got the idea of using corks to seal his wine after seeing Spanish brothers from his order using chunks of trimmed cork as stoppers for their water gourds. The large-scale revival of corks is closely bound up with the rise in the use of glass bottles for wine. As glassmaking techniques improved, bottles eventually became strong enough to be stoppered with cork. The first mass-produced bottles, sealed with pointed corks for ease of drawing, were bulbous in shape and had to be stored upright. When it was found that laying bottles down, which kept the corks wet, improved the ageing of wine, elongated bottles soon came onto the market, sealed with tight, straight-sided corks. This, in turn, necessitated the invention of the corkscrew.

Cork forest
A cork-oak plantation in the Alentejo region of Portugal, which produces half the world's natural cork.

CORK AND ITS MODERN RIVALS

After being harvested from the tree, the bark of the cork-oak is first dried and then boiled. The planks are then sawn into thin strips, from which the individual corks are cut. These are treated by being coated in paraffin and silicone. Traditional corks, which are prone to infestation by a parasite that can impart an unpleasant flavour to wine, now have to compete with alternatives made from reconstituted cork sawdust, as well as synthetic, plastic stoppers. Another threat is the growing trend for sealing wine bottles with metal screw tops.

A new type of medical treatment

In 1546 the French surgeon Ambroise Paré (1509–90) published his first work on the treatment of gunshot wounds. Written in French (not Latin), by a practitioner for other practitioners, this treatise laid the foundations of modern surgery, stressing the paramount importance of observation, experience and empirical analysis.

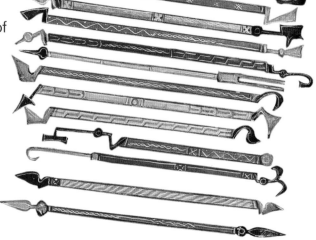

In 1537, in the latest round in the long-running Italian Wars, the French army of Francis I was besieging the city of Turin. Amidst the din of battle, as deafening explosions mingled with the piteous moans and screams of wounded men, a 28-year-old barber-surgeon was treating the terrible, lacerating wounds inflicted by bullets from arquebuses (an early form of rifle).

Medical luminaries
A 14th-century manuscript illumination showing the renowned French surgeon of the day, Guy de Chauliac (seated on the left), teaching alongside three great medical scholars of the past: Avicenna, Galen and Hippocrates.

A new approach to treating wounds

Following conventional practice, Paré applied compresses of boiling oil to the damaged tissue, an appallingly painful procedure. Cauterising the wound in this way was the only sure method of 'detoxifying' it of poison introduced by the gunpowder-driven projectile. At least that was what Paré had been taught. Presently, as more and more wounded men were brought to him, the oil began to run out, so Paré mixed up a concoction of his own, a 'digestive' (a dressing designed to make the wound suppurate) of egg yolks, rose oil and turpentine. He hoped this balm would prove

Fearsome tools
Scalpels and other instruments belonging to a 15th-century surgeon. To the modern practitioner, the notable absentee is an autoclave, vital for sterilising the instruments.

'gentle and soothing'. All the same, he could not sleep the whole night for worrying.

Rising at the crack of dawn, he immediately went to see how his patients were faring. Paré's own account describes what he saw: 'I found that those to whom I had applied my digestive medicament had but little pain, and their wounds were without inflammation or swelling, having rested fairly well that night; the others, on whom the boiling oil was used, I found feverish, with great pain and swelling about the edges of their wounds. There and then, I resolved never more to burn thus cruelly poor men with gunshot wounds.'

Learning through practice

This excerpt from Paré's notes sums up what was perhaps his great contribution to surgery: his awareness that nothing beats experience. Whether on the battlefield, in his surgery in Paris or at the bedside of the king of France, he was always seeking to add to his practical knowledge and to innovate. In 1552 he accompanied the Count de Rohan to the siege of Danvilliers in the role of field surgeon. It was on this campaign that he implemented his most innovative procedure: tying off blood vessels with ligatures during amputations.

Paré did not invent the technique – it was described in 14th century treatises, which may themselves have drawn on ancient Roman practice. But he was, as far as we know, the first to apply it. Before operating, he carefully thought through the procedure and consulted colleagues. As a precaution, during the operation he kept white-hot cauterising irons to hand, which were normally applied to the severed limb to prevent haemorrhaging. Cauterisation was horribly painful, produced severe scar tissue and was not terribly effective at staunching the flow of blood anyway.

After amputating the leg with a saw, Paré teased out the severed blood vessels using

crow's-beak forceps and tied them off using a strong double thread. He found he had no need of the white-hot irons. His technique of instant ligature for amputations has remained the standard procedure in surgery right up to the present day.

A symbolic figure

His innovations in battlefield surgery alone would have assured Ambroise Paré lasting fame, but his reputation as the 'father of modern surgery' rests also on his mission to share his knowledge with his peers. From publication of *The Method of Curing Wounds Made by Arquebus and Other Firearms* (1546) up until his death, Ambroise Paré wrote all his works not in Latin but in French, which was

Ordeal by heat
Cauterisation with a red-hot iron was the standard method of treating serious wounds in the 14th century.

Field surgery
An artist's impression of Ambroise Paré tying off the arteries in a patient's leg after amputation during the siege of Danvilliers in 1552.

THE SURGEON'S PROFESSION

Unlike physicians, most 16th-century surgeons had no university education, and many were unqualified 'barber surgeons' who used their instruments for more than a shave and a haircut. Regarded as mere artisans (the Latin term *chirurgicus* literally means 'a person who works with his hands'), they served an apprenticeship under a master surgeon. By the 13th century qualifications were beginning to be demanded in France and Italy. In addition to setting dislocations and fractures, surgeons' duties included extracting bullets from gunshot injuries, suturing and dressing wounds, amputating limbs, excising external tumours and bandaging hernias. They also operated on cataracts and performed trepanations in cases of cranial trauma. Delivering babies was still theoretically the domain of midwives, though skilled surgeons like Paré and the Italian Gabriello Fallopio (for whom Fallopian tubes are named) were well versed in obstetrics.

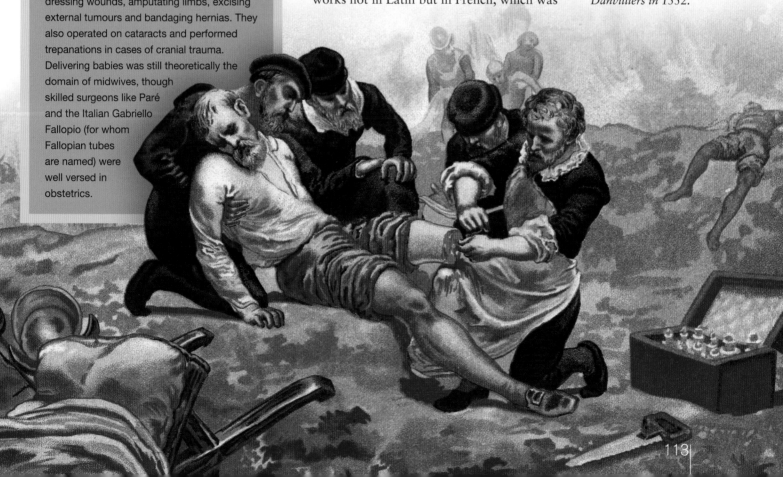

INDIA – AT THE CUTTING EDGE

Few scholars dispute that surgery first reached a high level of sophistication in India; similar standards were not attained in the West for many centuries. During the Brahman period (1000 – 500 BC), detailed descriptions in a surgical text known as the *Susruta samshita* indicate that Indian surgeons were already skilled in the excision of tumours, the extraction of gallstones and the removal of anal fistulas.

Stripped bare
The musculature of the face and neck is portrayed with remarkable accuracy in this 16th-century diagram.

Scream and bear it
Anaesthetics were not available until the 19th century. When this painting of a surgical procedure was made in the 18th century (above), patients simply had to endure the pain.

also the language he used in 1554 to present his thesis to the College of Surgeons in Paris. It was his firm conviction that medical knowledge should not reside merely in performimg operations, but in explaining successful procedures to other practitioners.

Surgery's slow evolution

Although he is justly celebrated as the leading surgeon of the Renaissance, Ambroise Paré benefited from the work of earlier surgeons.

These included Abulcasis of Córdoba, a Muslim surgeon of the 9th–10th century, whose important treatises on medicine were translated and expanded in the 11th century by the renowned medical school at Salerno in southern Italy. Other trailblazers were Lanfranchi of Milan, who in the 13th century made Paris one of the leading centres of medical teaching in the West, and Henri de Mondeville, a pupil of Lanfranchi and Professor of Medicine at Montpellier. These pioneers recommended pouring alcohol on wounds to make them antiseptic and covering wounds with dressings to prevent infection by airborne germs.

Drawing on this heritage, and driven by a new-found interest in the workings of the human body, 16th-century physicians began to make major advances. Another catalyst was the challenge posed by the terrible new destructive power of artillery. In Switzerland Felix Würtz (1518–74) condemned the contemporary practice of treating wounds by sprinkling them with powder from mummified corpses, and recommended that wounds should only be touched with clean hands. Likewise, the German anatomist Wilhelm Fabry of Hilden (1560–1634) greatly improved the amputation process by cutting off the blood supply with a circular band – a tourniquet – tied tightly above the point of amputation. The technique not only reduced the risk of haemorrhage but also helped to numb the leg.

PIONEER OF PLASTIC SURGERY

Gaspare Tagliacozzi (1545–99), Professor of Surgery at the University of Bologna in Italy, became famous for his facial reconstructions following amputation of the nose – not uncommon in a period when war, duelling and syphilis were rife. The nose reconstruction procedure was first used in 7th-century India, where the practice of cutting off the noses of adulterers was widespread. A skin graft was taken from the patient's arm and sewn over the wound until it healed. Tagliacozzi's treatment fell foul of the Catholic Church, which condemned it as a 'reprehensible interference in the work of the Creator', and plastic surgery was not rehabilitated until the 19th century.

VESALIUS AND A NEW ANATOMY

Even in the 16th century, Galen and Avicenna still cast a long shadow over medicine. Both diagnosis and treatment continued to be in thrall to their theory of the Humours, while their conception of anatomy, largely founded on glib analogies between animals and humans, was often wildly wrong. Dissection was not entirely in abeyance in the Middle Ages. Although the Church frowned upon the use of human corpses, in the medical schools that sprang up throughout Europe from the 13th century students were summoned once a year to attend dissection classes. Seated high on a rostrum, the Professor of Medicine would intone in Latin the anatomical texts of Galen, while his student assistant pointed out, one by one, the relevant organs for extraction by a (usually illiterate) barber-surgeon.

This was dissection of a sort, although it merely reinforced what was already known. More inquisitive minds began to shun religious taboo and ancient dogma and revive exploratory surgery on the human body. In Florence, Leonardo da Vinci (1452–1519) personally performed several dissections and drew the first anatomical plates based on practical observation. Later, Andreas Vesalius (1514–64), who had studied medicine at Louvain and Paris, criticised the contempt in which physicians held anatomy, which he saw as 'the most important and ancient branch of medicine'. Stepping down from the rostrum at Padua, where he held the Professorship of Anatomy, he eagerly got involved in dissections.

A fresh perspective

Vesalius's aim was to study the workings of the human body without preconceptions and through his dissections he gave rise to a groundbreaking work – *De Humani corporis fabrica* ('On the Structure of the Human Body'), which was published in 1543. The copper-plate engravings accompanying the work – the creation of which was personally overseen by Vesalius – refuted many of Galen's pronouncements on anatomy. Yet curiously, while Vesalius revolutionised the study of anatomy, he clung steadfastly to Galen's views on physiology. It was two of his successors in the Chair of Anatomy at Padua, Realdo Colombo and Fabricio de Acquapendente, who finally refuted Galen's doctrine, clearing the way for a thorough re-examination of the human body. Now that the true structure of the body had been laid bare, men like William Harvey in the 17th century would proceed to describe its functions.

Human musculature
An engraving from De Humani corporis fabrica (1543) by Vesalius (above). The illustrations were the work of the Flemish artist Jan Kalkar.

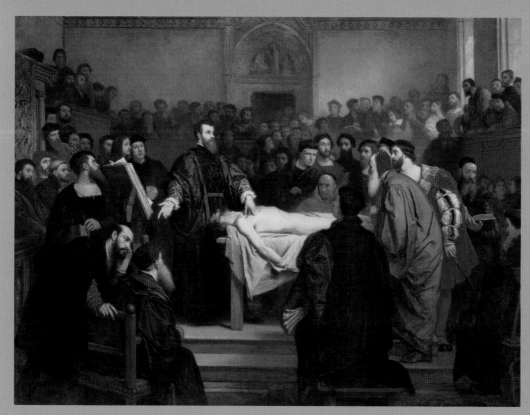

Anatomy lesson
A 19th-century painting imagines Vesalius lecturing on anatomy at the University of Padua.

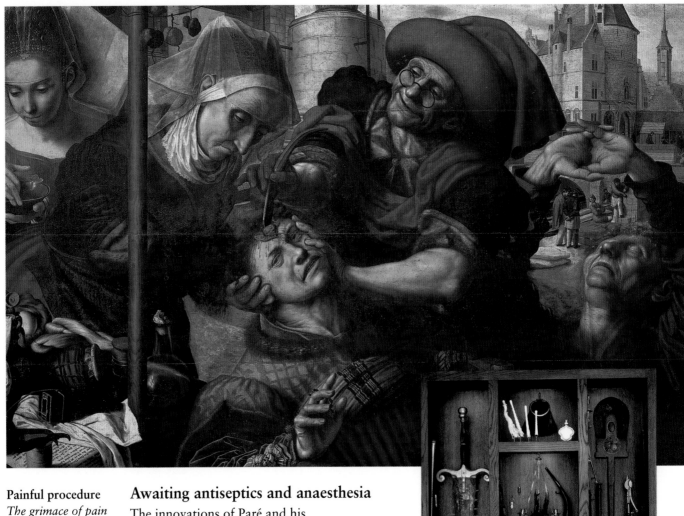

Painful procedure
The grimace of pain on the face of the patient in The Surgeon *(c1555) suggests that the artist, the Flemish painter Jan van Hemmessen, based his work on real life.*

Tool box
A case containing the instruments of a 16th-century surgeon (right).

Awaiting antiseptics and anaesthesia

The innovations of Paré and his contemporaries took a long time to become established practice. Surgery clung to the ancient methods for many decades, with the result that cauterisation was not wholly abandoned until the 17th century. This resistance to progress was compounded by even more insurmountable obstacles, such as the lack of any effective anaesthetics, which made every surgical procedure a ghastly ordeal for all concerned – the patient, surgeon and surgeon's assistants. Indeed, many patients did not survive the shock of surgery, while post-operative infections took a heavy toll until the introduction of surgical asepsis and antiseptics in the first half of the 19th century.

EXPANDING TOOLS OF THE SURGEON'S TRADE

For a long time, a surgeon's kit consisted of a limited array of instruments: a long, narrow surgical knife called a bistoury, scissors, a scalpel, saw and lancet. In the 16th century these were supplemented by crow's-beak, duck-bill and straight-ended forceps, slender catheters ending in a screw thread and tweezers with elongated blades, all of which were designed for extracting foreign bodies (particularly bullets) from patients. Examining and operating on the throat was facilitated by the invention (possibly by Paré) of the glossocatochos, which combined a mirror with an instrument for depressing the tongue. The periosteal elevator, with a hook in the middle, was developed for raising caved-in sections of the skull after penetration with a trephine (drill-bit). At the end of the 16th century, Peter Chamberlen invented obstetric forceps.

Artificial limbs 1560

In December 2000 archaeologists unearthed the 3,000-year-old mummified body of an Egyptian woman at the ancient city of Thebes. What was particularly intriguing was that the big toe of the right foot was missing, having clearly been amputated. In its place was a prosthesis made from three pieces of wood and held together by a leather sheath. The ancient Greeks and Romans were also familiar with artificial limbs, yet they hardly evolved at all in the Middle Ages, when simple stumps were used as false legs and hooks replaced missing hands. At best, a rich amputee might choose to sheathe an artificial leg in armour.

Iron arms and hands

With the revival of surgery and orthopaedics in the 16th century, prosthetic limbs became more sophisticated. In his *Ten Books on Surgery* (1564), Ambroise Paré described an artificial leg that he had devised and fitted to several amputees. It was made from a jointed piece of wood, clad with copper sheeting to improve its appearance. The wearer could bend and twist the leg and foot by operating a system of triggers, springs and hinges. Paré also introduced artificial hands and arms, both made of iron. The hand mechanism, which was activated by pressing a button concealed in the palm, allowed the user to open and close the hand and even to move the fingers in twos. The arms were jointed at the elbow. Such limbs allowed amputees to mount a horse, hold a pen or play cards. But they were heavy and unwieldy, and scarcely compensated for the major handicap of a lost limb. Even so, the basic principle remained unchanged until the 20th century.

Belated improvements

It was only in the aftermath of the Second World War that artificial limbs saw real improvement. Flexible feet made of neoprene foam were introduced in 1950, followed by a hydraulically driven knee 20 years later. Since then, great advances in materials such as plastics, polymers and carbon fibre have seen artificial limbs become ever lighter, while electronics and robotics have made them increasingly manipulable.

Iron hand
Artificial hands made by Ambroise Paré in the 16th century (right) incorporate some features that prefigure modern electronic prosthesis.

HANDICAPPED HERO

Artificial limbs – usually false legs made from wood – are mentioned a number of times in ancient Greek literature. In the 5th century BC, the playwright Aristophanes even wrote a part for a one-legged hero in his play *The Birds*.

Ahead of his time
A diagram of a wooden leg by Ambroise Paré shows he proposed that the leg be jointed to help the recipient walk with a normal gait.

In Paré's footsteps
French Paralympian Dominic André trying out a revolutionary new artificial limb developed by the Laboratory of Solid Mechanics at the University of Poitiers.

A self-taught genius

The name of Bernard Palissy will forever be associated with his incomparable glazed ceramics. But aside from being a potter, this free-thinker from France, also did pioneering work in geology and the life sciences.

Palissy the polymath
Keen intelligence and a clear sense of purpose shine out from this portrait of Bernard Palissy (c1565, right), a man deeply imbued with the Renaissance spirit of discovery.

The first significant chapter in Bernard Palissy's eventful life began in about 1530 in the town of Saintes, where this man of humble origins worked as both a glass-painter and land surveyor. The region around Saintes – the Saintonge in the far west of France, today in the *département* of Charente-Maritime – had been famous for its pottery since the early Middle Ages, but was now struggling to compete against the new tin-glazed earthenware (known as faience, or majolica) from Italy. Around this time Palissy, who was well versed in glassmaking, embarked on a career as a potter, spending 15 years uncovering the secret of Italian faience.

Man on a mission

Palissy laboured long and hard in his workshop, carefully measuring out silica sand, aluminium oxide and a variety of smelting agents, and adding different proportions of metallic oxides to vary the colour. Lead, boron, sodium and potassium were commonly used by potters to lower the melting point of the silica and to give the enamel glaze its smooth texture and particular lustre. After the glaze had been painted onto dry earthenware pieces baked at low temperatures came the tricky business of firing at an extremely high temperature. This meant waiting some 30 to 36 hours, plus the long drying time, to find out if the colours had come through the firing successfully as the glaze melted, or whether the glaze was of the high quality that he was after.

Time after time, Palissy raised his hopes only to have them dashed. He was getting close to success when he ran out of wood to fire his kiln. Undaunted, he proceeded to burn his furniture, then the floorboards. What he eventually achieved was a totally original glaze, a new material 'like no other Western pottery', as he claimed in his book, *An*

Attention to detail
Close observation of nature marks out all of Palissy's work. This small casting of a rabbit was designed as a 'figuline' for one of his famous platters.

Admirable Discourse on Pottery and Its Uses. In the complex typology of ceramics, experts in porcelain have even created the special category 'Palissy ware'.

Supremely gifted

By around 1550, Palissy was finally able to earn a living from his pottery. The first pieces he made were plates with a simple marbled glaze. These were followed by works that came to epitomise his pottery style – large, oval platters decorated with casts of plants and animals that he called 'figulines'. Typically depicting fish, lizards, frogs, snakes, leaves and seashells, they were moulded from the actual creatures. Palissy's celebrated 'rusticware' was designed both as luxury tableware and to adorn elaborate enamelled

grottoes. In 1556 the
Constable of France,
Duke Anne de Montmorency,
commissioned him to create a grotto
complete with flowing fountains for his
residence at the Château d'Écouen, north of
Paris. Palissy described the project in detail
in a memoir written in 1562–3, during his
imprisonment at the Conciergerie in Bordeaux
(the first of several terms in jail). His alleged
crime was to have taken part in riots staged
by his fellow Huguenots in the Saintonge.
Montmorency, his Catholic patron, pleaded his
case and even managed to secure him the title
of 'Inventor of the King's and Monseigneur le
Duc de Montmorency's Figulines'. After
Montmorency presented his protégé at the

Slice of life
*With its teeming animal and plant life, Bernard
Palissy's 'rusticware' astonished his contemporaries,
and still looks remarkably fresh and vibrant today.*

An enduring style
*Faenza in northern Italy became famous for
producing high-quality tin-glazed ware and gave its
name to a whole style of pottery. Faience was so
popular it was widely copied elsewhere in Europe.
These 17th-century apothecary's jars are
fine examples of the art.*

FROM GLAZED EARTHENWARE TO FAIENCE

Throughout the Middle Ages, the making of pottery in Europe was dominated by glazed earthenware, a technique practised since classical antiquity, which involves coating a terracotta object in lead sulphide (galena). During firing, the heat in the kiln vitrifies the compound into a thin layer of glaze that is transparent, glossy and waterproof. Around the mid 15th century, a new kind of ceramic ware was introduced to Italy from the Islamic Middle East via Spain. Coated inside and out with an opaque tin-based glaze, this pottery was known as faience, from Faenza, near Ravenna, where it was made. Its alternative name is 'majolica', from the island of Majorca, a staging-post on the route that Moorish traders used to bring their wares, including pottery, from Valencia to Italy.

learned men, that fossilised shells were the remains of marine creatures deposited by the sea in their present locations …' Palissy was making the revolutionary claim that fossils were neither the result of the Biblical Flood, nor some freak of nature. Intriguingly, another key figure of the Renaissance, Leonardo da Vinci, reached the same conclusion.

Natural science based on observation

Both keen observers of nature, Palissy and Leonardo sought to do it full justice in their respective art forms. The natural world furnished Palissy with animals and plants for his plaster casts and with the constituent minerals for his enamel glazes. His approach to nature was driven by his innate sense of curiosity. He could never have been satisfied with theoretical textbook explanations, even if he had been able to read ancient authors like Pliny the Elder. His approach was rigorously empirical. He was the first to give a correct account of the water cycle, when he stated that underground aquifers are the result of rainwater seeping down through the soil. He also refuted Aristotle's 'humus theory' of plant nutrition, which maintained that the soil itself provided the organic matter necessary for growth. Palissy claimed instead that plants somehow benefited from 'the salts of the Earth', which made him the first to recognise that plants get their nutrients from minerals.

Burning ambition
The image of the impoverished Palissy burning his furniture to maintain the temperature in his kiln has helped to foster the legend of the genius potter of the Saintonge.

Natural model
In a constant search for greater realism in his pottery, Bernard Palissy and his apprentices created exact plaster casts of natural objects and creatures; this mould (centre) is of a bumblebee.

court of Charles IX, the queen mother Catherine de' Medici commissioned a Palissy grotto for the gardens at the Tuileries Palace, which he created between 1565 and 1572.

A fertile mind

The slaughter of Huguenots in Paris in the St Bartholomew's Day Massacre of 1572 forced Palissy to flee to the eastern French city of Sedan, where he resumed his trade. While there, he wrote *An Admirable Discourse on Bodies of Water and Fountains, both Natural and Artificial*, which was published in 1580. This was a compendium of ideas on the natural sciences: paleontology, geology, hydrology and plant physiology.

Palissy expounded on his views in three conferences, held in Paris in 1575, which must have been tempestuous affairs. A century later, the philosopher Bernard de Fontenelle gave the following account of the gathering: 'This humble potter, who knew neither Latin nor Greek, was the first who dared to maintain … in Paris and in front of an audience of eminent

Too radical for his age

Palissy's ideas fell on deaf ears among his contemporaries. But later, in the 17th century, he inspired the Danish scientist Nicolas Stenon, the founding father of geology, while Edme Mariotte and Pierre Perrault, who developed the modern science of hydrogeology, confirmed his theory of the water cycle. In the realm of plant physiology, two centuries would elapse before the French scientist Antoine Lavoisier and the German Justus von Liebig corroborated Palissy's ideas on plant nutrition.

Palissy was fated never to receive the recognition he deserved during his lifetime. In around 1590, he died in a cell in the Bastille, where he had been imprisoned for refusing to recant his Protestant faith. In the 19th century he became a hero of the Romantic movement. Yet ironically, this only served to obscure his achievements as a thinker and for a long time his only legacy was his pottery.

LABOUR OF LOVE

Having long admired pieces by Bernard Palissy in the collection at his place of work, the Massé faience works near Tours in the Loire Valley, the potter Charles Avisseau decided, in around 1828, to try to rediscover the secret of the master's glazes. The experiment took him 15 years, the same time that Palissy had spent devising them in the first place. Avisseau's large platters in the style of Palissy sparked a revival of interest in this type of ceramic ware during the second half of the 19th century, not just in France but also in Britain and Portugal.

Condoms *c*1550

The condom was rediscovered in Europe in the mid 16th century by Gabriele Fallopio (1523–62), Professor of Anatomy at the University of Padua. Fallopio devoted much of his work to the human reproductive organs, providing the first truly accurate description of female genitalia and identifying the uterine tubes that now bear his name. In the proud tradition of his predecessors in the Padua chair, he did not confine himself to pure theory. Folk wisdom at the time ascribed the sexually transmitted disease of syphilis to various places – it was dubbed by some 'the French malaise', by others 'the Milan disease', among other names. Fallopio was concerned to stress the preventative role that the condom could have in combating the spread of syphilis, which was epidemic in Europe at the time. In his writings, he described the condom as a 'piece of linen cut to fit the member'.

An ancient precaution

There is evidence to suggest that condoms were known in ancient Egypt. By around 2000 BC, the Chinese were using condoms made from oiled silk. The legendary King Minos of Crete is said to have worn bandages impregnated with alum to protect his many lovers from his potent seed, reputed to contain scorpions and snakes.

The Romans were the first to make animal bladders into condoms. Protection against venereal diseases came in the form of pieces of sheep or pig intestine. The other role of condoms, as a mode of contraception, only came to the fore in the 19th century.

Ladies' man *The notorious seducer Giacomo Casanova (1725–98) is one of this male duo amusing a group of courtesans by blowing up condoms.*

Multicoloured
Modern condoms come in a variety of colours, styles and even flavours.

From linen to latex

In any event, after Fallopio, condom use became steadily more widespread, as attested by contemporary literature. Shakespeare cites a 'Venus' glove' in the play *Troilus and Cressida* (1602), while the French aristocrat Madame de Sévigné wrote a letter to her daughter in which she decried condoms as an 'armour against enjoyment, and a spider's web against danger'. In time, animal bladders made a reappearance, but the condom didn't really take off until the invention of the vulcanisation process using the sap of the Brazilian *Hevea* tree – latex – by Charles Goodyear in 1839. The Scottish chemist and raincoat manufacturer Charles Mackintosh was the to first mass-produce rubber condoms. Advances in rubber technology have seen the thickness of the modern condom reduced to a typical range of 0.09–0.3mm.

Serious message

A billboard on a road in Benin, West Africa, carries the stark warning that couples should use a condom to avoid contracting HIV/AIDS, a pandemic that has ravaged Africa in recent years.

NATIONAL PREJUDICE

In an attempt to ascribe anything sexual or decadent to their old enemies, the English invented the phrase 'French letter' for a condom, while the French dubbed them *Capotes anglaises* ('English hoods'). The term 'condom' may derive from a Dr Conton, a physician in the court of England's Charles II (r1660–85), who is thought to have improved their design.

Nuts and bolts c1550

Although screws had been made since ancient times, their manufacture was a fairly hit-and-miss affair. Fashioned from wood, with rudimentary tools, they were crudely finished and really only suitable for use in machines requiring large-diameter components, such as screw-jacks or presses for oil and wine – and later for printing.

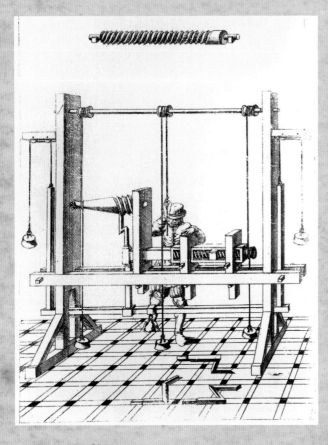

Metal screws

The second use of the screw, for joining things together, developed later. This function could only come into play once technology had evolved for cutting threads in metal and producing fixings strong enough to withstand major stresses. The first metal screws were made in Germany; they are mentioned sometime after 1405 in a work entitled *Bellifortis* by the military engineer Konrad Keyser. A later treatise, *De Re Metallica* (1556), by his compatriot Georgius Agricola, describes a wood-screw with a pointed tip. Gunsmiths and clockmakers adopted metal screws as a reliable way of joining pieces of metal so they could also be easily dismantled.

It was with an eye to ease of disassembly that, in the 16th century, a slot was first cut in screw heads for a tool to be inserted. Yet the long-handled screwdriver we are familiar with today was not invented until 1740. Thread-cutting by hand was a time-consuming and tricky task, which made screws expensive. In 1569 the French inventor Jacques Besson came up with a screw-cutting machine and such labour-saving devices were soon commonplace in workshops, especially armouries.

Screw + nut = bolt

In the mid-1500s, nuts were attached to screws (screws, that is, with flat ends and a shallow thread), effectively creating the nut and bolt. At first, nuts were crude handmade affairs, with the 'tapping' (the female thread cut in the centre of the nut) only engaging approximately with the thread on the bolt. In the Renaissance period, bolts were used on all kinds of mechanical devices, but screws, nuts and bolts only began to be mass-produced once they were made uniform and interchangeable.

Arms manufacturers led the way in the 18th century, but it was the next century before standardisation really took hold, with the publication of British engineer Joseph Whitworth's *A Uniform System of Screw Threads* in 1841. Today, nut, bolt and screw technology continues to evolve, with special materials and coatings for different types of fixing for particular jobs, and the development of electric screwdrivers and other tools for tightening.

An ingenious lathe
One of the many mechanical devices introduced by French inventor Jacques Besson in his Theatre of Instruments and Machines *(1569) is the first viable machine for cutting accurate, large-diameter wooden screws (left).*

Smart technology
Bolts now come in a huge range of sizes and types. A recent innovation is the Smartbolt®, with a disc on its head that changes colour when the correct tension is reached, a crucial factor in precision engineering jobs such as the assembly and servicing of helicopters.

The pencil 1565

In around 1565, a deposit of graphite was discovered at Borrowdale in Cumberland in the north of England. This dark-grey substance was oily and dirty to handle. Shepherds used it to mark their flocks, and people soon found that it left a clear mark on paper. If sharpened, it could produce quite legible writing. The only drawback was that it broke easily, a problem that was overcome by sandwiching the graphite between two half-cylinders of wood.

The principle of the pencil was described in 1565 by the Swiss Conrad von Gesner, but it was and Englishman, William Lee, who is thought to have been the first to come up with the idea of mounting a lead stylus (known since ancient times) in wood in 1504. At first, the spread of graphite pencils was hampered both by their high cost and by the fact that graphite was much in demand in cannon foundries, for lining the moulds.

A breakthrough came in 1760 when Kaspar Faber began producing pencils at his factory in Stein, near Nuremberg. To make them cheaper and more durable, Faber's pencils comprised a mixture of powdered graphite, sulphur, antimony and resin. In 1794, when England (a major supplier of graphite) was at war with Revolutionary France, the French authorities asked a young painter Nicolas-Jacques Conté to devise a pencil that did not require foreign imports. By mixing powdered graphite with clay and heating the paste to over 1000°C, Conté created a cost-effective crayon that still bears his name. He found that by varying the amount of clay he could make pencils harder (suitable for technical drawing) or softer (ideal for artists). Conté patented his invention in 1795, and his company still exists today, selling some 750,000 pencils daily.

Pencils ancient and modern
A German engraving (left) of pencil manufacture in Nuremberg in 1588, and a modern pencil (below) made by the French firm of Conté.

Royal commission
A beautifully detailed pencil drawing of Marguerite de Valois, Queen of France 1572–86, by François Clouet (1510–72), a Renaissance artist renowned for his pencil portraits.

EVOLUTION ⬡ FRANCE HB/n°2 Conté

MAN OF MANY PARTS

Though he is best known for inventing the crayon that bears his name, Nicolas-Jacques Conté (1755–1805) had other strings to his bow. Born into a peasant family, he went to Paris as a penniless young man in 1785 to study physics and mechanics. A gifted amateur artist, he supported himself through college by selling portraits. In around 1792, with France embroiled in the Revolutionary Wars, his work on observation balloons brought him to the attention of the Committee for Public Safety. In 1796, he accompanied Napoleon to Egypt and was later appointed editor of the *Description of Egypt,* an exhaustive series documenting the ancient and modern history of the country, which began in 1802.

Taking the guesswork out of navigation

Findings made during the great Age of Discovery had improved the map of the world considerably, but it was still not good enough to enable sailors to chart an accurate course. Then, in 1569, the Flemish cartographer Gerardus Mercator came up with a wholly new map projection.

Impressive array
Made by the London engraver Humphrey Cole in 1569, this compact set of scientific instruments, or 'astronomical compendium' (above right), may once have belonged to Sir Francis Drake.

Landmark map
A section of the Tabula Peutingeria *(below), showing the Adriatic, the Dalmatian coast, the heel of Italy, Sicily, part of North Africa and the Mediterranean.*

When he set sail from St Malo in the late 16th century, bound for the rich fishing grounds of the Great Banks off Newfoundland, French navigator Jean le Malouin was following a tried and tested sea route. Before him, Malouin had spread out a nautical chart criss-crossed with lines like those on medieval portolan charts. On this, he could easily trace the lines, or 'rhumbs' as they were known to sailors, that led straight to the coast of North America.

To the untrained eye the rhumb lines appeared a hopeless tangle; they radiated out from several centres around the edge of the map, each of which corresponded to a compass rose, whose 16 or 32 divisions gave the compass points. These roses were identical to the one on Malouin's magnetic compass. To set his course, he selected the rhumb that best matched his intended route. Then it was a matter of following the course indicated by the compass rose. En route, the navigator took regular readings with his magnetic compass to check that the ship was keeping to the bearing laid down by the rhumb.

Following the rhumbs

As a seasoned sailor, Jean le Malouin placed greater trust in his compass than in the map, using this to make adjustments to the ship's course. Indeed, if he had navigated rigidly by the straight, deceptively reassuring rhumb lines, he would have spent his days drifting aimlessly on the high seas. For when transposed from a flat map to the curved surface of the Earth, the rhumbs led nowhere. This paradox baffled the intensely practical men who plied the world's oceans. As it stood, the nautical chart that Malouin was using distorted angles; the rhumb lines never formed the actual angle with the various meridians that the captain had to cross in order to arrive at his destination. In other words, if a sailor followed the rhumb lines slavishly, he could not hope to stick to his intended course.

A mathematical approach

Gerardus Mercator was born in Flanders, which from the mid 16th century became the

---

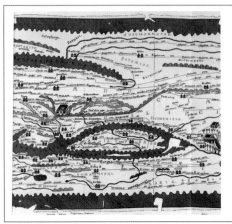

THE *TABULA PEUTINGERIANA* – A SEMINAL DOCUMENT

The *Tabula Peutingeriana* is a key document in the development of modern mapping. It is an *itinerarium* (a set of road maps) based on a census conducted by the general Marcus Agrippa for Emperor Augustus in the 1st century AD, which was redrawn by a monk in Colmar in around 1264. It shows some 50,000 miles (80,000km) of paved roads built in the Roman Empire for the movement of troops. Long forgotten, the *Tabula* was rediscovered in Worms by Conrad Celtes, librarian to Holy Roman Emperor Maximilian I, and published by Konrad Peutinger (1465–1547), Augsburg town clerk and a specialist in Latin inscriptions. The *Tabula* proved an invaluable resource; Agrippa's census had recorded the length of roads and distances between towns, enabling contemporary cartographers to correct their more recent but less accurate maps.

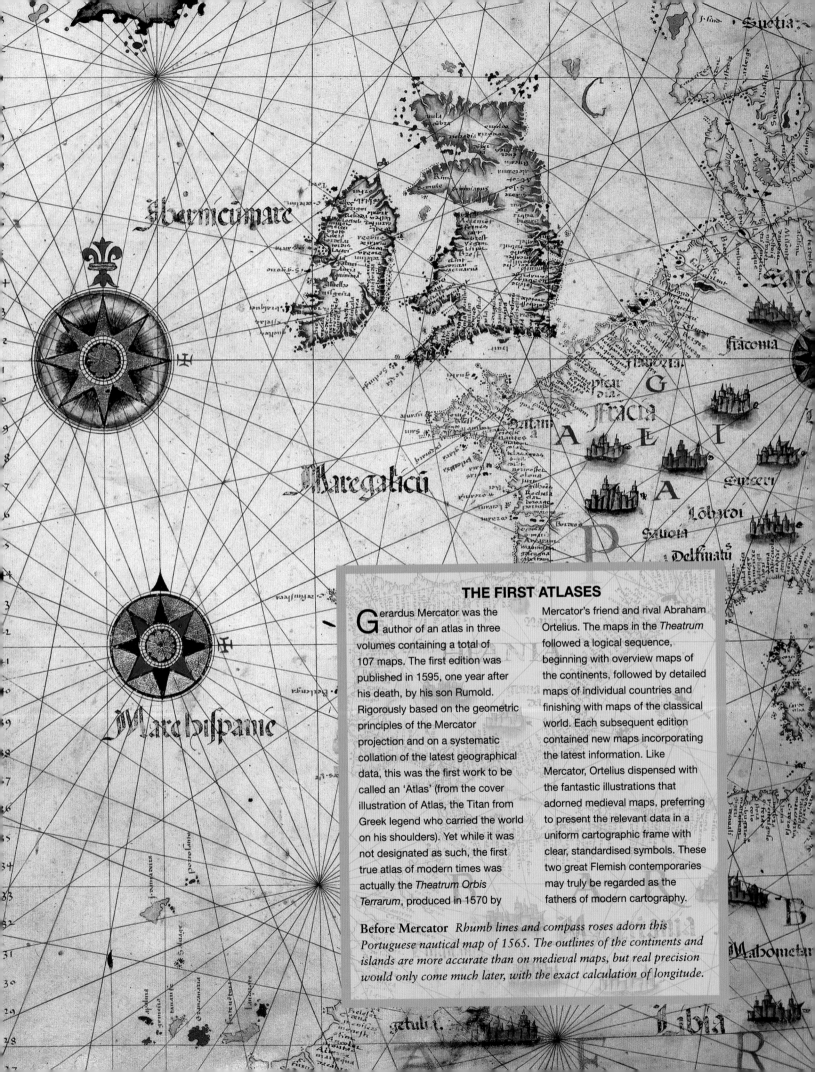

THE FIRST ATLASES

Gerardus Mercator was the author of an atlas in three volumes containing a total of 107 maps. The first edition was published in 1595, one year after his death, by his son Rumold. Rigorously based on the geometric principles of the Mercator projection and on a systematic collation of the latest geographical data, this was the first work to be called an 'Atlas' (from the cover illustration of Atlas, the Titan from Greek legend who carried the world on his shoulders). Yet while it was not designated as such, the first true atlas of modern times was actually the *Theatrum Orbis Terrarum*, produced in 1570 by Mercator's friend and rival Abraham Ortelius. The maps in the *Theatrum* followed a logical sequence, beginning with overview maps of the continents, followed by detailed maps of individual countries and finishing with maps of the classical world. Each subsequent edition contained new maps incorporating the latest information. Like Mercator, Ortelius dispensed with the fantastic illustrations that adorned medieval maps, preferring to present the relevant data in a uniform cartographic frame with clear, standardised symbols. These two great Flemish contemporaries may truly be regarded as the fathers of modern cartography.

Before Mercator *Rhumb lines and compass roses adorn this Portuguese nautical map of 1565. The outlines of the continents and islands are more accurate than on medieval maps, but real precision would only come much later, with the exact calculation of longitude.*

DIFFERENT TYPES OF MAP PROJECTION

● **Cylindrical projection,** as devised by Mercator, results from projecting the surface of the globe onto a cylinder. When cut from top to bottom and unrolled, the cylinder forms a flat, rectangular map. Since the cylinder is tangent to the globe along the Equator, the scale along this line is true. Distortion of scale is greatest at the northern and southern extremities of the cylinder (that is, the high latitudes). Today, cylindrical projections are used for nautical charts and world maps (now usually based on the Wagner projection, a refined cylindrical projection).

● **Conic projection,** first described by the Greek geographer Ptolemy in *c* AD 150, results from projecting the spherical surface of the globe onto a cone. If the cone is then cut along a meridian from the apex to the base and unfolded, the resulting map is fan-shaped. The cone touches the surface of the globe along a predetermined line of latitude, and it is at this point of contact (called the standard parallel) that the scale is truest. Far-flung parts of the globe do not usually appear on conic maps. Nowadays, conic projection tends to be used for relatively restricted areas, such as an individual country. The one most commonly employed today was devised by Johann Heinrich Lambert in the 18th century.

● **Azimuthal projection,** developed by Johann Lambert in the 18th century, results from projecting the surface of the globe onto a circular plane. There is no distortion in direction on such maps, with the 'azimuth' (the angle from a point on a line to another point) of every line, radiating out from the central point of the circle, being portrayed correctly. Scale is significantly distorted, however, only being accurate at the centre and growing increasingly deformed towards the periphery. Azimuthal projections are mostly used to show the hemispheres or a particular continent, or for maps centred on a pole, a small area or a city.

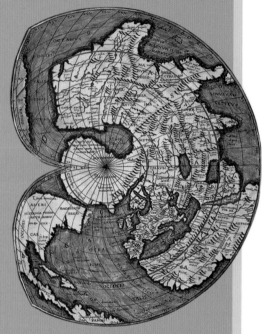

Navigational aid
A 16th-century Italian portolan chart using the Bonne projection, a variation of conic projection (left).

Ancient worldview
Ptolemy's conic projection on a map made in 1430 (below).

Mercator's Mappa Mundi
The cylindrical projection map of 1587 (below) involved distortion, but still gave a more accurate picture of the world than earlier maps.

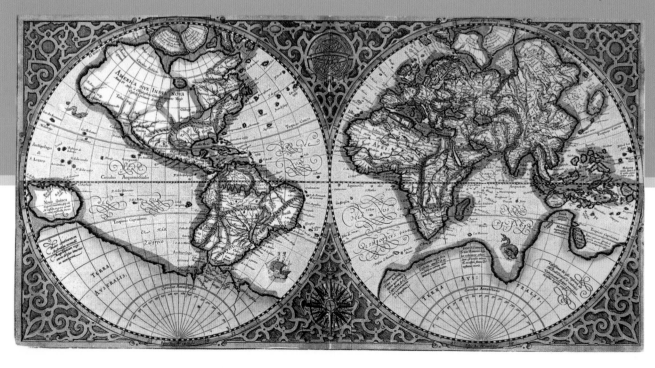

centre of European cartography. At the
University of Louvain he was tutored by
the Dutch mathematician and cartographer
Gemma Frisius, a pioneer of geodesy (the
science of measuring the shape and size of the
Earth). Frisius taught Mercator not only the
science of triangulation in cartography but also
the art of instrument making. A skilled engraver,
Mercator designed the spindles for a globe that
Frisius made in 1536 and later turned his hand
to making globes and scientific instruments
himself, while pursuing his cartographic
studies. To make navigation by magnetic
compass more reliable, he aimed to find the
best correlation between a ship's course on
the curved surface of the Earth and the
route shown on a flat map. In other words,
Mercator was determined to produce what
mathematicians call a 'conformal' map
projection – one that would not distort angles.

The Mercator Projection

The conical projection devised by Ptolemy
was clearly useless for Mercator's purpose.
In order to get rhumb lines on the map to
cross all meridians at the same angle (this
constant bearing is technically known as a
'loxodrome'), it was vital to ensure that the
meridians (the lines of longitude) should
always form a right angle with the parallels
(the lines of latitude). Mercator therefore drew
a network in which the meridians and parallels

were perpendicular to one another. Yet
bending the meridians – which in reality
converge on the poles – into parallel lines
identical to those of latitude entailed a major
deformation of the Earth's surface. Mercator
corrected for this distortion by setting the lines
of latitude at a greater distance apart from
one another the further they stretched away
from the Equator. The coefficient that he
employed meant that, at every individual
point location, the East–West scale is the
same as the North–South scale, but across the
map as a whole the scale varies enormously:
the deformation is at its greatest in the polar
regions, making Greenland appear as large as
Africa, when in reality it is 15 times smaller.
This served Mercator's purpose well, as these
regions were of only minor importance for
maritime navigation. By contrast, the areas
between the Equator and the polar circles
do not display anything like the same degree
of distortion. Mercator applied this method of
projection, known as 'cylindrical,' to a map
of the world produced on 18 separate sheets
that he published in 1569 – the first truly
practical navigational map.

Reliable nautical charts

Even so, Mercator's map only caught on a
century later, after the English mathematician
and navigator Robert Dudley published a
series of medium-scale nautical charts based on

Early navaids
*A map of Zeeland
(above) by
Abraham Ortelius.
The astrolabe
(below), the world's
first truly scientific
instrument for
navigation, was a
disc with degrees
of arc indicated
around its
circumference,
with sight vanes
on a rotating
pointer
called an
'alidade'.*

TOPOGRAPHIC SURVEYS AND TRIANGULATION

To meet the demand for ever more accurate maps, cartographers had to undertake reliable topographical surveys. Their key tool in this endeavour was the method of triangulation proposed in 1445 by the Italian architect (and theoretician of linear perspective) Leon Battista Alberti.

Triangulation consisted of dividing up the area to be measured into a network of triangles. To determine the position of a distant 'geographical object', such as a prominent natural or artificial feature, the surveyor first fixed two observation points forming the baseline of a triangle (a sighting was also taken later from a third point on this line, as a check). The surveyor then measured the angles to the object that formed the apex of the triangle by taking sightings from each endpoint of the baseline. Using basic trigonometry, he could calculate the lengths of the other two sides and the other angle of the triangle. Taking one of the sides as a new baseline, and selecting a new 'object' (the triangulation point), the surveyor then repeated the process, measuring the entire area to be surveyed as a series of zig-zagging triangles.

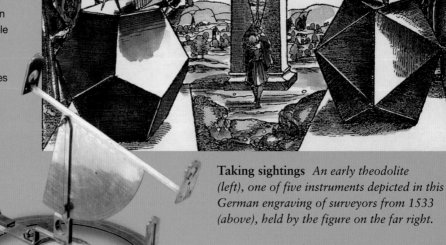

Taking sightings *An early theodolite (left), one of five instruments depicted in this German engraving of surveyors from 1533 (above), held by the figure on the far right.*

Safety at sea *John Harrison's H4 marine chronometer of 1759 (below) finally allowed sailors to fix their longitudinal position at sea.*

Sighting and measuring instruments

Alberti was the first to produce a map based on triangulation – his town plan of Rome in 1445. Maps like this gradually became more widespread from the 16th century onwards with the development of more sophisticated instruments for measuring angles. These instruments derived from the astrolabe used by astronomers, on which a pivoted bar called an alidade enabled the observer to take a sighting on a distant object and then measure its elevation above the horizon by means of a circular scale graduated in degrees. The first land surveying instrument – introduced in around 1555 by Arsenius Gualterus, a nephew of Frisius – was a simplified astrolabe incorporating a magnetic compass to help maintain a steady

direction. In 1571, the English surveyor Leonard Digges coined the term 'theodolite' for an instrument that combined the ancient inclinometer, employed by Hero of Alexandria in the 1st century to measure the gradient between two points, and the tangent scales used on artillery pieces. The instrument measured both horizontal and vertical angles. The modern theodolite, invented in the 18th century, comprises a movable telescope mounted within two perpendicular axes.

Pioneers of measurement

In 1669, the French astronomer Jean Picard used triangulation to make the first

accurate measurement of a degree of the Earth's meridian. This paved the way for the creation of the Cassini geodesic map of France in 1791. The 18th century also saw the invention of the marine chronometer by the English inventor John Harrison. His instrument finally solved the problem of how to measure longitude accurately, by comparing local time to the time at the ship's home port. Meanwhile, the sextant enabled sailors to take more precise readings of latitude. These important advances meant that the dimensions of the Earth could be measured as precisely as those of much smaller bodies.

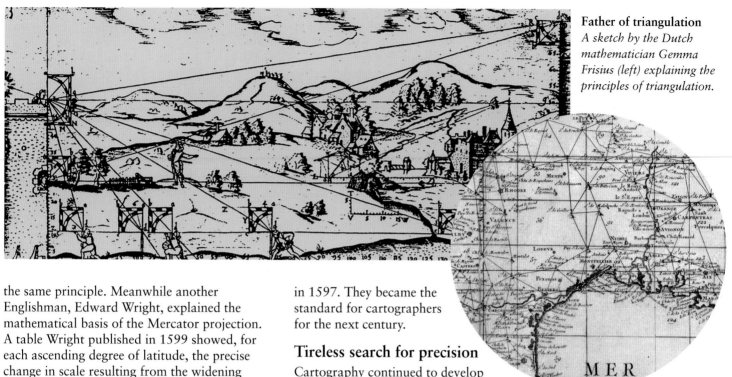

Father of triangulation
A sketch by the Dutch mathematician Gemma Frisius (left) explaining the principles of triangulation.

the same principle. Meanwhile another Englishman, Edward Wright, explained the mathematical basis of the Mercator projection. A table Wright published in 1599 showed, for each ascending degree of latitude, the precise change in scale resulting from the widening gap between the parallels. This made it possible to compensate for the deformation in distances resulting from the cylindrical projection.

Modern sailors still use charts based on the Mercator projection. Other projections, of the conic type, were developed from the 16th century onwards to map the Earth's land areas.

Triangulation and geodesy

The technique of triangulation, first described in 1445 by Leon Battista Alberti, soon became accepted as the only way to ensure an accurate representation of topographical relief features and precise measures of distance. The first significant application of triangulation to mapping was by Jacob van Deventer, who between 1536 and 1570 published a series of maps showing the towns and provinces of the Netherlands.

The first maps accurately identifying the towns, villages and rivers of England and Wales were produced by Christopher Saxton, a Yorkshire cartographer commissioned by Lord Burghley, adviser to Elizabeth I. Saxton began his detailed survey, county by county, in 1570 and his maps were eventually completed

in 1597. They became the standard for cartographers for the next century.

Tireless search for precision

Cartography continued to develop throughout the 19th century, as the colonial powers charted newly conquered territories and academic geographers moved towards a standardised approach. An international conference held in Washington DC in 1884 set the meridian that ran through the Royal Observatory at Greenwich as the world's prime meridian (0°). In the 20th century, new technologies were applied to mapping in the form of aerial photography and, later, geosurvey satellites. Processed by powerful computers, satellite imaging has not only increased accuracy, but also made mapmaking far faster and more cost-effective.

Increasing accuracy
Correct lines of longitude finally appeared on the geodesic map of France made by the Cassini family (above). This section shows the Mediterranean coast near the town of Montpellier.

Instrument of empire
An atlas produced for Bavarian schools in 1902 shows colonial possessions of European nations and principal shipping routes.

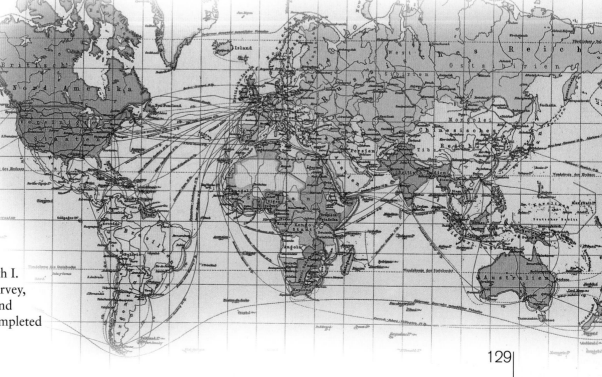

Astronomer between two worlds

From his observatory at Uranienborg, the Danish astronomer Tycho Brahe devoted his life to measuring the positions of the planets and stars. Using precision instruments of his own devising, he demonstrated the limitations of Ptolemy's geocentric system of the universe. Although Brahe refused to accept the idea that the Earth revolved around the Sun, his endeavours laid the essential groundwork for his successor, Johannes Kepler, to develop his radical theory of celestial mechanics.

Moveable instrument
A colour engraving of Tycho Brahe's 1582 triangular astronomical sextant. Tycho used this instrument at his Uranienborg observatory to measure the angular distances between stars. He took the sextant with him when he moved to nearby Stjerneborg and later, on leaving Denmark, to Prague.

On a cloudless, moonless night – the ideal conditions for looking at the stars –Tycho Brahe was pacing up and down on the terrace of his observatory. The astronomer gazed up at the sky and felt the thrill he always experienced at the natural spectacle unfolding before him. He rubbed his hands to keep warm; nights could be bitter out here on the tiny island of Hven in the Øresund, between Copenhagen and Elsinore. Around him, his assistants were geared up for another long session of observation. They had flocked to this remote spot from all over Europe, eager to have the chance to work with the famous astronomer. But although they had daily contact with him, they still felt overawed by this lumbering giant of a man, with his gruff manner and a false brass nose. Rumour had it that, in his youth, he had lost his real nose in a duel defending the honour of the great Greek astronomer and mathematician Pythagoras.

Now, in 1580, Tycho Brahe was renowned the length and breadth of Europe as the greatest astronomer of his day. Generous funding from Frederick II of Denmark had enabled Brahe to build the observatory at Uranienborg – the 'castle of Urania', dedicated to the muse of astronomy and astrology. This unique facility was entirely given over to the study of the stars and planets, and equipped with the world's most precise instruments, designed and built by Tycho himself.

Hooked from an early age

In 1560, while studying law in Copenhagen, Tycho Brahe witnessed a spectacle that would change his life forever: a partial eclipse of the Sun. He was captivated by the event, but what impressed him even more was that experts had predicted it. This marked the beginning of his obsession with astronomy. By day, he continued to work at the law, but his nights were given over to his new passion. The professors of mathematics at Copenhagen encouraged their talented student and urged him to read the most famous work on astronomy then in circulation, Ptolemy's *Almagest*. They also helped him to construct his first instrument, a celestial globe showing the positions of the stars.

In August 1563 another planetary event, a conjunction of Jupiter and Saturn, confirmed Tycho in his chosen career. He consulted a stack of celestial tables and almanacs to find

This was a groundbreaking discovery in a world that still clung to the Aristotelian view of the heavens as perfect and unchanging beyond the sublunary sphere. The next year, when the star came into view once more, Tycho published his first report on the phenomenon, *De Stella Nova* ('Concerning the New Star'), which caused a sensation and established his international reputation. It was the 1960s before this bright new star was finally identified as a supernova – the thermonuclear explosion of a massive star.

Temple of astronomy

In 1576 Frederick II granted Tycho the island of Hven and funded the construction of an observatory there. This was to be the site of most of Tycho's stargazing over the next 20 years. He now had the wherewithal to build the instruments he had long dreamt of, many of them improvements on designs from classical antiquity. One of the first installed at Hven, in 1576–7, was an azimuthal quadrant with a radius of 65cm, for measuring the altitude and the azimuth of stars. Meanwhile, Tycho's large brass equatorial armillary sphere enabled him to determine the declination and hour angles

Precious equipment
Tycho's brass armillary sphere (left), 1.6m in diameter, is now sadly lost. According to the German astronomer Johannes Kepler, this magnificent instrument alone cost the equivalent of 80 years of his salary.

Watcher of the skies
A portrait of Tycho Brahe made in 1600 and an engraving of his observatory at Stjerneborg (bottom).

out whether the occurrence had been predicted accurately, and was hugely disappointed to find that even the best prediction was very wide of the mark. And so he decided to devote his life to precise observation of the heavens – and to producing accurate tables.

Tycho's lucky star

Up until the age of 25, Tycho Brahe continued his education at various European universities, studying at Leipzig, Wittenberg, Rostock, Basel and Augsburg. He read everything on astronomy he could lay his hands on and observed the stars intensively. He also devised and built his first large instruments, including a wooden quadrant (a 90° sighting arc with a plumbline for the vertical) with a radius of 18 metres.

In around 1571, Tycho founded his first observatory in Denmark, at Skåne, and promptly made a sighting that proved a watershed in his career. On 11 November, 1572, he discovered a new star in the constellation Cassiopeia that shone even more brilliantly than Venus. He set about determining the star's exact position, a task that took him 18 months – the star was visible the whole time. He quickly ascertained that the light's position did not move one iota in relation to nine stars around it. In other words, the new star was far away, in deep space beyond the Earth's moon.

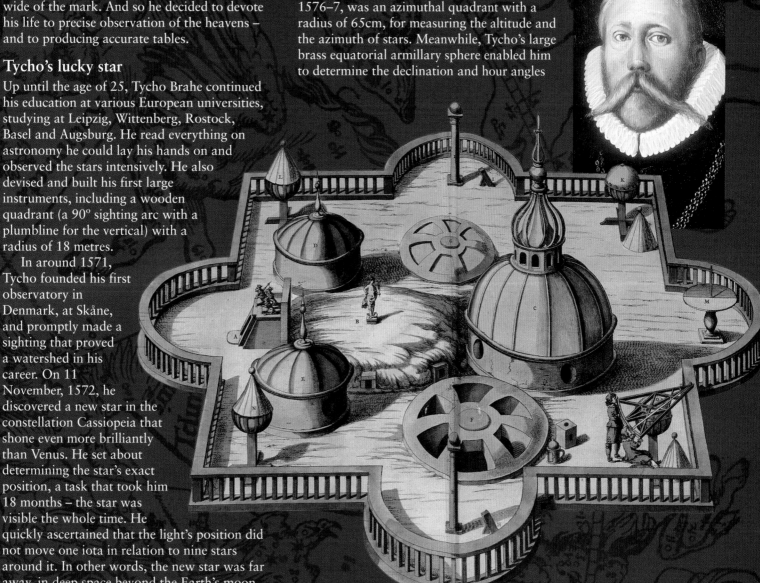

of celestial bodies. He also invented new instruments, such as an astronomical sextant for measuring the angular distance between stars. Light and portable, it had an accurate graduated scale and efficient sighting system.

Tycho's instruments furnished him with data ten times more accurate than that gathered by ancient astronomers. This was a magnificent achievement considering that he relied solely on the naked eye (optical instruments only became available to astronomers from 1610 onwards, with the arrival of Galileo's first telescope). Tycho owed the precision of his measurements not only to his well-designed instruments but also to his meticulous methodology, which remains a model of scientific rigour. This involved having the same measurement taken by different experimenters, correcting for atmospheric refraction, and monitoring results for their consistency.

Star signs
Zodiacal symbols such as Sagittarius (below) and the now-defunct Cornix ('the crow', 3–11 October, above) would have been familiar to Tycho. Astronomy and astrology were closely intertwined and Tycho prepared horoscopes for Christian IV of Denmark and Holy Roman Emperor Rudolf II.

Tireless observer of the heavens

Tycho was naturally keen to observe and measure the Great Comet of 1577. As with the supernova of 1572, he demonstrated that this event took place far out in space, at a distance roughly six times that between the Earth and Moon. This discovery shocked his peers, who still held to Aristotle's assertion that comets were atmospheric phenomena.

This was just one more example of the paradigm shift that was taking place in the science of astronomy, shaking people's faith in an unchanging firmament. Tycho's findings were later confirmed by a series of comets that became visible throughout the 1580s.

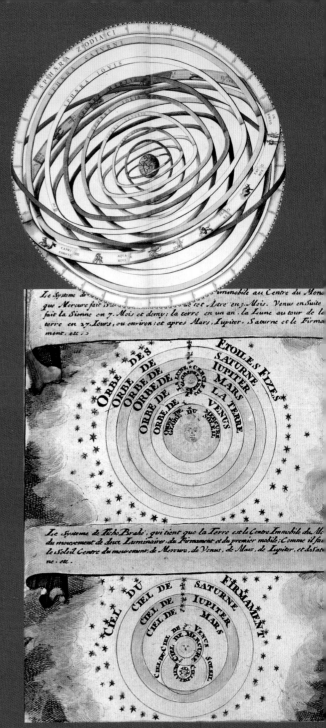

COPERNICUS AND THE HELIOCENTRIC UNIVERSE

Nicolaus Copernicus (1473–1543) was a polymath who knew canon law, economics, medicine and mathematics, but it is in the realm of astronomy that he gained lasting fame. The seminal treatise on which he worked for 30 years, *De revolutionibus orbium coelestium* ('On the Revolutions of the Celestial Spheres') only appeared after his death. Copernicus was loath to publish it in his lifetime, since what it proposed was totally at variance with Church doctrine. Copernicus put forward a new cosmology in which the Earth's position at the centre of the universe (a notion cherished ever since Ptolemy's *Almagest*) was usurped by the Sun. This meant that the Earth became a planet just like the rest, orbiting the Sun. It is unclear whether Copernicus came up with the idea of a heliocentric universe independently, or whether he drew inspiration from the 3rd-century BC Greek thinker Aristarchus of Samos or Arab astronomers from Maragheh observatory in Persia, who had devised a new cosmology in the 13th century. Whatever the case, Copernicus' work sparked an intellectual revolution that overthrew Ptolemaic astronomy based on Aristotelian physics. Later, it would fall to Kepler, Galileo and Newton to establish the theoretical basis of Copernicus' cosmology.

Conflicting cosmologies
The diagram (top) shows Ptolemy's conception of the universe with the Earth at its centre. This contrasts with the Copernican, Tychonic and Cartesian systems outlined in this 17th-century French engraving (above) .

In around 1588, Tycho published *On Recent Phenomena in the Aetherial World*, setting forth his view of the universe. He came down neither for Ptolemy's geocentric nor Copernicus' heliocentric cosmology. According to Tycho the planets revolved around the Sun, but the Sun in turn revolved around the Earth, now restored to its rightful place at the centre of the universe. Tycho also rejected the notion, current since antiquity, of solid celestial spheres carrying the stars and planets. A pivotal figure between ancient and modern

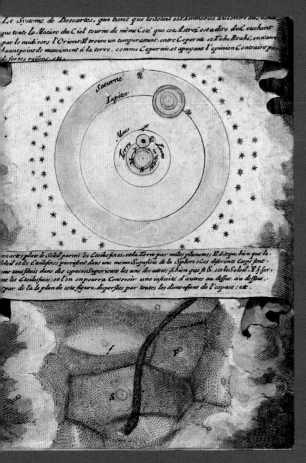

cosmological systems, Tycho effectively refuted certain archaic theories of the universe but still failed to blaze a trail for heliocentrism. Either for religious reasons, or because it ran counter to his astrological work, he refused to entertain the possibility of a Sun-centred universe.

For all that, his contribution to astronomy was immense. He left behind a catalogue of 777 stars, plotted over many years of observation. He corrected inaccurate astronomical tables and almanacs, and was the first to describe the Moon's irregular orbit around the Earth.

A worthy successor

But Tycho found himself at loggerheads with Christian IV, who came to the Danish throne in

1588. His funding dried up and in 1597 he left Uranienborg and set off on a long journey across Europe. In 1599 he settled in Prague at the court of the Holy Roman Emperor Rudolf II. On 3 June, 1600, a young German mathematician named Johannes Kepler visited the eminent Dane. Tycho spotted Kepler's talent and appointed him as one of his assistants, but this was his final inspired move; in October the following year, he fell ill and died. Kepler succeeded him as head of the imperial observatory, inheriting the huge archive that Tycho had built up, including his peerlessly accurate plottings of star positions. Using these, Kepler showed conclusively that planetary orbits are not circular, as Copernicus had thought, but elliptical. This was a seminal moment in modern astronomy, providing a vital springboard for the work of Isaac Newton.

Genius at work
A fanciful contemporary artist's impression (1598) of Tycho Brahe at work in his observatory, surrounded by his assistants (below). The curved instrument in the centre is a mural quadrant for measuring the Sun's position.

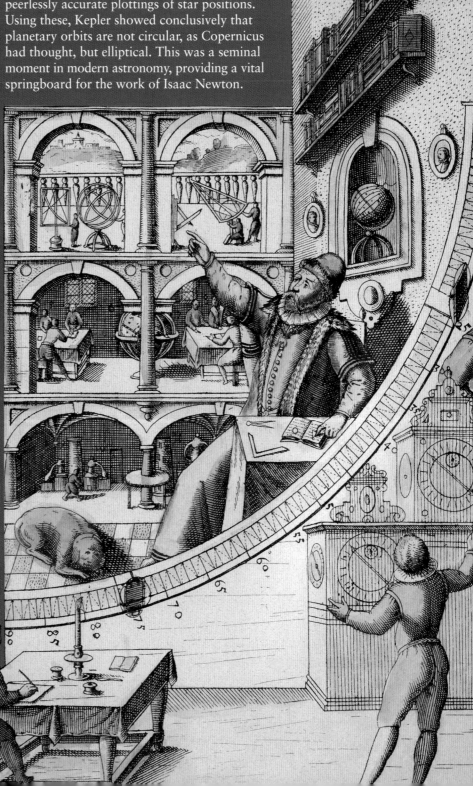

Prefabricated buildings 1577

The world's first known prefabricated building was Nonesuch House, erected on Old London Bridge in 1577. It was constructed around a timber framework, part of which was transported up the River Thames by barge from Flanders. The components of the building were re-erected on site, rather like a child's set of building blocks. Only sketchy accounts survive, but we do know that it was assembled without using a single nail, the beams and joists being held together with mortice and tenon joints and wooden pegs. It is unclear whether Nonesuch was a prototype or the work of experienced craftsmen well versed in the techniques of prefabrication. But by all accounts, the end result was a well-proportioned house with a frontage boasting seven arches. No trace remains of the building, which was destroyed by fire in 1623.

The concept of a prefabricated building was revived in the 19th century, as cast iron became a viable construction material. The most glorious example was the Crystal Palace, designed by Joseph Paxton to showcase the 1851 Great Exhibition in Hyde Park. Prefabricated buildings came of age in the 20th century, with the advent of steel girders and other components machine-made to high degrees of accuracy and standard templates.

Marvel of its day
The Crystal Palace (left), built in six months from glass and prefabricated cast iron sections, was a remarkable feat of engineering.

The shape of things to come
Old London Bridge (below), site of the world's first prefabricated building, Nonesuch House.

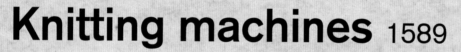

Knitting machines 1589

Legend has it that a Cambridge clergyman, William Lee (1563–1614), invented the world's first stocking knitting frame to spare his wife the drudgery of knitting. Operated by a pedal-driven belt, Lee's machine comprised a flat bed of tiny hooked needles, each attached to a loop of thread or yarn. At first, it was only capable of running out a coarse weft-knitted fabric, but Lee made various improvements until it could produce fine silk stockings. His invention appears to have been too far ahead of its time; Queen Elizabeth I bowed to the protests of English hand-knitters, who feared that the machine would make them redundant, and refused Lee a patent. His brother James, who inherited the business after William's death, finally succeeded in setting up the world's first fully automated stocking factory in England in 1620. In the interim, the Lees took their machine to France, where it thrived for a while around Rouen under the Huguenot King Henri IV. It fell into disfavour, until the trade was revived in the 1660s under Louis XIV.

Early automation *In the 17th century, machines like this (right) won English machine-made stockings a reputation for quality and durability.*

The water closet 1596

*G*ardez-loo! Medieval towns in England famously resounded to this cry, which came from the French *gardez l'eau*: 'Watch out – water!', as people flung open their windows and emptied chamber pots onto the street. People passing below had to be quick to avoid a soaking. In the Middle Ages, streets, fields and rivers were all polluted by human waste. Insanitary conditions were rife, with outbreaks of cholera common in towns. A small step forward came in the 14th century, as wealthy households began to replace chamber pots with commodes. The excrement was still collected in an open receptacle, as before, but this was discreetly hidden under an armchair whose seat was equipped with a strategically-placed hole. This made the user more comfortable, but scarcely improved hygiene.

The year 1596 saw a minor revolution in sanitary technology, in the form of the toilet-flush system invented for Queen Elizabeth I by Sir John Harington. His prototype water closet released a thin stream of water into a lavatory pan. Although this represented a significant step towards the modern toilet, it was far from being an optimal solution. The water flush kept the pan clean, but the waste simply dropped into a ditch beneath the house, a crude arrangement that allowed noxious smells to waft back up the pipes.

In 1775 the British watchmaker Alexander Cummings devised the first true flushing toilet, replacing Harington's thin stream with a cascade of water. He achieved this by setting a water-filled cistern above the pan, which the user emptied by pulling a lever that slid open a valve.

The problem of permeating smells was solved three years later by the inventor Joseph Bramah, who replaced the slide valve of Cummings' design with a hinged flap at the bottom of the bowl, and also added an 'S' bend to the waste pipe. These improvements meant that a small sump of water always lay at the lowest point of the system, thus preventing smells from rising. Yet even though toilets themselves had been largely perfected by the end of the 18th century, it would take another 100 years for them to come into their own with the supply of mains water and the building of sewage systems.

Sanitary solutions
A throne-like toilet seat from a Roman aristocrat's villa (right). The cutaway drawing (below) shows Harington's novel toilet-flush system; for all the ingenuity, in the absence of a proper sewerage network inventions like this were fated to remain one-offs.

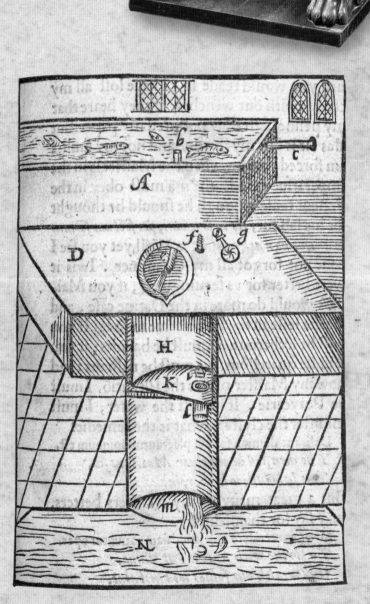

POSH PANS

Over the course of the 18th century, faience and porcelain were increasingly used in the manufacture of lavatory pans. Up until then, the pans were usually made from less suitable materials, such as wood or metal, which over time became impregnated with the smell of excrement.

Degrees of heat

With the invention of the thermometer temperature took on a new meaning, as the simple concepts of 'hot' and 'cold' were replaced by degrees of warmth and coldness. Later, with the addition of a graduated scale, thermometers were used to monitor body temperature and to make accurate recordings of weather.

Measuring with mercury
A 19th-century reconstruction of Galileo's mercury thermoscope. In the 18th century, after much debate, mercury finally became established as the principal thermometric liquid.

'He took a small glass flask, about as large as a small hen's egg, with a neck about two spans long [around 40cm] and as fine as a wheat straw, and warmed the flask well in his hands, then turned its mouth upside down into the vessel placed underneath, in which there was a little water. When he took away the heat of his hands from the flask, the water at once began to rise in the neck, and mounted to more than a span above the level of the water in the vessel. The same Signore Galileo had then made use of this effect in order to construct an instrument for examining the degrees of heat and cold.' These notes, written in 1638 by Benedetto Castelli, a friend of Galileo's, relate to an experiment supposedly conducted by the great Italian physicist in 1603. The apparatus that Castelli is describing was the ancestor of the modern thermometer.

A Greek invention

The ancient Greeks were the first to establish the principle of the thermometer, in the 3rd century BC, when mathematicians and engineers of the Alexandrian school – notably Ctesibius (fl285–222 BC) – began to investigate the nature of air. They were especially intrigued by two fundamental properties imputed to it; first, that fire condenses in air, and second, that the composition of air changes when it is passed through water. To verify this, Ctesibius and others would doubtless have constructed pieces of apparatus that indicated changes in air temperature. These instruments, known as thermoscopes, would probably have been considered little more than parlour games. Sadly, none of these early devices survive, although detailed

Elegant vessel
A combined thermometer–barometer, based on a 10th-century Arab design. As the air inside the flask expands with heat, it forces the water up the neck.

descriptions of them by disciples of Ctesibius, such as Philo of Byzantium and Hero of Alexandria, at least allowed later researchers to pick up the thread and develop the idea.

Thermoscopes were forgotten about for many centuries and only rediscovered in the 16th century with the appearance of a Latin translation of Hero's *Pneumatica*, which described machines running on air, steam and water pressure. This treatise came to the attention of the small group of scientists working with Galileo at the University of Padua, and in particular excited the interest of a young medical student by the name of Sanctorius Sanctorius (1561–1636).

The first graduated scale

Sanctorius took it upon himself to monitor the health of his patients, including himself, by measuring various vital functions. He had already begun to experiment with a 'weighing chair', a seat suspended from scales, which he sat in before, during and after every meal. In 1602 he unveiled the so-called 'pulsilogium', a pendulum-based device for taking the pulse, along with a thermoscope designed to measure the changing 'temperament' of his patients. This latter instrument was, it seems, identical to that of Galileo, as described by Castelli, except that Sanctorius included a graduated scale on the neck. He began by marking a minimum and maximum temperature, obtained respectively by cooling the glass bulb with snow and heating it with a candle flame, then he divided the space between into eight equal segments. Patients were instructed to put the bulb into their mouth, or hold it in the palm of their hand, while Sanctorius noted how far the water inside the bulb rose up the neck.

The procedure yielded some important findings, enabling Sanctorius to demonstrate that body temperature, which stays constant in a healthy person, rises by several degrees when they fall ill. Nevertheless, he still treated his patients in the old-fashioned Galenic manner, subjecting them to blood-lettings, enemas and purgatives in a vain attempt to restore the balance between the 'humours' (yellow bile, blood, phlegm and black bile) which were associated with different moods. Ultimately, he did not set much store by his thermoscope, which he mentions only once in his *Commentaria in artem medicinalem Galeni* ('Commentary on the Medical Procedure of Galen', 1612).

Extended apparatus
To measure oral temperature, Sanctorius invented several different mouth thermometers, including this long and cumbersome device (above).

A question of balance
Sanctorius was obsessed with measurement, but it enabled him to reach some useful conclusions: his 'weighing chair', for instance (left), proved that people excrete only a small fraction of what they consume.

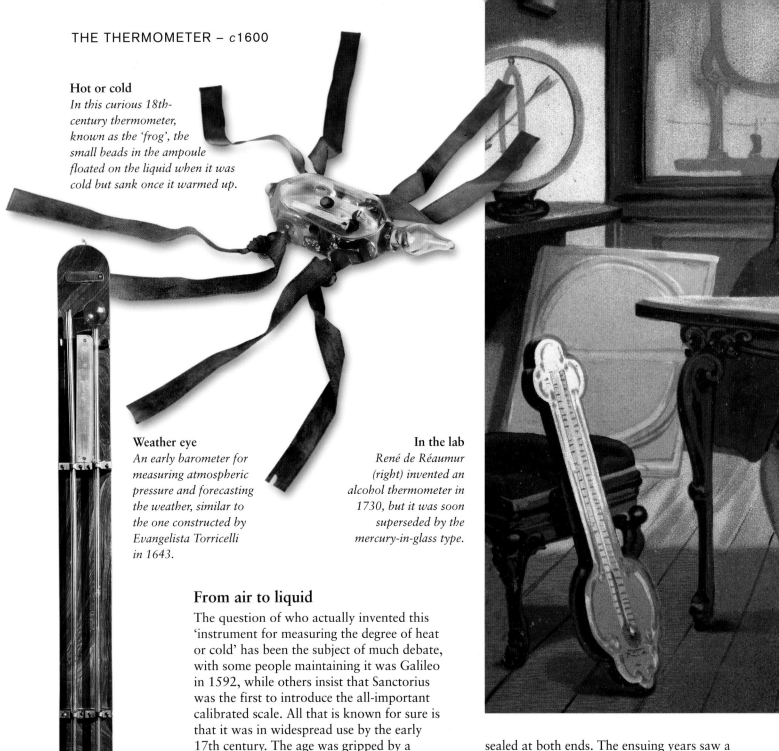

Hot or cold
In this curious 18th-century thermometer, known as the 'frog', the small beads in the ampoule floated on the liquid when it was cold but sank once it warmed up.

Weather eye
An early barometer for measuring atmospheric pressure and forecasting the weather, similar to the one constructed by Evangelista Torricelli in 1643.

In the lab
René de Réaumur (right) invented an alcohol thermometer in 1730, but it was soon superseded by the mercury-in-glass type.

From air to liquid

The question of who actually invented this 'instrument for measuring the degree of heat or cold' has been the subject of much debate, with some people maintaining it was Galileo in 1592, while others insist that Sanctorius was the first to introduce the all-important calibrated scale. All that is known for sure is that it was in widespread use by the early 17th century. The age was gripped by a mania for describing and measuring 'natural phenomena', and the thermoscope fitted the bill perfectly. Yet it had one major flaw: as the measuring tube was attached to an open receptacle, the apparatus was affected by variations not only in ambient temperature but also in air pressure. This is precisely what the physicist Evangelista Torricelli demonstrated in 1643, when he developed the first barometer, incorporating the first vacuum known to science.

Torricelli, whom Galileo invited to Florence that year, was greatly admired by the city's ruler, Duke Ferdinand II de' Medici, a gifted inventor in his own right. In 1654 Ferdinand attempted to improve upon the thermoscope by commissioning the first true thermometer, a glass tube filled with wine spirit (alcohol) and sealed at both ends. The ensuing years saw a lively debate between exponents of different thermometric liquids, when it was found that liquids do not all expand at the same rate. Scientists in Florence opted for alcohol, others insisted on mercury, and others still, following Newton, plumped for linseed oil.

A universal scale

Nor was the choice of liquid the only issue. Thermometer manufacturers all had their own methods of calibration, with different scales according to where the apparatus was to be used – for taking the temperature of the human body, say, or in the cellars at the Paris Observatory, or for recording the weather in London. The melting point of snow and the boiling point of water were often used to mark

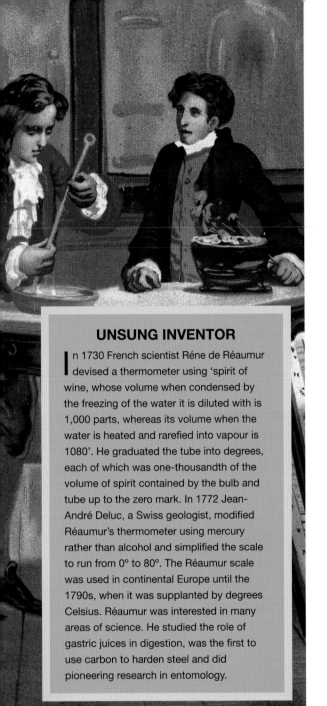

ABSOLUTE ZERO

To measure extreme temperatures, scientists use either alcohol thermometers, with a scale ranging from –80°C to 70°C, or electronic platinum resistance thermometers that can record temperatures up to 750°C. But one temperature point is beyond all measurement: absolute zero, –273.15°C. Absolute zero may not even exist in reality. It was set as the coldest temperature theoretically possible, at which all life would cease to exist.

Celsius or Fahrenheit?

Born into a family of Prussian merchants, Daniel Fahrenheit (1686–1736) was sent at the age of 15 to study commerce in Amsterdam. He became fascinated with scientific instruments and was much impressed by a thermometer made by the Danish astronomer Olaus Roemer. In 1714 Fahrenheit produced his own version. Following Roemer, he selected the temperature at which ice melts and the temperature of the human body as two key reference points, but he recalibrated Roemer's scale and added further fixed points. Thus, Fahrenheit's scale runs from 0°F at the bottom (the coldest winter temperature in his native Danzig, equal to –18°C) to 212°F at the top (the boiling point of water, 100°C). The melting point of ice was 32°F, while 96°F was reached 'when the thermometer is held in the mouth or under the armpit of a man in good health' (this core body temperature was later revised to 98.6°).

By contrast, Celsius took the freezing and boiling points of water as the main fixed points for his scale. Initially, the scale indicated boiling point as 0° with freezing point at 100°C, an arrangement that had a distinct advantage in that it did not involve minus figures, which people were still struggling to come to grips with. The scale was effectively reversed in 1744, the year of Celsius' death, by the Swedish botanist Carolus Linnaeus. Following this change the Celsius scale was widely adopted, except in Anglo-Saxon countries which opted to retain Fahrenheit. Today, the Fahrenheit scale is largely redundant outside the USA.

The 'degree of heat or cold' was thus succeeded by the thermometric degree, which in turn was replaced by degrees Celsius. Meanwhile, the thermometer became part of everyday life, appearing in a wide variety of forms, from the familiar medical thermometer to thermometers in cars to heavy-duty instruments used by vulcanologists in order to measure the temperature of magma.

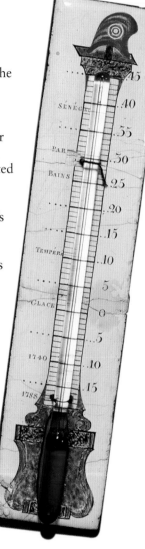

Changing style
As the thermometer became an everyday household item, it came to be decorated to suit the fashion of the day. On this example from the French Revolutionary period, the scale is surmounted by the Phrygian cap, a symbol of the Revolution.

UNSUNG INVENTOR

In 1730 French scientist Réne de Réaumur devised a thermometer using 'spirit of wine, whose volume when condensed by the freezing of the water it is diluted with is 1,000 parts, whereas its volume when the water is heated and rarefied into vapour is 1080'. He graduated the tube into degrees, each of which was one-thousandth of the volume of spirit contained by the bulb and tube up to the zero mark. In 1772 Jean-André Deluc, a Swiss geologist, modified Réaumur's thermometer using mercury rather than alcohol and simplified the scale to run from 0° to 80°. The Réaumur scale was used in continental Europe until the 1790s, when it was supplanted by degrees Celsius. Réaumur was interested in many areas of science. He studied the role of gastric juices in digestion, was the first to use carbon to harden steel and did pioneering research in entomology.

---

the top and bottom of the scale, but the number of divisions between varied wildly. The direction in which the scale should be read also differed from one thermometer to the next: 0° might indicate extreme cold or extreme heat. By the mid 18th century, more than 60 different scales were in use.

This was the situation when Anders Celsius (1701–44), a professor at Uppsala University in Sweden, appeared on the scene. Celsius had inherited an aptitude for mathematics from one of his grandfathers, but he followed the other (and his father) into a career in astronomy, which required him to conduct meteorological observations. He soon began to appreciate – like scientists Daniel Fahrenheit and René de Réaumur before him – the need for a universal temperature scale.

Snapshot of a Renaissance city

Venice was the wonder of the age in the 16th century. The pride of this cosmopolitan floating city, which dominated trade between East and West, was the Arsenal, birthplace of the most powerful fleet in the world. Venice could boast a celebrated university, along with renowned publishing houses and a thriving banking industry. The 'Most Serene Republic' was a cultural magnet that attracted artists and intellectuals from far and wide.

State pomp and power
A detail from Departure of the Bucentaur to San Nicolò on the Lido *(1768), a painting by Francesco Guardi. The inset (top right) shows the winged lion of St Mark, patron saint of Venice.*

King without a crown
Doge Leonardo Loredan (r1501–21) in a portrait by the Venetian painter Vittore Carpaccio. The doges of Venice had great power, being elected for life by the aristocracy.

On Ascension Day, 1537, a huge flotilla of small, brightly coloured boats turned out in St Mark's Basin to escort the *Bucentaur*, the lavish state barge of *La Serenissima* – the Most Serene Republic of Venice. Outside the Doge's Palace (the *Palazzo Ducale*) the quayside was packed with people; a huge crowd had been gathering there since early morning. Suddenly, the Doge himself appeared on the magnificent Gothic-arched colonnade that ran around the palace, accompanied by members of Venice's Great Council and her ambassadors (Venice was the first western state to appoint foreign envoys).

The dignitaries made their way slowly through the milling crowd to the barge. Led by a Flemish conductor, musicians from St Mark's Basilica struck up a madrigal, a musical form invented in Italy in the 14th century. The *Bucentaur* and its accompanying flotilla left the Basin and headed for the Lido. Their destination was the port of San Nicolò on the Adriatic. There Andrea Gritti, like the 81 doges of Venice who had performed the ceremony before him, cast into the sea a

Triumph of commerce
A modern view of Venice (left), looking down the Grand Canal, the city's main waterway, to the Church of Santa Maria della Salute and, beyond it, the Customs House.

Shipbuilding tradition
A naval shipyard in 16th-century Venice (bottom). During the Middle Ages and after, Venice was not only the main commercial port of the Adriatic (indeed, of the whole Mediterranean), but also maintained a powerful navy as a defence against the other great power of the region: the Ottoman Empire.

golden ring blessed by a bishop, intoning the words: *Desposamus te, mare, in signum veri perpetuique domini* ('We wed thee, sea, as a sign of our true and everlasting sovereignty').

The sea – Venice's friend and foe

Venice owed the sea a great deal, not least its booming maritime trade, but it was also a source of problems, such as the constant erosion that threatened the Lido. Trees were regularly felled there, and earth and sand removed as part of an ongoing programme of preserving the salt marshes, but this had damaged the island's ecosystem. Many rivers emptying into the lagoon had been diverted, such as the Brenta in 1452, to stop them silting up the channels to the Adriatic, but this also prevented their alluvial deposits from helping to compensate for the coastal erosion.

The Venetian Senate appointed 'water experts' with a roving brief to visit trouble spots and determine the degree of longshore drift, monitor tide levels and assess the state of the city's canals. According to tradition, men from the lagoon city of Chioggia were engaged to carry out the necessary repairs. Though they had only rudimentary equipment – punts, spades, baskets and adzes – over time they

EUROPE'S BUSIEST SHIPYARD

The Venice Arsenal was founded in 1104 by Doge Ordelaf Falier, and enlarged several times in its history in response to the demands of trade and war. In the Middle Ages, it was the largest industrial enterprise anywhere in Europe. It employed over 16,000 workers in its heyday, turning out ships on a production line (an entire ship was once completed in a single day). These vessels were sold at auction to the city's wealthy noblemen.

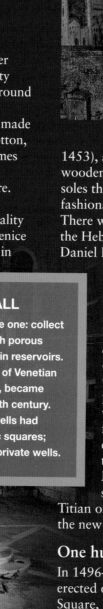

WHEELER-DEALERS

Well versed in foreign exchange, Venetians bought different commodities with different currencies. They used silver to trade with the West, paid Eastern merchants in gold, and bartered salt with local farmers from the Veneto, who supplied the city with agricultural produce. As in Genoa and many other European ports, clearing-houses in Venice later turned into leading merchant and investment banks.

City of culture
A Venetian printer in his workshop (top right). As Venice grew more prosperous and powerful, so its reputation as a centre of culture spread. By the 16th century, the city was home to a booming printing and bookselling trade.

Public works
The demand for fresh water in a city surrounded by the sea was met by sinking wells in Venice's squares (campi), as here in the San Polo district.

became highly adept at building breakwaters and managing water flow. By 1200 the Venetian lagoon was the largest seawater lake in the Mediterranean. The impressive coastal defences on the Lido – palisades, oak pilings, jetties, groynes – ensured that the three main inlets into the lagoon (San Nicolò, Malamocco and Chioggia channels) remained open.

Major hub of trade

St Mark's Square was a hive of activity, attracting traders and visitors from all over Europe. Foreign buyers, pilgrims to the city and locals – Venice had a population of around 100,000 in the 1500s – milled around the market stalls, admiring the coloured silks made by the dyers of the Canareggio district, cotton, spices, Russian furs and amber and perfumes imported from the East.

All the latest fashions could be had here. Spectacles with lenses crafted by Venetian glassmakers, fine needlepoint lace (a speciality of the Byzantine Greeks who flocked to Venice after Constantinople fell to the Ottomans in

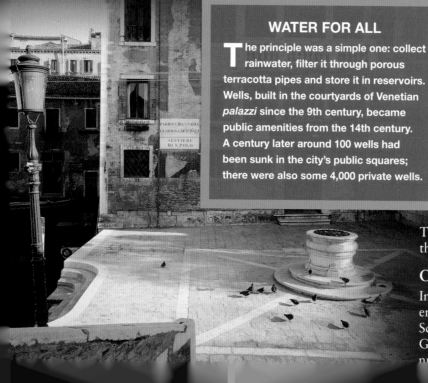

WATER FOR ALL

The principle was a simple one: collect rainwater, filter it through porous terracotta pipes and store it in reservoirs. Wells, built in the courtyards of Venetian *palazzi* since the 9th century, became public amenities from the 14th century. A century later around 100 wells had been sunk in the city's public squares; there were also some 4,000 private wells.

1453), and Venetian 'chopines', shoes with wooden or cork heels and tall platform soles that were the must-have accessory for fashionable ladies in Renaissance Europe. There were even rare books on sale, such as the Hebrew-language volumes printed by Daniel Bomberg, a native of Antwerp who set up shop in Venice in 1511.

Artists were much in evidence. Unlike foreign painters, who were retained by royal courts, the artists of Venice were commissioned on a strictly *ad hoc* basis. Some were in great demand by doges and noblemen – Giovanni Bellini painted a famous portrait of Doge Leonardo Loredan, while his brother Gentile painted the frescoes in the *Palazzo Ducale*. Less exalted artists were forced to hawk their works on St Mark's Square. Many tried to emulate the great figures such as the Bellinis, Vittore Carpaccio, Titian or the young Tintoretto by employing the new technique of painting in oils.

One huge building site

In 1496–9 a magnificent clocktower was erected opposite the cathedral in St Mark's Square, by Gian Paulo Rainieri and his son Giancarlo. The gilded clockface showed the numbers 1 to 24 in Roman numerals and the

Bessarion (1403–72) finally found a fitting home in the Biblioteca Marciana, which Sansovino built on St Mark's opposite the Doge's Palace. This magnificent public library attracted scholars from all over the world.

A world-class university

In the early 15th century Padua came under Venetian control and its famous university became Venice's official seat of higher learning. Its alumni included Copernicus, Vesalius and Galileo. Teachers from Padua also gave private lessons to young noblemen in Venice itself. Some of these scholars came from far afield – the schools of grammar and calculus, for example, employed German, Portuguese, French and Spanish masters – and the city took a portion of their salaries in taxation. This lively intellectual scene created a market for academic publishing, and Venice became one of the main centres of printing in Europe.

Dining in style

On his return from the *Sposalizio* ceremony, the Doge treated his guests to a banquet. A table covered with white linen was set with fine china plates, knives, forks (introduced to Venice in the 11th century by the Greek wife of Doge Domenico Silvio), and crystal glasses made on the island of Murano. Beside each place setting was a napkin folded into the shape of a bird. At the 1537 feast, the fine art of Venetian dining greatly impressed the ambassador of François I of France, Cardinal Georges d'Armagnac. As the day drew to a close and candles were lit, Armagnac prepared for an audience with the Doge. Venice was under threat from the Ottomans and France would be called upon to support her ally. The very existence of the city that everyone since Petrarch acclaimed as the wonder of the modern world was at stake. *La Serenissima* was at the peak of her power, but the storm clouds were gathering.

Venetian weddings
An aerial view of St Mark's Square in the 16th century (left). Every year, on Ascension Day, the Doge would embark from here to celebrate the city's symbolic marriage to the sea (Lo Sposalizio). *The Venetian painter Tintoretto (1518–94) took* The Marriage at Cana *as the subject of one of his canvases, a detail from which is shown below.*

12 signs of the zodiac. At the time, the city was one immense building site. Venice is made up of around 100 small islands, intersected by 150 canals and linked by more than 400 bridges. These islets had been laboriously reclaimed from the lagoon by sinking wooden palisades into the silt of the lake-bed to make a caisson. Water was then pumped out and sturdy tree-trunks rammed into the mud to take the foundations of buildings. Literally thousands of pilings supported the weight of the stone buildings above. In public squares and alleyways, workmen replaced the original surface of compacted mud with flagstones or fired bricks, which incorporated an ingenious drainage system for collecting rainwater.

La Serenissima in the 16th century was caught up in a vast programme of urban renewal. In the Rialto quarter, an old timber bridge was replaced in 1591 by the elegant single-span stone bridge still seen there today; the nearby market, destroyed by fire in 1514, was completely rebuilt. The renowned architect Jacopo Sansovino was hired to rejuvenate St Mark's Square. The impressive library bequeathed by the Greek scholar Cardinal

Watery city
The glory of Venice rests entirely on wooden pilings sunk into the bed of the lagoon (left), foundations that have stood the test of centuries.

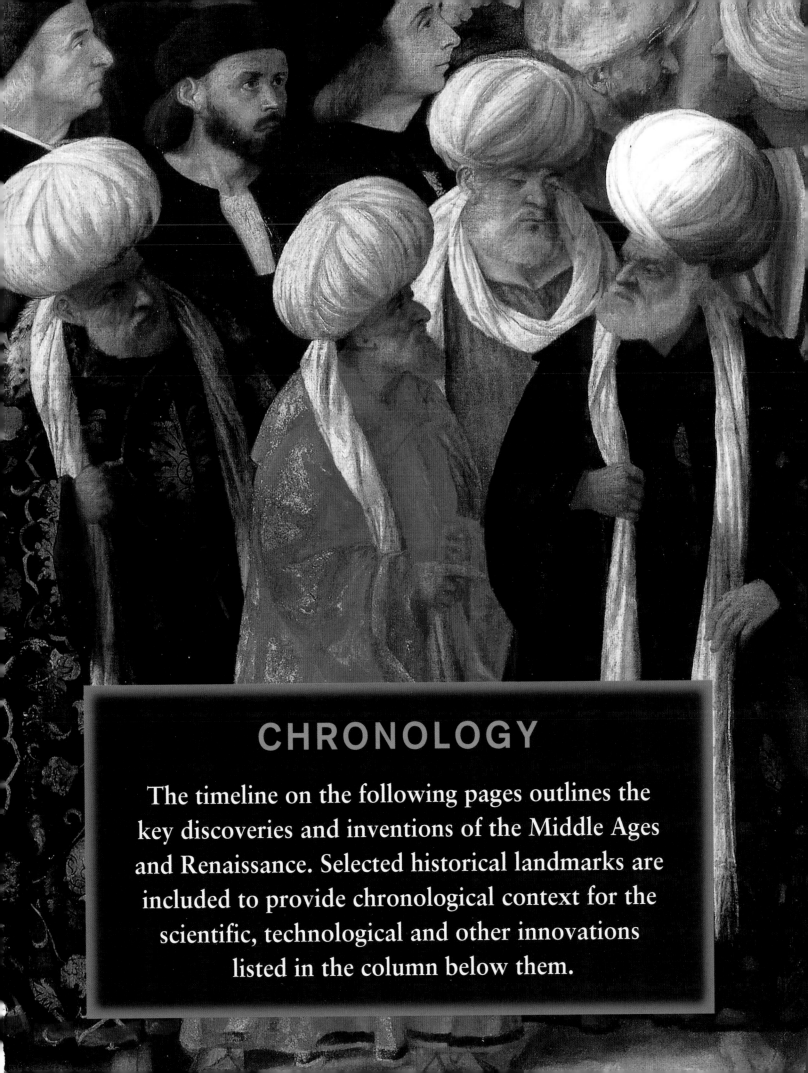

CHRONOLOGY

The timeline on the following pages outlines the key discoveries and inventions of the Middle Ages and Renaissance. Selected historical landmarks are included to provide chronological context for the scientific, technological and other innovations listed in the column below them.

900

EVENTS

- Emergence of a feudal system in Europe
- Foundation of Cluny Abbey (910)

INVENTIONS

- Playing cards first appear in China
- Use of horseshoes recommended by Byzantine Emperor Leo VI
- Woodblock-printed edition of *Classics of Confucianism* is published in China
- Scholar Gerbert d'Aurillac brings Arabic numerals and the astrolabe to the West
- The principle of anti-viral vaccination becomes known in China
- A camshaft is first used in the mechanisms of windmills
- Revival of the postal system in the West
- The Vikings discover and colonise Greenland

1000

- Confucianism adopted as the official ideology of the Chinese state (1020)
- William the Conqueror wins the Battle of Hastings (1066) and orders the compilation of the Domesday Book (1086)
- Development of a system of communal government in Italy (1085)
- First Crusade (1095–99)

- The shoulder collar becomes established in Europe as part of the harness for horses, which from this period on are used for heavy work such as ploughing and hauling carts
- Persian physician and philosopher Avicenna (Ibn Sina) compiles all the medical knowledge of the age in his *Canon of Medicine*; translated into Latin by Gerard of Cremona in the mid-12th century, Avicenna's work becomes the standard textbook for European medical faculties until the 17th century

- The Benedictine monk Guido of Arezzo invents modern musical notation ('staff notation')
- A Chinese work, the *Wu Ching Tsung Yao*, mentions the use of a magnetised iron fish suspended in water, the ancestor of the magnetic compass
- The Byzantine wife of the Doge of Venice introduces the fork as a dining implement
- First known use of movable printing type, made from terracotta blocks in China

1100

- Founding of the Venice Arsenal (1104)
- University of Paris founded (1120)

- Use of the mouldboard plough, invented by the Celts, spreads throughout northwestern Europe, playing a major part in the agricultural revolution that begins at this time
- The centreline or sternpost rudder, known to the Chinese since the first century, replaces lateral (side-mounted) rudders on Atlantic oceangoing vessels
- First mention in Europe of the magnetic compass, long familiar to Chinese and Arab sailors
- Windmills are introduced to Europe; unlike earlier Persian windmills, they have sails mounted on a horizontal (not vertical) axis

▶ Ancient Chinese movable type

▲ A horse's shoulder collar in use, as shown on the Bayeux Tapestry

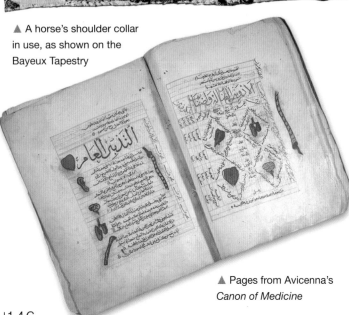

▲ Pages from Avicenna's *Canon of Medicine*

▼ A mouldboard plough

1150

- Conquest of Egypt by Saladin (Salah-al-Din, 1171–93)
- Saladin captures Jerusalem (1187)

1200

- Crusaders to the Holy Land found the Latin Empire (1204)
- Genghis Khan becomes supreme leader of the Mongols (1206)
- King John is forced to sign the Magna Carta (1215

1250

- The House of Habsburg assumes control of the Holy Roman Empire (1273)
- Mongol Khans comes to power in China and establish the Yuan Dynasty (1274)
- Founding of the Ottoman Empire (1283)
- Edward I summons the 'Model Parliament' (1295)

- Construction of dykes as sea defences in Friesland (the Netherlands)

- Used for the first time at the Abbey of St Denis, near Paris, cross-ribbed vaulting gives rise to Gothic style in architecture, which spreads rapidly throughout western Europe

- The first papermills are established in Europe

- The shoe, which the Crusaders brought back from the Middle East, is widely adopted in Europe

- Screw-jack technology, which gives rise to more efficient lifting gear on building sites, is described by Villard de Honnecourt

- Forehead yokes are in use in Europe to harness oxen teams

- Franciscan missionaries Giovanni de Piano Carpini and William of Rubruck journey overland to Central Asia (Mongolia)

- Grisaille stained-glass first produced

- Tin plate, an alloy of steel and tin, is manufactured in Bohemia

- The spinning-wheel, originally used in India and Persia, is introduced by the Arabs to Europe, where it soon begins to rival the spindle and distaff

- The first spectacles, thought to have been invented by Salvino degli Armati of Florence, are used to correct long-sightedness

- Pierre de Maricourt expounds his theory of magnetism

- The English theologian and philosopher Roger Bacon, who was schooled in Oxford and taught in Paris, advocates experience and reasoning as methods of learning; among his many achievements, Bacon explains the precession of equinoxes and tides, shows the Julian calendar to be inaccurate, and discovers the secret of gunpowder (first invented by the Chinese)

- Creation of the *Carte Pisane*, the oldest known Portolan chart

- Italian adventurer Marco Polo travels across Central Asia and China

- First recorded use of the wheelbarrow in Europe

▲ Chinese river junk with a centreline rudder

▶ Cross-ribbed vaulting in the nave of the Abbey of St Denis

▲ Roger Bacon conducting an experiment with gunpowder, as imagined by a 19th-century illustrator

▲ A medieval shoe

1300

1350

1400

EVENTS

- The city of Tenochtitlán is founded by the Aztecs (1325)
- Start of the Hundred Years' War (1337)
- The Black Death ravages Europe (1348)

- The Mongols are expelled from China by the Ming (1368)
- Timur the Lame (Tamerlane) conquers Persia (c1370)
- Peasant's Revolt in England (1381)

- Beginning of the Renaissance in Italy
- Venetian victory over the Turkish fleet at the Battle of Gallipoli (1416)
- The English win the Battle of Agincourt, ending the 100 Years' War (1415)

INVENTIONS

- The cannon is widely adopted in Europe; updated and improved, its firepower makes warfare far more deadly

- Weight-driven mechanical clocks make their first appearance in European cities

- The first blast furnaces are set up in Europe to manufacture blown glass and cast iron

- Lace is made in Flanders and France

- The gunpowder rocket first appears in Europe

- Chinese admiral Zheng He undertakes a series of major voyages of discovery

- Architect and sculptor Filippo Brunelleschi demonstrates the principle of single-point linear perspective; another Florentine architect, Leon Battista Alberti, sets down rules for the use of linear perspective by artists

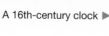

A 16th-century clock ▶

▲ Chinese junk belonging to the fleet of Admiral Zheng He

▼ Medieval cannons firing on a besieged city

The Coronation of the Virgin by Fra Angelico, an early example of the use of linear perspective in painting ▶

1425

- The Christian kingdom of Castile makes massive inroads into Moorish Spain (1430)
- Construction of the dome of Florence cathedral (completed 1434)

1450

- Constantinople falls to the Ottoman Turks, ending the Byzantine Empire (1453)
- Start of the Wars of the Roses in England (1455)
- Marriage of Ferdinand and Isabella links Aragon and Castille in Spain (1469)

- Manufacture of the first portable firearms
- According to Renaissance art historian Giorgio Vasari, the Flemish painter Jan van Eyck invents oil painting (in fact, he adds oil highlights to an egg tempera base coat)

- Leon Battista Alberti produces the first map based on triangulation
- German inventor Johannes Gutenberg produces the first printing press, ushering in modern printing

- Nuremberg locksmith Peter Henlein manufactures the first portable clock ('watch')
- Magnetic compasses are perfected in the West, with their needles mounted on compass roses

- The caravel is widely used by European seafarers on their voyages of discovery
- Gutenberg's 42-line Bible is printed and published
- Faience pottery is introduced to Italy from the East via Moorish Spain

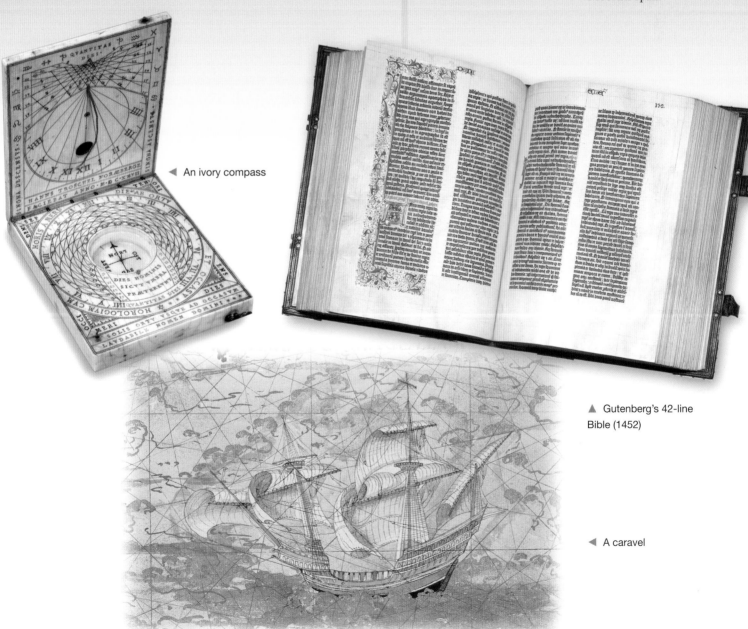

◀ An ivory compass

▲ Gutenberg's 42-line Bible (1452)

◀ A caravel

1475

1500

EVENTS

- Start of the Spanish Inquisition (1480)
- The Christian reconquest of Spain from the Moors is completed with the capture of Granada (1492)
- The Treaty of Tordesillas divides discoveries in the New World between Portugal and Spain (1494)
- Start of the Italian Wars (1494)

- Beginning of the African slave trade (1505)
- Beginning of the Protestant Reformation (1517)
- Spanish conquest of the Aztec Empire (1521)

INVENTIONS

- Portuguese seafarer Bartolomeu Dias becomes the first European to sail round the Cape of Good Hope; a decade later his compatriot Vasco da Gama completes the journey to India and the East

- The tower mill, with a movable cap, first appears in Europe

- German mathematician Martin Behaim makes the first known terrestrial globe, divided into 360° of longitude and featuring the coastline of Africa as charted by Portuguese expeditions

- In the service of Spain, Genoese explorer Christopher Columbus crosses the Atlantic and reaches the Americas

- Earliest written evidence of whisky distillation in Scotland

- Venetian mathematician Luca Pacioli establishes the principles of double-entry bookkeeping

- First rolling mills constructed in Europe

- Seafarers Pedro Cabral and Amerigo Vespucci explore the coast of South America

- Geographer-monk Martin Waldseemüller christens the continent discovered by Christopher Columbus 'America'

- Chinese invent the modern toothbrush, made from the bristles of wild boar

- Wallpaper first appears in England, from where it soon spreads to continental Europe

- Leonardo da Vinci dies in France (1519); the legacy of this remarkable polymath includes paintings that helped to revive the art of portraiture and revolutionised the depiction of landscape, as well as a huge portfolio of scientific drawings and notes with designs for advanced machines such as helicopters and tanks

- A ship from a fleet that set out under the command of Ferdinand Magellan completes the first circumnavigation of the globe

- Spectacles with glass lenses become widespread

- Italian publisher Alde Manucce produces the world's first paperback book

Terrestrial globe (1568)
by Johannes Praetorius
of Nuremberg ▶

▼ One of the earliest nautical charts of the Pacific Ocean

▼ Early accountants at work

1525

- Outbreak of the Peasants' War in Germany (1525)
- Founding of the Mughal Empire in India (1526)
- The Spanish overrun the Inca Empire (1533)
- The Society of Jesus (Jesuit order) is founded (1540)

- The turn-wrest mouldboard plough is widely adopted by European farmers

- The cork for sealing bottles, long used in ancient times in Mediterranean countries, is rediscovered in Europe

- Diamonds first used in glasscutting

- The heeled shoe becomes fashionable in Europe

- Painting on canvas becomes popular among Venetian painters

- First documented use of the nautical astrolabe

- French navigator Jacques Cartier explores the St Lawrence River in Canada

- Flemish physician Andreas Vesalius publishes *De Humani corporis fabrica*, which revolutionises people's understanding of human anatomy

- Posthumous publication of *De revolutionibus*, a work by the Polish astronomer Nicolaus Copernicus, which expounds his heliocentric view of the universe

- French barber-surgeon Ambroise Paré publishes his first work on battlefield surgery, written in French, and lays the foundations of modern surgery

1550

- Russia begins its conquest of Siberia (1556)
- Roman Catholic Church publishes its first list of banned books, the *Index Vaticanus* (1559)
- England loses Calais, its last bastion in France (1558)
- Thousands of French Huguenots slain in St Bartholomew's Day Massacre (1572)

- Oil painting supplants egg tempera

- Jointed artificial limbs are devised by Ambroise Paré; they remain in use essentially unchanged until the 20th century

- Flemish mapmaker Gerardus Mercator lays the foundations of modern cartography by devising a form of map projection that makes it possible to navigate accurately with a magnetic compass

- First modern atlas published by Abraham Ortelius

- English inventor Leonard Digges creates a surveying instrument that is the precursor of the theodolite

- Italian doctor Gabriele Fallopio recommends the prophylactic properties of the condom

- Development of accurate screw threads cut on lathes improves the consistency of nuts and bolts, which are increasingly used in the assembly of metal components

- The graphite pencil, thought to have been invented by the Swiss Conrad von Gesner, replaces the lead pencil used since ancient times

▲ Early theodolite

▲ A case of surgical instruments

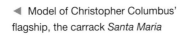

◄ Model of Christopher Columbus' flagship, the carrack *Santa Maria*

151

1575

1600

EVENTS

- Adoption of the Gregorian Calendar across most of Europe (1582)
- Mary, Queen of Scots, is beheaded (1587)
- The English defeat the Spanish Armada, heralding the decline of Spanish naval power (1588)

- Edo (Tokyo) is made the new capital of Japan (1603)
- Scottish and English thrones are united under James VI of Scotland (James I of England, 1603)
- The Gunpowder Plot is uncovered (1605)
- Founding of the city of Quebec (1608)
- Pilgrim Fathers land in America (1620)

INVENTIONS

- The oldest prefabricated building (Nonesuch House) is erected on Old London Bridge

- In his *Discours admirable*, French master-potter Bernard Palissy gives the first accurate explanation of the water cycle, and puts forward pioneering ideas concerning palaeontology and plant nutrition

- At Uranienborg and later Prague, Danish astronomer Tycho Brahe compiles a catalogue of 777 stars and refutes the notion of the unchanging heavens accepted since the days of

Ptolemy; while Tycho never adopts a Copernican view of the universe, his work paves the way for Johannes Kepler's revolutionary new astronomy

- English inventor William Lee invents the world's first stocking frame knitting machine

- The flushing water closet is devised by the English engineer John Harington

- Dutch navigator William Barents (Willem Barentsz) pioneers polar exploration

- English surgeon Peter Chamberlen introduces the obstetric forceps

- Copperplate engraving becomes more widespread for illustrations in printed books

- First use of the tourniquet, by German surgeon Wilhelm Fabry of Hilden

- Building on earlier work by Galileo, Italian scientist Sanctorius Sanctorius invents the first true thermometer

- Galileo undertakes the first astronomical observations using a telescope

- Dutch scientist Hans Jansen invents the first microscope, a key moment in the advance of scientific knowledge

- German astronomer Johannes Kepler formulates his first laws on planetary motion

An enamelled dish by Bernard Palissy ▼

▲ Tycho Brahe's astronomical sextant

An Arab thermometer/barometer ▶

Old London Bridge, site of the world's first prefabricated building ▼

1625

- New Amsterdam (New York) founded (1626)
- Construction of the Taj Mahal in Agra, India, begins (1631)
- Founding of Prussian state (1640)
- Start of English Civil War (1642)

- English physician William Harvey describes the circulatory system and establishes that the heart pumps blood around the body
- French philosopher and mathematician Blaise Pascal invents the first calculating machine
- Umbrellas made of waxed canvas become popular
- The phenomenon of atmospheric pressure is investigated and described by various scientists

▲ Anatomical drawing from Vesalius' *De Humani corporis fabrica*

1650

- Beginning of Dutch colonisation of South Africa (1652)
- Scientific societies founded, including the Royal Society (1660) and the French Academy of Sciences (1666)
- Hudson's Bay Company founded (1670)

- Dutch scientist Christiaan Huygens constructs the first pendulum clock
- English scientist Robert Hooke invents the wheel barometer for measuring atmospheric pressure
- Italian Marcello Malpighi proves the existence of red blood corpuscles
- German chemist Johann Joachim Becher discovers ethylene
- The beam balance is invented by French engineer Gilles Roberval
- English doctor and astronomer Isaac Newton develops the reflecting telescope
- French mathematicians Fermat and Pascal give the first systematic solution to a problem concerning the laws of probability
- Jacques Marquette and Louis Jolliet explore the Mississippi Basin
- Tea goes on sale in England
- Tobacco smoked to ward off the plague

Huygens working on his pendulum clock ▼

1675

- Revocation of the Edict of Nantes (1685)
- *Habeas corpus* established as a fundamental legal principle in England (1679)
- The Indian city of Calcutta (modern Kolkata) is founded (1690)

- Huygens invents the first watch with a spiral spring regulating the movements of the balance
- Danish astronomer Olaus Roemer measures the speed of light
- Dutch biologist Louis Dominicus Hamm is the first to identify human spermatozoa and their role in reproduction
- French engineer Denis Papin invents the pressure cooker
- English engineer Thomas Savery designs the first water pump to run on steam pressure
- Isaac Newton formulates the law of universal gravitation, which forms the basis of modern astrophysics

▲ Fob watch by the French clockmaker Breguet

Index

Page numbers in *italics* refer to captions.

Picture credits

THE ADVENTURE OF DISCOVERIES AND INVENTIONS
The Middle Ages – 1000 to 1600
is published by The Reader's Digest Association Limited,
11 Westferry Circus, Canary Wharf, London E14 4HE

Copyright © 2009 The Reader's Digest Association Limited

The book was translated and adapted from *Vers la Renaissance des Inventions*,
part of a series entitled L'ÉPOPÉE DES DÉCOUVERTES ET DES INVENTIONS,
created in France by BOOKMAKER and first published by Sélection du Reader's
Digest, Paris, in 2005.

Translated from French by Peter Lewis

Series editor Christine Noble
Art editor Julie Bennett
Designer Martin Bennett
Consultant Ruth Binney
Proofreader Ron Pankhurst
Indexer Marie Lorimer

Colour origination Colour Systems Ltd, London
Printed and bound in China

READER'S DIGEST GENERAL BOOKS
Editorial director Julian Browne
Art director Anne-Marie Bulat
Managing editor Nina Hathway
Head of book development Sarah Bloxham
Picture resource manager Christine Hinze
Pre-press account manager Dean Russell
Product production manager Claudette Bramble
Production controller Sandra Fuller

Copyright © 2009 The Reader's Digest Association Far East Limited
Philippines Copyright © 2009 The Reader's Digest Association Far East Limited
Copyright © 2009 The Reader's Digest (Australia) Pty Limited
Copyright © 2009 The Reader's Digest India Pvt Limited
Copyright © 2009 The Reader's Digest Asia Pvt Limited

We are committed to both the quality of our products and the service we provide to our
customers. We value your comments, so please feel free to contact us on 08705 113366
or via our website at **www.readersdigest.co.uk**

If you have any comments or suggestions about the content of our books, you can
email us at **gbeditorial@readersdigest.co.uk**

CONCEPT CODE: FR0104/IC/S
BOOK CODE: 642-003 UP0000-1
ISBN: 978-0-276-44515-6
ORACLE CODE: 356400003H.00.24